The Saxon Mirror

THE MIDDLE AGES SERIES

Ruth Mazo Karras, Series Editor
Edward Peters, Founding Editor

A complete list of books in the series
is available from the publisher.

The Saxon Mirror

A *Sachsenspiegel* of the Fourteenth Century

Translated by Maria Dobozy

PENN

University of Pennsylvania Press

Philadelphia

10 9 8 7 6 5 4 3 2 1

Published by
University of Pennsylvania Press
Philadelphia, Pennsylvania 19104–4011

Library of Congress Cataloging-in-Publication Data
Sachsenspiegel, English
The Saxon mirror : a Sachsenspiegel of the fourteenth century / translated by Maria Dobozy.
p. cm. — (The Middle Ages series)
Includes bibliographical references and index.
ISBN 0-8122-3487-1
1. Sachsenspiegel. 2. Law—Germany—Sources. I. Dobozy, Maria. II. Title. III. Series.
KK205.6.S2313 1999
340.5'5'094321—dc21 98-51171
CIP

Contents

Translator's Preface

Aside from Roman and canon law, Eike von Repgow's *Sachsenspiegel* was probably the most important legal text for all of late medieval Central Europe. It not only committed to written form a set of customs accepted by the German-speaking areas of the empire and its ethnic minorities for more than three hundred years but also influenced the legal systems in Prussia, Silesia, Poland, Ukraine, Hungary, and Bohemia. Although scholars of medieval Europe acknowledge its influential role, surprisingly it has never before been translated into English. In fact, until now very little information about the *Sachsenspiegel* has existed in English for students or scholars.

The following translation of the *Sachsenspiegel* came about because my colleagues in history and literature encouraged me to make this seminal text available in English. Initially, I was quite daunted by the conceptual legal framework of the medieval collection of laws and customs (custumal), but I persevered, wanting this book to be accessible all those who desire to deepen their knowledge of German culture and history. This translation is based on the text of the illuminated manuscript (Cod. Guelf 3.1 Aug.2^0) housed in the Herzog August Bibliothek in Wolfenbüttel, Germany. It contains unique illustrations that, in tandem with the text, give us a formalized yet unidealized glimpse into the daily activities of the Saxons and the operation of the legal system. I have attempted to provide a faithful English translation of the text that I hope will open up this truly multidimensional cultural document and manuscript to the English reader interested in any aspect of medieval German civilization and culture.

Many libraries and individuals have helped make this translation possible. I am indebted to the National Endowment for the Humanities and the University of Utah Research Committee for their support of my research in Münster, Germany. The director of Department 231 of the *Sonderforschungsbereich* "Träger, Felder, Formen pragmatischer Schriftlichkeit im Mittelalter" at the University of Münster, Germany, Prof. Dr. Ruth Schmidt-Wiegand, and her staff, especially Dr. Dagmar Hüpper, deserve special thanks for their gracious generosity while I worked at the department. I have benefited immensely from discussions with them. Sincere thanks also go to Madelyn D. Garrett, curator of rare books in the J. Willard Marriott Library, University of Utah, and to the entire staff in Special Collections for doing everything in their power to fulfill my needs. I also thank Dr. Wolfgang Milde and the directorate of the Herzog August Bibliothek for making the manuscript available to me and granting permission to reproduce the illustrations. The University of Utah Undergraduate Research Opportunities Program must also be thanked for supporting my research assistant, Scott VanDam, while he assisted me in the translation of the "Table of Contents."

Others who aided and abetted my work at critical stages are Paul Brand, Hartwig Mayer, Charles Nelson, Lambertus Okken, Peter von Sivers, Alan McGill Smith, and Donald Smith. I owe them grateful thanks for all their corrections, suggestions, and support.

This book is dedicated to the memory of my parents.

Abbreviations

In references to the Wolfenbüttel manuscript and this translation Roman numerals indicate books I–IV, and the Arabic numbers indicate the chapters.

Du	Dutch
G	German
E	English
MHG	Middle High German
OE	Old English
ME	Middle English
LG	Low German
fol.	folio
c.	column
l.	line
n.m.	masculine noun
n.n.	neuter noun
n.f.	feminine noun
v.	verb
refl.	reflexive
adj.	adjective
pl.	plural
D	Dresden (M 32, Dresden State Library)
H	Heidelberg (Cpg 164, University of Heidelberg)
O	Oldenburg manuscript (CIM 1410, Landesbibliothek Oldenburg)
W	Wolfenbüttel (Cod. Guelf. 3.1 Aug.2^0, Herzog August Library, Wolfenbüttel)
BMZ	*Mittelhochdeutsches Wörterbuch*. Ed. Georg Benecke, Müller, and Zarncke. New York and Hildesheim: Georg Olm, 1986 [1854].

Buch	*Der Sachsenspiegel als Buch*. Ed. Ruth Schmidt-Wiegand and Dagmar Hüpper. New York and Bern: Lang, 1991.
DWB	*Deutsches Wörterbuch*. Ed. Jacob and Wilhelm Grimm. Leipzig: Hirzel, 1854. (First edition unless otherwise noted.)
Eckhardt *Lndr*	*Sachsenspiegel Landrecht*. Ed. Karl August Eckhardt (Monumenta Germaniae historica. Fontes juris Germanici antiqui, n.s., vol. 1 pt. 1). Göttingen: Musterschmidt, 1973 [1933].
Eckhardt *Lnr*	*Sachsenspiegel Lehnrecht*. Ed. Karl August Eckhardt (Monumenta Germaniae historica. Fontes juris Germanici antiqui, n.s. vol. 1 pt. 2). Göttingen: Musterschmidt, 1973 [1933].
Facsimile D	*Die Dresdner Bilderhandschrift des Sachsenspiegels*. Ed. Karl von Amira. 2 vols. Leipzig: Hiersemann, 1902.
Facsimile H	*Die Heidelberger Bilderhandschrift des Sachsenspiegels. Kommentar und Anmerkungen*. Ed. Walter Koschorreck. 2 vols. Frankfurt am Main: Insel Verlag, 1970.
Facsimile O	*Der Sachsenspiegel, Landrecht und Lehnrecht, nach dem Oldenburger Codex picturatus von 1336*. Ed. August Lübben. Amsterdam: Rodopi, 1970 [1879].
Facsimile W	*Eike von Repgow: Sachsenspiegel: Die Wolfenbütteler Bilderhandschrift Cod. Guelf. 3.1 Aug.2⁰*. Ed. and trans. Ruth Schmidt-Wiegand. 3 vols. Berlin: Akademie Verlag, 1993.
HRG	*Handwörterbuch zur deutschen Rechtsgeschichte*. Ed. Adalbert Erler and Ekkehard Kaufmann. Berlin: E. Schmidt Verlag, 1971–.
Lexer	*Mittelhochdeutsches Handwörterbuch*. Ed. Mathias Lexer. Stuttgart: Hirzel, 1992 [1876].
LexMA	*Lexikon des Mittelalters*. Munich: Artemis Verlag, 1980–.
Lübben	*Mittelniederdeutsches Handwörterbuch*. Ed. August Lübben. Darmstadt: Wissenschaftliche Buchgesellschaft, 1990 [1888].
Ostsiedlung	*Die deutsche Ostsiedlung des Mittelalters als Problem der europäischen Geschichte: Reichenau-Vorträge 1970–71*. Ed. Walter Schlesinger. Sigmaringen: Jan Thorbecke, 1975.
PL	*Patrologiae Cursus Completus: Series Latina*. Ed. Jacques-Paul Migne, Paris: Migne. 1844–64.
TBI	*Text-Bild-Interpretation: Untersuchungen zu den Bilder-*

	handschriften des Sachsenspiegels. Ed. Ruth Schmidt-Wiegand. Munich: Fink Verlag, 1986.
VL	*Die deutsche Literatur des Mittelalters, Verfasserlexikon*. Ed. Kurt Ruh and Gundolf Keil. 2nd rev. ed. New York and Berlin: De Gruyter, 1978–.
ZfdA	*Zeitschrift für deutsches Altertum und deutsche Literatur*
ZRG GA	*Zeitschrift der Savigny-Stiftung für Rechtsgeschichte, Germanistische Abteilung*

Plate 1. The enemies of God and the Law kicking the lawbook and Eike underneath it (Cod. Guelf. 3.1 Aug.2°, folio 85r, IV 84). (Reproduced by permission of the Herzog August Bibliothek, Wolfenbüttel, Germany)

Introduction

THE *SACHSENSPIEGEL* (1235) BY Eike von Repgow marks the beginning of German jurisprudence.[1] It is not only one of the earliest custumals in the German language but also, because of its rich transmission and widespread reception, the single most significant document of its kind in the history of German laws, customs, and material culture. Indeed, the *Sachsenspiegel*'s influence was felt in German territories for more than three hundred years, until the reception of Roman law in the sixteenth century. In some areas, such as Prussia, it remained valid until the General Landlaw was established in 1794.

Far from being strictly a set of legal rules, the *Sachsenspiegel* was built upon the interrelatedness of language, religion, literature, morality, and aesthetics; for this reason, it re-created then as it does now the very structure of society. Consequently, this lawbook is unique because it opens a window onto medieval communities and the concerns of all their inhabitants, including serfs, free peasants, women, children, and ethnic minorities. Just as laws and customs intertwine inextricably with the beliefs, events, and activities of daily life, so does this lawbook encompass medieval Saxon society. It did this so successfully that it almost immediately came to be used as an authoritative reference work. The *Sachsenspiegel* makes available information on any number of fundamental human experiences such as work, play, birth, death, and such social issues as inheritance and property conveyance, status of women, family structure, community organization and administration, minorities, ethnic diversity, multilingualism, and crime.

The term *Sachsenspiegel* refers to a set of legal customs first put into book form by Eike von Repgow between 1225 and 1235. Even though Eike's original German text has not survived, we must credit him as the initiator of vernacular legal prose that spread throughout German-speaking lands. At the time Eike was writing, he had no comparable vernacular model.[2] Nevertheless, Eike produced a relatively systematic and remarkably comprehensive text covering most aspects of legal custom in Saxony.

In preparing the lawbook, Eike had no model, and the book had no clear predecessor. The fact that we know the author's name allows us to reconstruct some of the local circumstances in which the lawbook was conceived in order to understand better its content and purpose. The *Sachsenspiegel* enjoyed immediate success by being reproduced in a great many manuscript versions. Although Eike's own text did not survive, the manuscript transmission reveals that his concept and execution of the custumal became the model for all subsequent lawbooks. This manuscript tradition allows us to trace revisions of and additions to the content, but the multiple versions also force the translator to select one version among several for translation. These issues concerning the author, scope and content, context, and reception of the *Sachsenspiegel* manuscripts, as well as the choice of the Wolfenbüttel manuscript (1358–62) for translation, will be discussed below.

The Author and His Book

To locate our author, we must look to the Saxon territory east of the Elbe River. According to the *Sachsenspiegel* manuscripts, the cultural and legal entity of Saxony in the thirteenth century consisted of the Duchy and Palatine County of Saxony, the Landgravate of Thuringia, the newly settled Marches of Brandenburg, Meissen, and Lusatia, and the County of Aschersleben (III 62) (Map 1).[3] The manuscripts conceive of the cities of Goslar, Minden, Paderborn, Verden, Lübeck, Schwerin, Havelberg, Brandenburg, Meissen, and Nordhausen as belonging to Saxony (III 62) (Map 2). Slightly to the east of center in this circle was Magdeburg, the growing hub for jurisprudence in Saxony. By the mid-thirteenth century, Magdeburg was well known for its college of *Schöffen*, to whose decisions many judges resorted in difficult cases.[4]

By the year 1150, a family had settled in the area between the rivers Saale and Mulde just southeast of Magdeburg and named itself after the village of Repgow (present-day Reppichau) between the towns of Dessau and Köthen (Map 2). This family belonged to the class of *Schöffenbarfreie*, the lowest level of nobility eligible to perform the judicial function of determining judgments.[5] The author of the *Sachsenspiegel* was most likely a member of this family because the name "Eike von Reppichowe" (also "Heico von Repechowe") appears in several charters from 1209 to 1233, thereby placing him in contact with Count Heinrich of Anhalt, Margrave Dietrich of Meissen, and Landgrave Ludwig of Thuringia (*VL*, vol. 2, c. 400). Eike was also closely connected to Count Hoyer of Falkenstein, who was the advocate of the ecclesiastical foundation in Quedlinburg; they are listed together in the entourage of Count Heinrich of Aschersleben in 1215 and 1219 (Nowak, 6). For a layman, Eike received a solid education in the seven liberal arts, possibly in nearby Magdeburg, for he learned Latin and was highly familiar with the Bible and canon law. Because his family owned a house in Magdeburg, and the *Schöffen* in Magdeburg were the first to read and use the *Sachsenspiegel*, it is possible that Eike acquired his extensive knowledge of law in that city (Kroeschell, "Licht," 236).

Eike began writing his custumal at the behest of Count Hoyer shortly after 1220. According to the rhymed preface, Eike first compiled his text in Latin and then was asked to rework it in German.[6] People like Hoyer and Eike must have perceived that the oral repository of legal and social information was no longer adequate for maintaining and perpetuating public duties. In the rhymed preface, Eike's uncertainty about the reliability of an orally transmitted customary law is revealed when he states that he writes his book for the next generation: "dat min scat under der erde / mit me nicht verwerde, / Van Goddes halven diu gnade min / scal alle der werlde gemene sin" [so that my knowledge shall not disappear with me under the earth and the favor given me by God shall belong to the entire world] (rhymed preface, Eckhardt, *Lndr*, l. 155–58).[7] Even if we recognize this statement as a commonplace, it may also be true. Hoyer and Eike must have felt that too few judges adequately understood the legal rules and customs, making it necessary to record the customary laws and their operation in writing for young men about to take up legal duties. Based on Eike's rhymed preface, the purpose of his vernacular project was to collect and preserve the inherited legal rules as a reference tool for everyone: "en ander merket aver dar bi, / Dat nemannes mut / bat dar to ne stut, / Wo he de lude gemene / grot unde klene / Rechtes brechte in kunde, / na deme he sek verstunde, / Denne dut de mut min; / des geve ek to orekunde dit bukelin" [But it should also be noted that no one has given a thought to bringing the law to people in general, to the powerful as well as the weak, so that they can understand it for themselves. Consequently, I have determined to do it, and document it with this book] (l. 212–220). It is obvious that a single manuscript would have filled the needs of only a very few who would perhaps inquire about legal customs, but we know that it was customary for a judge to seek a judgment on a particular point from a well-respected judge, or Schöffe, and also from the college of Schöffen in Magdeburg. Perhaps a judge like Hoyer gained additional authority and was

Map 1. Europe, showing the region of Saxony according to the *Saxon Mirror.* The maps, therefore, have been drawn to indicate not the actual historical territorial borders, but rather the undefined regions mentioned in the *Saxon Mirror.*

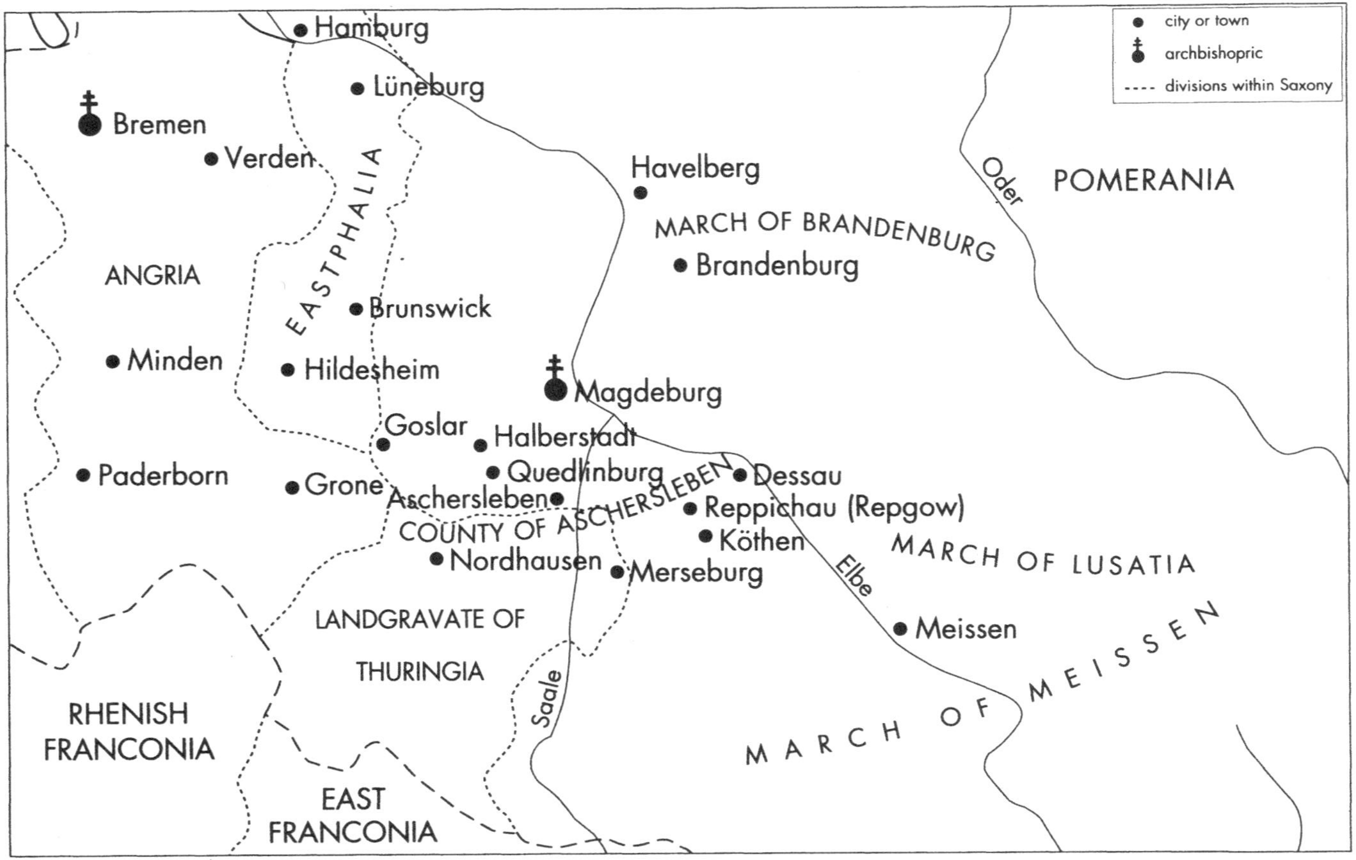

Map 2. Detail of Saxony, its territories, archbishoprics, and towns, according to the place-names in the *Saxon Mirror.* Not all places mentioned in the text are included. The map has been constructed to render the territory of Saxony as the *Saxon Mirror* describes it and does not attempt historical accuracy.

consulted because he held Eike's book. Contemporary scholars point out that a text was needed because custom was changing rapidly, but few other factors that led to the writing of the lawbook are known.[8]

After Eike completed his first German version, he apparently produced a revised version but did not change the organization. Judging from the manuscript tradition, his first and second versions had an intended unity marked by a sequential numbering of five books; they were framed by the two prologues that iterated the purpose of the lawbook and a short epilogue that justified the work against detractors (IV 84; Homeyer, *Rechtsbücher* 6–15). One prologue and the epilogue were dropped from some manuscripts. Eike has been attributed with writing lines 97–280 of the rhymed preface in which he identifies himself and names his work. After the first two German versions attributable to Eike, a third and fourth German redaction were also created. By the late thirteenth century, the manuscript tradition of the third redaction began to divide the lawbook anew, this time into two discrete parts: general territorial law and feudal law. The prologues and rhymed preface were kept. In the same period a new, inclusive compilation was made adding numerous new customs (novellas). This fourth German redaction, continuing the bipartite division of the territorial and feudal law, is extant in a great many manuscripts, including the Wolfenbüttel manuscript, the source of the present translation (see "Choice of Text" below).[9]

The general territorial or rural law (*Landrecht*) applies to all men and women and to rural life in general, but it specifically concerns the peasants' activities. Although it deals with personal rights and obligations, family relations, real and movable property, criminal acts, and judicial procedure, it is not organized according to modern categories. Instead, the *Sachsenspiegel* texts proceed associatively, moving from theme to theme, and digress where Eike or a redactor apparently felt the need to supply background information, elaborate on a point, or add novellas.[10] The lawbook outlines class order and hierarchy and discusses the relations of freemen with respect to clan obligations, marriage, and the possession and transfer of real property, as well as crime and its punishment. It also details specific legal procedures, frequency of hearings, and the selection, privileges, and duties of members of the judiciary.

The second, more concise part of the lawbook contains the feudal law (*Lehnrecht*) which delineates the legal customs governing relations and feudal land tenure among the nobility in Saxony. It is thought to have been written before the territorial law (Kroeschell, "Licht," 239). This section was also freely applied in other German-speaking parts of the empire. The lawbook does not specifically address either city and municipal codes or canon law. Instead, the structure and issues in the two-part custumal are driven by the rural and agricultural concerns that were shared widely throughout the German territories. The many manuscripts and the popularity of the *Sachsenspiegel* texts furnish ample evidence that the book was conceived broadly enough to be valuable to a wide audience both inside and outside the German-speaking parts of the empire.

Eike's personal contribution is more than a mere collection of legal rules because these rules are encased in a narrative based on biblical wisdom and political theory. The clarity and breadth of the custumal indicate that Eike had theoretical interests and reflected upon the origins and workings of legal custom before setting down his interpretation. The custumal in its earliest forms profited not only from Eike's knowledge of the Bible and canon law—he incorporated papal decretals and Gratian on inherited custom of law (Johanek, 405)—and from his familiarity with German literature,[11] but also, and most important, from his extensive experience with legal procedure. Whether he actually served as a *Schöffe*, we do not know, but it is clear that he was not a legal scholar and was not formally trained in jurisprudence according to the practice of the Italian law schools. He instead offered readers a narrative shaped by his own personal perspectives (Kroeschell, "Rechtsaufzeichnung" 351). For example, in discussing legal jurisdiction, he is not afraid to support the emperor in the dispute between the primacy of empire or papacy (I 1). When he reconsiders the customs of serfdom or bondage, he presents his own vivid argument in the form of a *quaestio*[12] to prove that such practices are not supported by biblical tradition and, regardless of long-standing custom, are also not good legal custom (III 43).[13]

Since Eike's lawbook is both a theoretical and a practical guide primarily compiled from the actual practice of law, his designation, *Sachsenspiegel* (Saxon Mirror), exactly suits the text.[14] In medieval terms, the appropriate classification or title for this type of guide is "mirror" (G *Spiegel*; L *speculum*), hence the title of my translation, *The Saxon Mirror*.[15] The mirror genre examines the metaphysical and intellectual dimensions of subjects such as virtue, law, and rulership. Such mirrors, written in Latin, informed and instructed the next generation. Eike's lawbook fits this tradition, but, significantly, it also marks the first such instructional prose text to appear in the vernacular. Eike borrowed the concept from the earliest well-known twelfth-century mirror, Honorius Augustodunensis's *Speculum eccle-*

siae, in which the Bride of Christ looks in a mirror to find those faults in herself that might be objectionable to Christ:

Huius tabellae sit nomen: Speculum Ecclesiae. Hoc igitur speculum omnes sacerdotes ante oculos Ecclesiae expendant, ut sponsa Christi in eo videat quid adhuc sponso suo in se displiceat, et ad imaginem suam mores et actus suos componat.

[Let this list be called 'The Mirror of the Church.' Let all priests, therefore, present this mirror before the eyes of the church so that the bride of Christ may see in it what displeases her spouse in her and compose her own behavior and deeds according to that image.] (Migne, *PL*, vol. 172, c. 815–16)[16]

The mirror is thus a device for measuring practice against the ideal concept, thereby enabling the viewer (i.e., listener or reader) to correct flaws. Eike explains in the rhymed preface that his text should have the same title because it functions in like manner: "Spegel der Sassen / scal dit buk genant, / went Sassen recht is hir an bekant, / alse an eneme spegele de vrowen / er antlite scowen" [This book is called the Saxon mirror, since Saxon custom is given here in the same way that ladies observe their faces in a mirror] (rhymed preface, Eckhardt, *Lndr*, l. 178–82).[17]

As a metaphor for text, the mirror becomes the mediating component of the cognitive process by which reality (i.e., what one sees in the mirror) is reflected in order to be gauged against the ideal. Put another way, the text mirrors daily activities in the temporal world within the frame of eternal justice. Eike instructs the reader in this process by presenting the concept of legal custom in three dimensions: literal, ethical, and metaphysical (Kisch, "Biblical," 39). At the literal level, customary law is concerned with regulating events and providing remedies. At the moral level, law encompasses both rights and duties. Individuals improve themselves morally when they fulfill their legal responsibilities and learn right conduct. This means that customary law, education, and morally proper conduct are interdependent parts of a single whole. At the metaphysical level, Law finds its source in God, as stated in the first short prologue: "Got is selber recht, dar umme is im recht lip" [God is Law itself, therefore, justice is dear to him].[18] This ontological premise establishes an explicit, metaphysical foundation for legal custom for the first time in a secular, vernacular lawbook (*VL*, 2, c. 402; Kisch, *Sachsenspiegel*, 21–26). Moreover, it grounds all of Saxon custom in God-given law, thereby giving Saxony a definite place in salvation history (III 45).[19] This premise is evident in the opening words of the first prologue, where Eike appeals to God for insight: "Des heiligen geistis minne der sterke mine sinne das ich recht unde unrecht der sachsen bescheide noch gotis hulden unde noch der werlde vrumen" [May the love of the Holy Spirit sharpen my mind so that I may pronounce what is lawful and unlawful among the Saxons for the grace of God and the benefit of the world].[20] Once God has been invoked, if the text is to function like a mirror, then any judge or *Schöffe* would be able to glimpse the eternal law by consulting the book. In fact, the mirror "directs man beyond his temporal world to the real, eternal world" (Shinn, "Function," 62). Thus those who refer to the book when a complicated case arises come to know the customary law and, therefore, God by means of the mirror that is the text.

Accordingly, if we view the *Sachsenspiegel* texts in this way as a theoretical book, we find that it was considered a mirror of virtues. To the extent that it asserts the divine foundation of law, it follows that all who are involved in supporting the legal custom are participating in moral betterment. Support for this interpretation comes from the Franciscans, who showed almost as immediate and lively an interest in the custumal as they did in mirrors of virtues: they are known to have played a significant role in its dissemination in Magdeburg and Augsburg (Johanek, 416; Kroeschell, "Rechtswirklichkeit," 7).

As a mirror, Eike's book does not present specific cases. Instead, it teaches about the legal customs and procedures in the same way that mirrors of princes inform young rulers-to-be about the basic concepts and methods of rulership. The *Sachsenspiegel* texts thus offer a comprehensive framework that defines legal custom, explains legal procedures, and stipulates the conditions under which the reader should apply this knowledge to individual cases.

Scope and Content of the Custumal

The mirror metaphor is especially appropriate because it illustrates that the scope of the concept of custom for the mirror, like legal tradition, can reflect any aspect of human activity. Being inseparable from all other social institutions, oral traditional custom includes all the habits, rules, and mores that regulate social relations between individuals and groups in society from the village level to a large social-political entity such as the territory of Saxony. It is a set of rules for social conduct that evolved over time.

In order to understand the metaphorical framework in which people thought about legal rules according to the terminology of the *Mirror*, we must also look to the key Middle High German (MGH) term *recht* (n.)

and its connotations. This concept is decidedly different from modern assumptions concerning law. *Recht* translates as "law," but even our modern English term, as abstract as it is, has a much narrower range of meanings and is insufficient to convey the several aspects of *recht*. For example, *recht* can be accurately translated as "justice," "right," "righteousness," "rectitude," "uprightness," and "lawfulness." The complexity of this term must be recognized and understood because all of these connotations indicate a very different way of thinking about law and justice at a time when legal custom was oral and all actions had a moral component. Such a broad set of connotations makes it very difficult for us not to foist our own modern categories onto the text unless we look at the family of terms and metaphors connected with "law." As a result, the translation of the word in each instance depends on which aspect or connotation the translator considers to be essential to the passage.

At its very foundation, the original adjective coming from Germanic **rehta* (adj.) found in all the cognate languages meant "straight" or "unbent." It described the correct, straightforward way of doing things in terms of the customs or rules people lived by. In other words, customs were experienced as actions and behavior, not as a set of abstract rules. A number of nouns and verbs expressing central concepts of law also derive from the adjective. If *recht* (n.) is "lawfulness," then *unrecht* (n.) is "lawlessness." Hence, phrases such as *nach recht* indicate the proper, and therefore legal, way to do things.[21] Further, if *recht* (n.) translates as "right" in the moral sense, then its opposite, *unrecht*, means "wrong." The process by which a conflict or unlawful conduct is corrected or righted is the *gericht* (n.), or "court hearing." Amira phrased it thus: "Das gekrümmte Rechtsverhältnis wieder in die Richte zu bringen ist Beruf des 'Gerichts'" [The task of the court is to straighten out a 'bent' legal relationship] (*Germanisches Recht*, vol. 2, 148). *Recht* (adj.) also yields the noun *richter*, meaning the "judge" who sets the matter straight; his activity is *richten* (v.), "to make straight." Thus, what creates justice is the judge's authority to bring about the conditions for a judgment (i.e., to preside over a trial). A violation of the legal rules (primarily a felony) is called *ungericht* (n.), which in a literal sense meant something bent or made crooked. Although the literal meaning of *recht* as "straight" is no longer obvious in the *Saxon Mirror* because the text uses these words specifically as legal terms, its moral connotations continue to resonate.

These terms also can be found in modern German *Gerechtigkeit*, meaning "justice," and in *rechtschaffen*, which can be rendered as "upright" and "righteous." The English equivalents are actually cognates deriving from the same common Germanic source. They certify a fundamental metaphor dividing the world into right and wrong before the reception of Roman law in Germany and England. The basic metaphor of setting aright was also perceived in the twofold duty of the judge: first, to hear a case so that a judgment could be reached speedily, and second, to arrange some type of restitution for the injured party (II 25) that would correct the lawless situation and return it to its original, proper condition. The metaphors associated with these legal terms are therefore simply the first step in defining customary law and do not even begin to exhaust the concept.

Customary law as a concept in the *Sachsenspiegel* texts is extremely broad. *Recht* naturally applied to all people because everyone was expected to live according to the unwritten rules. At the same time, the term *recht* also referred to the rights and privileges of individuals acquired and upheld by long-standing custom. In addition, since no privilege exists without a corresponding responsibility or duty, *recht* also meant the duty of community members to know legal custom and to participate in the legal system in order to maintain justice in the community. Julius von Planck's summary elucidates the breadth of legal custom:

> Was zunächst das Wissen vom Recht angeht, so wird das deutsche Recht durch die Vorstellung beherrscht, dass durch die bestehende Rechtsordnung alle Vorkommnisse des Lebens im Voraus fest bestimmt und geordnet seien, dass es also überall nur darauf ankomme, den bestehenden, richtigen Rechtssatz aufzufinden.
>
> [As far as knowledge of law is concerned, the view in German law is that the established customs had already organized and accounted for all events of life with the result that the single procedure in every case is to determine the existing, *correct* legal rule for each situation.] (Planck, 87, emphasis in original)

According to Planck's assessment, everyone participated in all aspects of legal custom, thus implying that the participatory process itself is what creates justice. This evaluation is consistent with the *Saxon Mirror*, which notes the responsibility of the community members in a maxim formulated in terms of *recht*: "Wo der man recht vordert, da sal he rechtis phlegen unde helfen" [Wherever a man demands justice there must he answer to the law and foster it] (I 60). The text also makes clear what this maxim required of people—community cooperation. In the rural community, the freemen composed the judiciary; they were required to attend the regular court hearings and were called upon by the judge when necessary to render a judgment, which was then confirmed by consensus (I 18). Without the contribution of the members and a consensus on a judgment, there is no customary law. If these are the conditions necessary for customary law to exist in oral tradition, then how does the creation of a written lawbook alter customary law?

Even though customary law may have been long transmitted in oral form, once a lawbook like Eike's is written, the characteristics of orality are superseded—if only gradually. A written text actually made it easier to check on consistency in handing down legal judgments, and once consistency was recognized as valuable, it eventually conferred normative character on the lawbook. In other words, the concept of precedent only became possible once written lawbooks were created (Lieberwirth, *Entstehung*, 15). Of course, the potential of such correctives was only gradually recognized. Meanwhile, the oral traditional nature of legal custom continued. In fact, many stylistic and syntactic elements of the *Sachsenspiegel* texts—including the use of maxims, pronouns without antecedents, and phrases such as "now hear" are typically oral and continue even as late as the fourteenth century.[22] As for the oral nature of legal procedure, it was scarcely affected.

Legal procedure was experienced as formal spoken language accompanied by prescribed gesture (II 4). Oral practice continued in all procedures of the law court, including pleas, contracts, payments, transfers, oaths, and appeals. Evidence was also oral, as it had to come from a guarantor, an eyewitness, or a witness who recalled information from memory, since written records were rare. Legal practice was thus forced to remain oral as long as a support system of written documentation and court records was largely unavailable.[23] Moreover, the fact that Saxon customs were suddenly written down did not necessarily result in their being completely delimited.

For these reasons, custumals are not to be read as we read modern written codes, that is, with the expectation of a fixed, systematic presentation. Several of the earliest *Sachsenspiegel* manuscripts already exhibit a great deal of variation, suggesting that no reader or copyist thought of the text as an unchanging, prescriptive system. Instead, scribes and their patrons treated the lawbook as a flexible guide that they could adapt to their own needs because they frequently made changes that deviated from acknowledged local or territorial custom outside of Saxony (see "Reception" below). The lesson here is that a custumal is best understood today in the context of its oral traditional foundation. This means one must know what not to expect: a custumal is not a legislated code of law in the modern sense, has no normative function, is not fixed, and is not an exhaustive account of legal custom.

It is not my intention here to deny the fixity and authority of a written lawbook. It is, however, equally important to recognize that although custom in text gains authority because its physical form changes little, the set of accepted legal rules was, at that time, far more extensive than any custumal. In other words, the contents of the lawbook did not exhaust customary law. In this sense it is correct to say that the law of tradition and custom remains the foundation of Eike's text. He himself speaks of a tradition that has no single source: "Dit recht hebbe ek selve nicht irdacht, / it habbet van aldere an unsik gebracht / Unse guden vorevaren" [I did not invent this law myself; it has been handed down to us by our benevolent ancestors] (rhymed preface, Eckhardt, *Lndr*, l. 151–53). Typical of the *Saxon Mirror* is an elementary trait of orality in the concept that customary law is unconfined or unlimited by a text. It is this particular concept that accounts for its flexibility. Even so, one need not assess this fundamental orality as leading to a contradiction between the desire for a lawbook on the one hand and distrust of the written form on the other. Instead, the *Saxon Mirror* operates as part of the slow, uneven transformation from orality to literacy in all aspects of culture.

Also contributing to the flexibility of the *Sachsenspiegel* texts is the fact that customary law, like all human institutions, is constantly in flux. Consequently, it is best to view the written custumal with more than 450 manuscript versions as participating in that flux. We have thirteenth-century texts that are thought to resemble Eike's original closely, and we also have numerous manuscripts of the expanded fourth redaction (see "Reception," "Choice of Text" below). Each *Sachsenspiegel* manuscript freezes one moment in the evolution of the judicial system and is not an exhaustive nor necessarily accurate record of custom. What is more, it need not be. Lacking the precise formulation of a code, their unsystematic, open-ended organization allows for much of the flexibility of the legal tradition as practiced by the judiciary.[24]

As mentioned above, this open-endedness meant that the lawbook was merely a subset of a customary law that was complete and existed in the oral tradition beyond the book. Eike acknowledges this concept and signals its implications in the first prologue:

> bitte ich czu helfe alle gute lute di rechtis gern ab keine rede begeine di min tumme sin vormide, unde da dis buch nicht von en spricht das si das noch rechte bescheiden noch irme sinne so sis rechste wissen.
>
> [I request the support of all law-abiding people who desire justice. If they encounter a legal dispute that I have omitted from this book because of my limited knowledge, I request that they reach a determination according to justice to their best knowledge and discretion.]

Eike is not concerned about having omitted a part of the law; rather, he warns that he may have omitted an example of a particular type of dispute and is asking his readers to apply legal custom based on their community's knowledge, which is not exhausted in the book. In fact, the texts never use the term *recht* to refer to a written document. With this all-encompassing legal tradition in mind, Planck's point about procedure ("the single procedure in every case is to determine the right law for each situation," cited above) elucidates the basic premise of the lawbook: the essential and critical part of judicial procedure is the proper application of legal rules to each particular case. Hence we find the unspoken conviction that customary law is universally applicable and at the same time cannot be completely contained within a text.

Since customary law is not a clearly defined text or code, its application is based on individual judgment and interpretation. Put another way, customary law is a social phenomenon, like language: it exists in individual application but is invalid unless the community of speakers—in this case the members of the judiciary—acknowledges its meaning. The judge may not determine a judgment. He needs a decision from the judgment finders, who must determine which custom applies to the specific situation. This procedure required the judgment finder to make a determination according to his own best interpretation of the legal rules. However, determining a judgment was not arbitrary. The majority had to agree to each judgment before any final determination could be reached in a case (I 18, 19; Planck, 99). Since legal judgments required the consensus of the members of the judiciary, it is clear that the responsibility for legal decisions rested with the community and not with the individual. Consequently, the analogy with language illustrates that the system evolved requiring a consensus among the judiciary for each judgment because custom exists only in the community. If consensus fails, then customary law fails because it did not apply to a given situation. Each time a case was tried, the custom had to be reestablished, and thus individual settlements and judgments had no normalizing function.

Viewing customary law in thirteenth- and fourteenth-century Germany in terms of the heritage of the oral tradition—that is, in terms of the continued flexibility of both customary law and its textual means of transmission—is more precise than studying the texts alone. This approach is also more consistent with the concept of custom portrayed in the *Sachsenspiegel* texts than is Fritz Kern's older interpretation that folk law is simply the "good old law" inherited from the forefathers and maintained because it is good (Kern, 23–29).[25] Instead, custom is defined as an inherited, constantly reevaluated and modified yet agreed upon set of habits that fits any occasion and brings about just settlements.

Reiner Schulze summarizes a discussion concerning a redefinition of customary law as "habits of law" that stresses the essential orality and social existence of these habits. As he explains, the term *customary law* is inadequate:

> "Rechtsgewohnheiten" wären vielmehr als Bestandteile einer Kultur zu begreifen, in der Rechtsentwicklung und gerichtliche Streitentscheidung weithin noch nicht durch Gesetzgebung und Rechtswissenschaft vorgeprägt sind und nicht auf den damit verbundenen, schriftlichen Dartellungsweisen des Rechts als Gesetz, als Begriff und als System beruhen.
>
> [Rather, "habits of law" should be understood as components of a culture in which the development of laws and legal settlements are not at all as yet predetermined by legislation and legal theory and also do not depend upon any written formulation of law as code, concept, or system.] (13)[26]

Thus customary oral traditional law, however different from contemporary systematic law, is the inherited foundation upon which the subsequent legal developments in Germany have been built (Dilcher, "Rechtsgewohnheit," 27).

The *Sachsenspiegel* texts are the earliest evidence of a gradual transformation from oral legal custom to systematic, codified law in German legal history (R. Schulze, 14). In general, the innovations in these texts most likely resulted from political expansion, population growth, increase of social stratification, legal enactments, and accommodations to canon law occurring since Carolingian times (Dilcher, "Rechtsgewohnheit," 27).

Because we have no written custumals from the tenth to the thirteenth centuries—between the Latin codes of the seventh to ninth centuries and the earliest *Sachsenspiegel* texts—we must rely on the contrasts between *Sachsenspiegel* and the Latin, Carolingian *leges* in order to discover the significant innovations in the legal system put forth in the *Sachsenspiegel* texts. It is possible in the space of this introduction to list the developments and innovations presented in the *Mirror*, but not to discuss the many factors that brought about these changes. The Latin codes produced by each of the tribal groups (Burgundians, Lombards, Franks, etc.) after they gained control of Roman towns and settlements exhibit a dependence on Roman law. The only two early codes showing limited Roman influence and therefore reflecting Germanic customs, are the *Lex Salica* of the Franks, written in

Latin, and the Anglo-Saxon laws written in the vernacular (Drew, 25). However, one later set of laws, the *Lex Saxonum* [Saxon Law] of 945 pertains directly to the history of Saxon customs. This text marks the beginning of the integration of Saxons into the Frankish empire and Roman church and is therefore the text in which the greatest similarity between the Carolingian and thirteenth-century legal custom might be expected. Nevertheless, a comparison yields a distinct lack of continuity. The similarities are few: where the *Lex Saxonum* devotes 77 percent of the text to crimes, the *Sachsenspiegel* texts devote only 26 percent. New in *Sachsenspiegel* texts are items pertaining to procedure that define the requirements and duties of offices such as judge, bailiff, advocate, and the manner of their appointment. Approximately 44 percent of the text is devoted to these items whereas the *Lex Saxonum* lacks procedural topics completely (Theuerkauf, 416–20). With this study, the earlier thesis postulating a continuity of legal concepts that might be traced in German legal history has been rejected (R. Schulze, 12; Theuerkauf, 419). Because we have no other written evidence of Saxon customs, we may accept those topics and concepts that are not recorded in the Saxon law but are discussed in the *Sachsenspiegel* texts as innovations even though we cannot date their inception.

The following discussion focuses on four specific, fundamental, and far-reaching developments. The first, and perhaps the most obvious, development is the explicit integration of Christianity by accommodating German legal custom to the legal thought of the canonists;[27] second is the establishment of territorial law; third, the expansion of a complex judiciary with the king remaining the highest dispenser of justice; and fourth, the formation of a criminal code.

Integration of Christianity into custom was the necessary result of religious conversion, but the second fundamental change was actually an innovation: the concept of territorial law resulted from a new type of legal thinking. The early system of *leges* had been built on personal law in which each individual was held to the laws and procedures of his ancestors no matter whether he lived under Roman or any other rule. I refer to this personal law as tribal law because, in effect, it represented the customs of the tribes. Franks were tried under Frankish law, and Burgundians and Saxons under their own. Only later, as kings gained greater and more centralized administrative control, did tribal laws gain territorial jurisdiction.

The next step in tribal law becoming territorial law was spurred by German colonization of the east. Rolf Lieberwirth points out that Eike wrote his custumal in clearance lands, where new rules were being made as settlements spread (*Entstehung*, 17). This area attracted colonists from several different German-speaking regions, and when they came, they all brought their own customs and dialects with them.[28] These variant customs gradually were melded into one set of rules for all. Once this process was recognized—that is, by the time the *Mirror* was written—territorial law was an established concept. At the same time, legal custom continued to respect personal or tribal law in specified instances (I 17, 19; III 69, 71, 73).

The third but most radical change is the grounding of Law and Justice in God and the secular state (and with it, the expansion of the judiciary). No longer were the forebears the primary source of law. If the oral customary tradition had previously needed no state sanction and no legislation or objectified code behind it, by the thirteenth century it did. At this time the concept of legal custom came to be firmly rooted in the state ("Deutsches Recht," *LexMA* 3, c. 777–81). From the outset, the *Saxon Mirror* points to God as the source of law and justice, and ascribes the specific, secular application of law to imperial governance that began with Constantine and Charlemagne, who gave certain laws and privileges to the Saxons (second prologue). The passage does not imply, however, that all laws derived from the king. The statement that presents the king as judge above all people and promulgator of laws further emphasizes that the administration of justice was delegated from a central point (III 26), which means that all judicial authority came from the king. He delegated his royal judicial authority to the judges and thereby gave them the right to preside over a superior court. The king's court was the highest and ultimate court of appeals.

The Carolingian *leges* report the existence of the king's court and the court of the hundred only. In contrast, the *Saxon Mirror* records a proliferation of magistrates and courts, sometimes with overlapping jurisdiction, as well as a new complexity in the system (Lieberwirth, *Entstehung*, 15). These tribunals included the royal court, the count's court, the *Schultheiss*'s court, and, finally, the local court. The king delegated his judicial authority to the prince, and the prince, in turn, to his count, who then delegated that authority to his *Schultheiss*. Only the highest three levels of judges presided over capital crimes. The local judge appears not to have had superior jurisdiction.[29] The fact that the number and level of courts below the royal court increased means that the court system adapted to accommodate greater social stratification.

The *Mirror* speaks little of the prince's court and focuses instead on the count's court and its relation to other courts. The count presided over the superior court—called the "blood" or "high" court—that had jurisdiction over criminal acts punishable by death or mutilation but the text says very little about mutilating punishments (II 16, 17). In defining the superior court, the underlying concept was the shedding of blood; if the wound inflicted drew blood, the suit belonged in the high court, and the penalty equally could require the blood of the perpetrator if convicted.[30] The count's court in particular had jurisdiction over civil cases involving all freemen, including those at the level of the lower nobility. The judges of a superior court also included the *pfalzgraf, landgraf*, and certain advocates (III 52). At this level the judge dealt with all disputes regarding property in full ownership not subject to rents or duties (allod) (I 59).

The count's court convened three times a year at a fixed location. To hold a legal hearing, the count had to have in attendance his *Schultheiss*, the *Schöffen*, and the court officer or bailiff (III 61). The judge presided over the hearing, the *Schöffen* determined the judgment, and the bailiff enforced the decision (III 56). The count's appointed *Schultheiss* was actually more than a court officer. He appears to have represented the count as judge when he presided over cases postponed by the higher court in order to pursue fact-finding or to determine a final settlement. His singular function in Saxon custom, however, was to hear complaints against the count himself (I 59, III 52). The *Schöffen* in the count's court were responsible for applying the law. Their charge was to know the legal custom well, hand down rulings in the course of building a case, and determine the final judgment. Because the *Schöffen* formed a select group, it was extremely difficult to challenge their judgment unless one belonged to the same class (II 13).

A lower court with a locally elected judge also plays a significant role in the *Saxon Mirror*. This local judge presided over the lower court having jurisdiction over all petty crimes and red-handed deeds (I 55–57) carrying a sentence of lesser corporal punishment (e.g., flogging and cropping hair), as well as all the disputes of free small landholders and tenants. Exactly which cases the local judges actually tried remains unclear in the text, and not enough external information exists to clarify the local judge's jurisdiction.[31]

Another problem is the lack of precision in the text itself, especially with the simple word "judge." The *Sachsenspiegel* texts themselves fail to distinguish between the levels of courts because they use the term "judge" without stipulating whether the court being referred to is a count's, a *Schultheiss*'s, or a local judge's court. Consequently, since *richter* (judge) occurs in the text with high frequency but without qualification, it is very difficult to ascertain what level of judge presides over a specific civil suit in the general territorial laws of the *Saxon Mirror*. To be sure, a hearing of the superior court was normally designated by the phrase "royal judicial authority" (*ban*) but this qualifier does not always appear. Only the illustrations distinguish with any regularity between local judge, count or king using the formal idiom of costume symbolism. The images represent the king with a crown, the count with his identifying head covering and the local judge with his hat. These drawings cannot be used as a definitive guide, however; when the pictures are consulted to aid in interpreting the text, one must take into account that the illustrators may have misinterpreted the text.

This many-tiered court system engaged a large number of people in the judiciary. According to the general territorial law, the judiciary consisted of a judge, *Schultheiss*, bailiff, the *Schöffen*, the village headman, and the freemen who participated in the legal system at the village level. Freemen were required to attend a specified court according to their legal status and that was determined by type of land they held: the free landowners attended the count's court, the free peasant landholders went to *Schultheiss*'s court, and the free tenants and sharecroppers to the local judge's court (I 2). We may conclude from this evidence that the court jurisdictions were also defined by the social and legal status of their judiciary and litigants. The division between high and low courts was not simply one of jurisdiction over grave versus petty crimes, but rather one in which the rights given by social status were recognized and guarded. The lower courts only dealt with civil suits brought by freemen with or without land holdings, and not with any suit against nobles of any level. Similarly, the princes of the realm attended and brought suits only to the king's court. However, an appeal of a judgment at the count's court apparently was taken directly to the king's court.[32]

In the lower court, the entire village — that is, all the free landed men — composed the judiciary. Their most important function was to make determinations as the hearing proceeded. These decisions, including a final judgment, were made by consensus. This judgment could then be challenged by an individual in the judiciary, but only with support of the majority. In practical terms, this meant that a dissenting villager who found that a different rule needed to be applied in the particular situation had to convince his neighbors that their decision was incorrect and that his own application of the legal rules was better (II 13). Appeals of a final judgment or verdict from any court could be taken to the king. The village headman played a special role in the judiciary; he made indictments in cases of assault, open threats, or failure to attend a court session (I 2, 13), and he also served as witness in the count's court.

All the able-bodied members of a village or judicial district were responsible for responding to the hue and cry to protect the community in case of natural disaster and to pursue a criminal when a crime was committed. If the offender was caught in flagrante or with signs of the crime on his person, he was tried immediately. If the local judge was unavailable, provisions allowed an interim judge to be elected on the spot for a summary trial (I 56).

The fourth significant development noted in the *Sachsenspiegel* is a rudimentary penal code generated by the direct action of the German rulers. Not content merely to delegate responsibility within the justice system, they also gave vital impetus to the formation of a system of criminal law. In the wake of the papacy's *pax dei* movement, they took an active role in promulgating a series of truces and peace ordinances in their own right. Each of the peace ordinances was valid for a specified period of time only, but they exerted an unmistakable influence on local laws and provided a new, overarching framework for dealing with criminal acts.

Much earlier, the Germanic judicial system had provided a forum for peaceful settlement of claims for personal injury and criminal acts. To achieve a settlement between parties and avoid a feud, it was necessary to have a procedure for proof of a deed and its perpetrator, and a means to assess damages and make restitution. When no physical proof of guilt existed, accusations and claims were proved or disproved by compurgation which permitted a man in good public standing to absolve himself of accusation with a "cleansing" oath, in conjunction with the supporting oath of his kin or "oathhelpers." Criminal acts such as homicide were treated as civil suits for damages (Drew, 33). To settle such suits and avoid a blood feud, the laws provided a fixed scale of composition or tariff amounts called wergeld. The wergeld tables were fixed according to the value of each individual based on his or her social and legal status. For homicide, the dead man's total wergeld has to be paid to his family; for personal injury, a scale determined the amount paid. The laws do not state what happened when one of the parties refused the decision of the court or could not pay the wergeld. Scholars have suggested that the inability to pay wergeld tariffs caused many families to fall into servitude (Drew 50).

By the thirteenth century, the influence of royal and territorial peace ordinances was being felt. Heinrich's Truce (*Treuga Heinrici*) of 1224 already had contributed directly to Eike's *Sachsenspiegel*, which incorporated its list of criminal punishments. In later versions such as the Wolfenbüttel manuscript, additional penalties were added from the Imperial Landpeace of Mainz (*Mainzer Reichslandfriede*, 1235). This document was copied into the Wolfenbüttel manuscript beginning on the very first folio as a preamble to the custumal. This position of primacy gives the impression that the lawbook was promulgated by the king and consequently lends the *Mirror* the authoritative and normative character of a code.[33]

The *Saxon Mirror* specifically mentions the *Imperial Landpeace*, too (II 66). At first these peace ordinances were intended to eliminate blood feuds, and to do so they designated certain days and places free of violence, and protected certain people (women, children, Jews, priests) at all times.[34] Soon, however, the idea of a limited peace grew into the concept of a general peace and its violation (Hirsch, *Gerichtsbarkeit*, 85); this gradual change in thinking forced a steady shift from a wergeld system of composition to a system of criminal law (Bar, 99). In addition, the stated penalties gradually established the new principle of public and equal punishment regardless of class; physical correctives then began to replace composition payments in cases where the amount of wergeld had been based on class (Bar, 99; Scheele, *Delikte*, 59). Committing a crime and breaking the peace at the same time made the crime more serious and therefore subject to additional fines or penalties (I 69; II 10).

The rudiments of the new penal code also required a set of legal procedures. The *Sachsenspiegel* texts describe procedures that deal with claims for injury, criminal charges, and procedures for repayment of a debt. Because the *Lex Saxonum* did not record such information, and because the *Saxon Mirror* shows the two systems coexisting (Theuerkauf, 420), we cannot determine exactly what changes took place or when, but we do know that physical punishment began replacing wergeld for homicide and other grave crimes. In addition to recording the criminal punishments, the *Saxon Mirror* retains composition tables such as those in the Germanic laws in which the listed wergeld amounts reflect legal and social status (III 46). The *Saxon Mirror* refers to the wergeld of animals in spite of the fact that the *wer* in wergeld means "human." The older laws had specific terms for the value of beasts, but this semantic shift demonstrates that terms had become archaic by Eike's time. The tables themselves categorize animals according to their usefulness as food and for labor (III 52). Apparently, as the system transformed itself from a composition to a penal system, it needed to retain the wergeld tables as a means for assessing damage and punitive payments.

The *Saxon Mirror* focuses heavily on violent crimes discovered soon enough for the community to pursue the culprit, a focus lacking in the thirteenth-century southern German translations of Eike's text, the *Deutsch-*

enspiegel [German Mirror] and *Schwabenspiegel* [Swabian Mirror]. The advantage of such cases is that the felon is known, and the evidence is still available to convict him easily. The many court procedures outlined in the *Saxon Mirror*—bringing charges (I 66), bringing charges against a person who is absent (I 67) or against a dead man (I 64), challenging someone to a trial by battle (I 50; III 34), when witnesses are required (II 22; III 19), when a spokesman is disallowed (III 30), how to judge crimes (II 13)—reveal both a traditional and a completely new approach to the process of reaching a judgment. The traditional and habitual reliance on compurgation with the aid of oathhelpers continued to be important. This older concept of proof was established on formal rules and requirements. For example, supplying the required number of oathhelpers brought one closer to winning the decision, and it was essential to be formally correct in word and gesture. This emphasis on formal procedure partially explains the rather detailed descriptions of procedure; for example, for transforming limited outlawry into imperial outlawry (I 71),[35] determining a judgment (II 18), and appealing a judgment (II 13). Many of the chapters referred to here not only outline procedure, but also provide the exact words to be used.

Even in Carolingian times the courts had relied heavily on concrete evidence, especially for red-handed deeds. In the old system people had not been concerned that compurgation and cleansing oaths might be unsuccessful means for discovering facts. The new approach attested to in the *Mirror* signals an attempt to ascertain factual information by placing increasing dependence on witnesses, whose testimony was understood as a means of establishing facts (Kroeschell, *Rechtsgeschichte*, 268).

Other procedures for reaching an acceptable judgment existed as well, including the three ordeals of carrying the glowing iron, thrusting an arm up to the elbow into boiling water, and fighting against a hired champion.[36] The word "ordeal" (OE *ordâl*) originally meant like G *Urteil* a "judicial decision" or "verdict." According to the *Saxon Mirror*, the trials of boiling water and hot iron were reserved only for defendants whose legal capacity was limited because of a previous conviction or a disreputable profession. Unlike the other two ordeals, the trial by combat carried no stigma and could be used by those who enjoyed full legal rights. To settle a civil or criminal dispute, any man could challenge to a trial by combat any person who was his equal or was lower by birth (I 43, 63; III 35). The text also mentions an ordeal by water that was used to determine who had a rightful claim to a property when other means had been unsuccessful (III 21; IV 44).

Any convicted felon charged with a second offense suffered serious legal disadvantages that led to the ordeals. The compurgation system permitting cleansing oaths as one important means of arriving at a judgment was not available to a second offender. This greatly curtailed his ability to win his case, because the legal capacity of a person to clear himself with an oath would have been withdrawn before the earlier punishment, and even if the person were able to make a money payment in place of physical punishment, he never regained all his previous rights. The most serious penalty was the permanent loss of all rights, called "attainder," which made it nearly impossible for someone previously convicted to defend himself in court if he were ever again accused of a crime (II 14). The *Mirror* also deals with the community's inability to carry out punishments. If a convicted felon slipped away and did not comply with the court decision, outlawry was the judge's only method of bringing him to justice. Outlawry was an attempt to prosecute someone who has become a fugitive from the law by temporarily revoking his legal rights and refusing him shelter.

The *Saxon Mirror* occupies a middle place in the transition from old composition remedies to the developing list of punishments. Even though the *Mirror* recorded this transformation when it was not yet complete, the evidence affirms that the landpeace enactments promoted three important legal developments. First, there was a shift from protecting certain places, objects, and individuals to a direct listing of punishable offenses. Two other shifts also took place: a move from composition to physical punishment for criminal acts regardless of social rank, and a strong tendency to eliminate legal recourse of individuals to feud and revenge, which previously had been allowed (Scheele, *Delikte*, 58).

It is easy to interpret the construction of this penal code as a process by which people in medieval Germany gradually came to distinguish between civil and criminal law, but this merely reflects the outcome; namely, the relatively clear modern divisions.[37] Indeed, the changes involve a thorough reassessment of the concept of crime and the means of dealing with it. First, the notion that an act could be redeemed through payment based on the social status of the victim shifted to one in which physical punishment was inflicted on the malefactor regardless of his or her status. A compensation payment evidently was no longer considered an adequate settlement. Along with a new concept of crime came a shift in responsibility for providing justice and dealing with an offender. Instead of a crime becoming a source of a private family vendetta or being settled by payment to the victim, it was referred to an expanded state justice system with community enforcement of penalties.

The development of a system of criminal punishments relied on an appropriately organized justice system with an adequate number of judges and magistrates able to enforce sentences. In the *Saxon Mirror*, the system is regulated by the royal court as the ultimate court of appeals. We know that during the eleventh and twelfth centuries the number of judges increased and that many court jurisdictions began to overlap, but because we know little about actual legal practice in the lower courts, how this came about and whether their numbers were adequate is not known (R. Schulze, 16). The text also refers to the superior and lower courts, which may indicate that the justice system was able to deal with the rudimentary penal code. Given the elaborate set of punishments and composition tables for those with rights and for those whose rights had been curtailed in previous convictions, it would not have been possible to support customary law and administer justice without an organized state justice system. However, it is just as important to recognize that what the lawbook contains may be partly actual practice and partly an ideal that the author or redactor wished to see put into practice.

Even though it may contain legal rules that were simply desirable, but not yet put into practice, or no longer in practice, the *Saxon Mirror* is still a sensitive barometer of social values. The customs were grounded in the daily, material affairs of Saxon agrarian communities, and because they regulated land rights, community cooperation, and neighborly relations, they reveal a great deal about social priorities. One priority was the protection of women, children, and clergy from violence, another was the protection of the rights of ethnic groups such as the Wends already living in the region, and immigrants such as the Swabians.

When Eike wrote the *Sachsenspiegel*, Saxony east of the Elbe River experienced unique conditions because it was still being actively colonized. Colonization created new rules and privileges concerning the peasants' ownership and inheritance of real property and the size of their landholdings. The purpose of these advantages was to entice settlers from the western German territories to the new clearance lands (Rösener, 229). And the settler came—clearing forests, draining marshes, and laying out fields on the fertile loess plains that allowed for larger and more productive fields than in the west. The colonists tended to arrange their houses in a cluster, at least close enough so that their fields were beyond the house and yardland, and beyond those fields were the pasturage areas and forests where the animals grazed (Rösener, 47).

The colonists who cleared the land often managed to gain several privileges for themselves. First, they gained heritable rights to their landholdings and also to the buildings on the property (II 21). They also held the right to use their land without any manorial dependence of the type known in western Germany. For these holdings they owed only standard dues and limited service obligations (II 58) and were frequently exempted from the death tax (heriot) to the lord. Furthermore, limits were placed on when and how a tenant could be expelled from his leasehold (II 59). These landholders thus gained some degree of personal freedom and are referred to by scholars as "free peasants."[38] The *Saxon Mirror* also substantiates the greater degree of freedom for villages that had special communal and jurisdictional rights (I 60; II 55) such as electing the judge to preside over the local court (I 56, Rösener, 229). In addition, each village held meetings with its headman regarding its own affairs and made improvements based on majority decision (II 55).

The text mentions these privileges as having been established in clearance lands (III 80) yet does not provide enough detail to define a village as a commune. What the text also fails to reveal is the extent or uniformity of these privileges. One must therefore assume that the privileges of peasants varied from place to place. Nevertheless, the generalization can be made that peasants in Saxony enjoyed greater freedom than those anywhere else in Europe (Rösener, 231).

A peasant with a wife, children, and dependents (including servants) lived in a house with stalls for livestock and a fenced yard for geese and chickens (II 50, 53). Beyond the yard was a vegetable and fruit garden. Immediately adjacent to one family's yard and fence was the next family's house and yard. Rules for safety and maintaining good neighborly relations were based on common sense but were made explicit. To reduce the risk of fire danger, a person's ovens had to be three feet from the neighbor's fence; for reasons of health and aesthetics, his cess pits had to be enclosed and located at least three feet from the neighbor's property (II 49, 51). Although each family grew garden produce for its own use, a portion of it, and of the crops and livestock, had to be paid in tithes, each on a specified day (II 48). The village community paid a herdsman to take all the grazing animals to the pastures (II 54). Since pasturage was very important as the primary means of feeding the animals, each family had rights to the common grazing areas. These rights were carefully protected, and anyone using the wrong section of grazing land was fined (II 48).

In addition to producing enough for their own household, peasants sometimes had to cultivate the lord's fields. In the three-field system of crop rotation used in fourteenth-century Saxony, the work of all the peasants had to be centrally organized according to the village headman's (and occasionally the lord's) directions. Even when services were not demanded, as in a manorial system, each peasant needed to know which of the fields were his to plow and which would lie fallow. The *Saxon Mirror* provides remedies in the event that a peasant plows the the wrong field, which means that such mistakes were frequent and that a great deal of coordination was required for the three-field crop rotation to function (II 46). In fact, the three-field system was a significant impetus in the creation of rural communes in the colonial clearance areas because it forced people to coordinate their work (Rösener, 157).

Because Saxony was settled by Germans and Dutch from several dialect areas, their dialects inevitably coalesced to produce a new one called East Middle German.[39] The several tribal identities of the settlers also were blended until differing customs were accommodated. By the thirteenth century, Saxon customs acknowledged the region's multiethnic and multilingual character. The *Saxon Mirror* describes the special protection within customary law given to minorities, women, Jews, and others, and it also recognizes and respects the legal rules of the other German territories, including the recently colonized Marches in the east. Since a few non-Saxon customs are given consideration in the *Sachsenspiegel*, it seems likely that the colonial areas permitted the many settlers from western regions such as Swabia or Franconia to adapt gradually (I 29, 30). For example, every person had the right to hear the complaint or charges brought against him or his ward (who might be a woman) in his own language (III 71). The language of every judicial hearing was German, but the Wends could have translators. The Wends also lived under their own laws within Saxony (III 73).

All women and children normally had the protection of a guardian who represented them in any legal action, but the *Mirror* assigns them additional safeguards and rights as well (I 11, 23, 32). For example, minors and the physically and mentally handicapped were eligible to inherit (I 3, 4, 5), but their guardians were not always the legal heirs. Because a guardian had to account for the ward's assets to the legal heir, he could not squander them. Other legal rules ensured that heirs were not disinherited unlawfully (I 32). Minors could not be beaten or given severe criminal sentences even if they committed serious injury or homicide (II 65); instead, the child's guardian was required to pay the indemnity fine or the wergeld (II 65).

Although women were disadvantaged before a court of law because they could not speak for themselves but needed a guardian to speak for them (II 63), they also had rights protected by custom. A woman had the right to initiate a suit in court concerning a charge of rape (II 64), and she also had the right to own real property (I 45), to claim her morning gift upon her own oath once she was widowed (I 21, 46), and to prosecute her guardian directly if caught stealing from her or otherwise misusing her assets (I 41, 44). If she proved her case, the court would assume guardianship and grant the woman control of her real property. No one could remove a widow from land legally designated for her lifelong use (I 21; III 74, 75), and no one could evict a pregnant widow from her property (III 38). Despite these safeguards, women still were left vulnerable in terms of their legal status. The wergeld value of women was far less than that of men. Each woman received 50 percent of her husband's wergeld and compensation (III 46), and each girl and unmarried woman was allotted half the compensation allowed for men of her status (III 46).[40]

The father of the peasant household was the guardian of the wife (III 46), children, and dependents (I 11, 23). He provided for them by caring for the oxen and horses and by working in the fields plowing, sowing and reaping the crops. The grain crops were so precious that theft of grain was a capital crime (II 37). When yields were low the community faced famine, but when yields were high, the father still had to deliver a portion of his harvest in rents and tithes to the lord. Originally paid in kind, these dues were often commuted to money payments. The *Mirror* provides a calendar of due dates and a scale of money payments along with a detailed explanation of how the ground rents and tithes, when paid in kind, were measured and collected (II 58).

Inheritance—namely, the transfer of property—was probably the most important issue for families and kin groups. Family members inherited up to the seventh degree of consanguinity (I 3).[41] Real property owned or held in tenancy could be passed on to an heir or heirs. Freeholds and leaseholds were inherited along with their buildings (II 43), but if someone other than the person with right of possession built on the land, the buildings could not be inherited (II 21, 53).

Movable property was also of great interest. The personal nature and economic value of a woman's dowry and personal belongings necessary for her role as homemaker (including geese and chickens as well as household items) are indicated by the fact that these items were inherited by the woman's closest female blood relative if she had no daughter (I 5, 24). The military outfit of a knight—including his horse, armor, camp cot, washbasin, sheet, and blanket—reflected his role and status in society and could be inherited only by his closest male blood relative if he had no son (I 22). The concept behind these and similar laws is kinship, one of the basic building blocks of a community, and these laws reveal that in fourteenth-century Saxony, the extended family was as significant a social and legal bond as marriage. The division of certain goods as belonging to the male line and others to the female line appears to support the thesis that there was indeed a household division of labor between men and women. It appears that the husband used tools and animals, worked the fields, and prepared the raw materials for the family's survival. The wife's domain appears to have been the yard, where she tended the geese, chickens, and sheep. Working with raw materials that had been made available by her husband, she in turn made them into goods directly usable by humans such as food and clothing. All the animals she owned and was responsible for were eaten, and the sheep provided wool which she turned into cloth. (Kuchenbuch, 159–62).

Context and Reception of the *Sachsenspiegel*

The creation of a written custumal was not an odd idea in Eike's time. A movement toward codification emerged following Gratian's decretals (ca. 1140), which induced people to commit to writing customary laws in the second half of the twelfth century. These custumals, written in Latin, were often produced by jurists educated in the law who were also knowledgeable about its practice. The important "Tractatus de legibus et consuetudinibus regni Angliae," previously attributed to Ranulph de Glanville, was written in 1187 as part of this movement (Hall, introduction). In the thirteenth century a vernacularization led by the *Mühlhäuser Rechtsbuch* and *Sachsenspiegel* also began to spread to France, where the codification of customs reached a high point at the end of the century with the *Coutumes de Beauvaisis* by Philippe de Beaumanoir. During this same period, laws normally presented orally were committed to writing in Norway (*Borgarthingslög*), in Sweden (*Westgötalagh*), and in Iceland (*Grágás*) (*Medieval Scandinavia*, 383–86). The laws of these northern lands were scarcely touched by Roman or canon law. But of this entire movement, the German lawbooks, specifically the *Sachsenspiegel* and the *Sächsisches Weichbild* (an adaptation for a municipal context), had considerably broader, even international influence. Within Germany, the southern territories adjusted the *Sachsenspiegel* to fit the local customs and accommodate some Roman and canon law not current in Saxony. Outside of Germany, Eike's work, together with a collection of *Schöffen* judgments, enjoyed excellent reception in central Europe, including Poland, Ukraine, Prussia, and Silesia.[42] The High German translation, the *Schwabenspiegel*, influenced law in Hungary and in Bohemia, where it became the foundation of Czech law (*LexMA*, 7, c. 519–21).[43]

The date of Eike's original text is based on internal evidence. Eike took into consideration the *Treuga Heinrici* of 1224, which gives us the terminus post quem. Similarly, Eike's failure to consider the *Imperial Landpeace of Mainz* of 1235 means that the manuscript must have been completed before that time. It may easily have taken him a decade to assemble fully his text, and there are indications in the earliest manuscript groups that he continued to amend his work and may well have produced a second version.[44]

Planned as a repository of legal custom, Eike's text did not originally have the status of binding law and is, therefore, not a legal code. However, the rapid, widespread and thorough reception of the *Sachsenspiegel* by means of manuscript copies and translations in cities and territories beyond Saxony swiftly transformed the compendium into the authoritative model code copied and adapted throughout German-speaking areas, including the Netherlands. Even the *Weistümer* (collection of court decisions) indicate that the *Sachsenspiegel* was viewed not only as authoritative but even as deriving from royal authority.[45]

Of the large number of extant manuscripts, none are earlier than 1290–1300, leaving us with no direct access to Eike's original. The Harff manuscript is dated 1295. The Quedlinburg manuscript and the Berlin fragment were both written at the end of the thirteenth century. All in all, by the end of Middle Ages more than 450 complete or partial manuscripts had been created (Schmidt-Wiegand, "Einführung," *Facsimile W*, 3). From the first appearance of Eike's text, the need for a written, systematic presentation of custom was obvious, and this need is the most convincing explanation for its overwhelmingly rapid appropriation and adaptation.

To understand the significance and influence of Eike's text, we must sort out the various manuscript groups it spawned in just the first hundred years as German society was discovering the value of written, prose vernacular documentation. The manuscripts proliferated and metamorphosed in several ways: through translation into several dialects and languages, through copying and adaptation for use in several territories, and through innovative glossing and commentary. Consequently, the early manuscript versions document the beginnings of vernacular lawbook writing as oral culture was being transformed into a literate culture. The literate vernacular culture gained enormously from the writing of the lawbook in German. Although legal language was in flux from 1200 to 1400,[46] Eike's expressions and his book's exemplary reception sheltered the language from foreign influence. When elements of Roman law were incorporated, the native language accommodated them without resort to excessive numbers of loan words. The written lawbooks, supported by political stability within the empire (with respect to foreign intrusion), ensured that all Germans could participate in the entire judicial process because they guaranteed the use of vernacular in the courts. Consequently, the impact of medieval written legal texts is felt to this day—Germans still use a mainly German-based vocabulary to conduct their legal affairs,[47] whereas English speakers must resort to French lexical stock.

The cities were the most influential in the reception and distribution of the *Sachsenspiegel* because their residents were the first to copy, cite and incorporate parts of the text in their city ordinances. The *Schöffen* in Magdeburg were citing Eike's book in their Latin decisions as early as 1235. Almost immediately thereafter, the vernacular *Magdeburger Weichbild* absorbed applicable sections of the lawbook as part of its city code.[48] The *Sachsenspiegel*'s reception in terms of area was astonishing for its time. Since Magdeburg was a center for production of written laws and ordinances, it also became the central transmission point for the *Sachsenspiegel* (Lieberwirth, *Entstehung*, 37–38). Within the first sixty years, the reception spread in all directions. In the west the *Sachsenspiegel* was known in Cologne and Hamburg, to the east, in Görlitz, Breslau (1261), Silesian cities like Neumarkt, Cracow in Poland, and even in the extreme northeastern Marienburg, the governing center of the Teutonic Knights. Toward the south it went directly to Augsburg.

The southern city of Augsburg accomplished the same disseminating function as Magdeburg had farther north. The fact that by 1274–75 the High German translation, the *Deutschenspiegel,* had been completed is evidence that Eike's work was immediately considered applicable beyond Saxon territory. By referring constantly to *teutzelant* (Germany), the translator extended the book's jurisdiction to all the German-speaking areas (Johanek, 413; Kroeschell, *TBI,* 7). The *Deutschenspiegel* was produced one year before the Augsburg city code (*Augsburger Stadtrecht*, 1276), which quotes it. Another High German version, the *Schwabenspiegel,* appeared that same year. Meanwhile, the process of duplicating the *Sachsenspiegel* manuscripts and incorporating them into city laws also introduced changes as parts of the text that did not fit or appeared outdated were eliminated.

The *Schwabenspiegel* translation follows the text of *Sachsenspiegel* quite closely although it makes specific changes regarding legal rules and details in which Saxon and Swabian custom differed. The *Sachsenspiegel* itself had already acknowledged the differences in procedures for appealing a judgment (I 19) and in rights of inheritance (I 17). Between 1272 and 1292 Konrad von Oppeln translated it into Latin for use in the eastern parts of the empire.

Even though the *Sachsenspiegel* was gaining a normative and authoritative influence, writers in different parts of Germany persisted in altering the text and even reorienting its political perspective. For example, the *Deutschenspiegel* differs from the *Sachsenspiegel* in its discussion of the source of Law. Whereas the *Sachsenspiegel* defines customary law as God-given first and as a legacy of central authority traceable to Constantine and Charlemagne second, the *Deutschenspiegel* stresses more strongly that it is promulgated by kings (*chunige pracht*). This emphasis represents a movement toward understanding customary law as *kaiserrecht*; that is, law enacted and promulgated by imperial authority. The *Schwabenspiegel* translation takes this development a step further. Influenced by university-trained jurists, it incorporates sources of canon law that are similar to and seem to underpin German legal custom, whereas the *Sachsenspiegel* itself shows little direct influence (Johanek, 416) and instead supports the two-sword theory (I 1). It is no surprise then that on the issue of papacy versus empire the *Schwabenspiegel* subordinates the emperor to the pope. Thus, from a comparison of these texts, we discover distinct regional differences in customs, attitudes, and political orientation.

Adjusting to regional demands and keeping pace with social and juridical changes over the course of approximately three hundred years were not the only metamorphoses of the *Sachsenspiegel* textual transmission. With heavy use, questions of interpretation arose almost immediately because the lawbook, like any set of legal customs, occasionally needed to be clarified. Evidently, explication of the laws and principles was not a simple task, for interpretive aids were gradually developed.

When a text requires explication and interpretation, the usual solution is a gloss, and for jurists, glosses had become an essential tool. A set of glosses was first compiled for the *Sachsenspiegel* by Johann von Buch (ca. 1325) according to the principles of learned jurisprudence.[49] As did some of his contemporaries, Buch interpreted I-III 81 of the territorial law as a privilege given by Charlemagne to the Saxons; he attributed III 82–86 to the Ottonians, and III 87–91 to Frederick I. These attributions provided

Buch with the justification for comparing Saxon customary laws with canon and Roman law (Lieberwirth, *Glosse*, 8). He was also responsible for the bipartite division into the general territorial and feudal law that we know from all later manuscripts. Being a university-trained jurist, his primary interest was to correlate as much of the *Sachsenspiegel* as possible with canon law in order to harmonize contradictions between the two. In his version of the *Sachsenspiegel*, he defined concepts, explained contradictions, and added specific cases as examples in order to call attention to developments since Eike's time. From the way he explained his project, we learn a most significant fact: a judge had to perform his duty in accordance with *written law*, which in turn required a source book that could not be easily misinterpreted (Johanek, 421–22). This comment validates the conclusion that by the fourteenth century, the concept of a binding vernacular written law was firmly established among jurists at least.

Just thirty years earlier, and just sixty years after Eike wrote his text, the *Sachsenspiegel* had acquired a remarkably ingenious glossing and amplification system. It consisted of a set of colored illustrations keyed to specific passages in each chapter. Although a few other illuminated lawbooks exist in Germany, the pictures here make visible, augment, and elucidate the text continuously throughout the entire codex. Here we have a singular and fascinating instance of the integration of picture and word within a reference book intended for practical application. Only four such illuminated *Sachsenspiegel* codices survive. The Oldenburg manuscript, 1336 (CIM 1410, Landesbibliothek Oldenburg = O) is the only one written in Low German; the others—Heidelberg, 1294–1304 (Cpg 164, University of Heidelberg = H); Dresden, 1295–1363 (M 32, Dresden State Library = D); and Wolfenbüttel, 1358–1362 (Cod.Guelf 3.1 Aug.2⁰, Herzog August Library = W)—are written in East Middle German, a dialect spoken further south (Schmidt-Wiegand, "Mitteldeutsche Bilderhandschriften," 95). All are thought to derive from a single archetype created in the March of Meissen (ca. 1291–95)[50] from which two separate text-picture branches, Y and N, sprang. Since these branches subdivide the text into three or five books, respectively, we can determine that the postulated N manuscript (ca. 1314) gave rise to O with five books, and the Y (ca. 1300) with the tripartite division gave rise to the texts of H, D, and W (Schmidt-Wiegand, "Kreis," *Facsimile W*, vol. 3, 1–16). Today scholars agree that W is a reliable although not exact copy of D.

All the codices rule the page in two columns, with the text in one column (usually the right) and the pictures in the other. In H, D, and W, a large margin under the text has been left blank and is occasionally used for an additional picture or an expanded scene that runs across the bottom of the page. The column of illustrations contains four and sometimes five separate registers without line or frame divisions. These registers are carefully arranged in a synoptic fashion so that each of the colored drawings corresponds to and amplifies a particular section of text. Enlarged, color-coded capital letters found in both text and picture guide the reader from specific paragraphs to the appropriate picture registers and vice versa. The illustrations are quite precise to the extent that they reproduce accurately much specific information presented in the text. Depending on the legal points made in the text, the pictures may illustrate scenes and activities both outside and within a court of law. Most important, the pictures reveal cultural details such as legal gestures, court benches, and reliquaries necessary for carrying out justice but to which the text rarely refers.

The current opinion among philologists who are most concerned with the texts themselves is that the set of images accompanying the text has its own internally consistent symbolic system but also augments the text.[51] In these instances, the author and scribes of the *Sachsenspiegel* manuscripts may have assumed that these details were common knowledge. In contrast, the illuminators may have desired to make explicit a gestural semiotic tradition that had not yet been fixed in the pictorial medium. Each picture is carefully planned and placed to illustrate in sequence each chapter of the lawbook so that one finds two media, each with its own symbol system, enriching the other. The very richness and complementarity of the illustrations is intended to emphasize the dignity of customary law (Ott, "Bemerkungen," 41).

The illustrations make these manuscripts all the more valuable for studying the Middle Ages because the artists represented everyday people, tools and implements, and activities. In most illuminated manuscripts it is rare to find ordinary scenes depicted without an allegorizing tendency. This manuscript's pragmatic approach and attempt at concreteness in presenting aspects or applications of the legal text allow the illuminations to function as explicative commentary. Norbert Ott has already demonstrated the complexity of the multilevel symbolism in the illuminations ("Rechtsikonographie," 122–24); but art historians do not yet fully understand how these images relate to the text.

Choice of Text for this Translation

Unfortunately, Eike's original work of 1225–35 is lost to us. Even with the wealth of extant *Sachsenspiegel* manuscripts at our disposal, our sources and methods are inadequate to retrieve Eike's original language and content in a way that would even approximate modern editorial standards. More than 450 complete and fragmentary manuscripts prohibit the creation of a critical edition. The earliest manuscript dates no earlier than the end of the thirteenth century, and all the extant manuscripts are many years and several copies removed from the original manuscript. Furthermore, many editions of the *Sachsenspiegel* have been printed since the sixteenth century. With all the permutations, translations, glosses, and metamorphoses of the *Sachsenspiegel* texts available, it is clear that "the" *Sachsenspiegel* as a unique, discrete text does not exist. It is neither *a* single "text" nor *a* single "source."

Because *Sachsenspiegel* texts were copied and consulted in so many places throughout the German-speaking parts of the empire, each manuscript represents an adaptation to new and shifting requirements of an evolving society and judicial system. Hence, many individual texts are represented by the term *Sachsenspiegel*. I use *Sachsenspiegel* to mean the several-hundred-year-old tradition of the entire species of lawbook realized in all its adaptive diversity. For the purpose of reading a text or a source, we must then seek out and specify a single manuscript or a manuscript group. In this case, the Wolfenbüttel *codex picturatus* is the source of my English translation. When referring to the translation or to the manuscript itself, I use the title *Saxon Mirror*.

Given the plethora of manuscript groups and editions in the entire tradition, what criteria should be applied in choosing a text to translate? One must first select a specific time period or geographic region and then determine which editions or manuscripts are most representative and valuable within those parameters. As mentioned above, the illuminated group is the most fascinating. But why use a manuscript rather than an edition? A representative manuscript is more reliable than an edition because it is a genuine artifact and source of information. Editorial principles have changed, and we now give much more credence to each manuscript.[52] We are less willing to amend or revise; instead we conserve much that appears to be incorrect or incomprehensible.

Today we also have the advantage of recognizing the pitfalls of a reconstruction of Eike's text, such as that attempted by Karl August Eckhardt. His text of the general territorial law and feudal law (1973) has been commonly cited in the absence of a critical edition, but it is misleading. Eckhardt compiled a patchwork text by combining several manuscripts and attempted to reconstruct Eike's original dialect even though we have scarce documentation for dialect usage during Eike's lifetime in the Quedlinburg area.[53] This means that the edition, which is supposed to be read as if it were Eike's text as he finished it, is simply a linguistic and textual artifact created by Eckhardt in the 1930s. It never really existed in this form in the thirteenth century.[54] With his fabricated reconstruction, Eckhardt has presented an unreliable and undatable text to historians, linguists, and legal historians who wish to trace the content of the lawbook, the development of its legal terminology, the speed and impact of Eike's reception, and its implications for intercity and territorial relations throughout Germany. These questions can normally be answered dependably on the basis of dialects and terminology reflected in chronology of dated manuscripts, but Eckhardt's edition has eliminated numerous specifically datable linguistic markers and created questionable new ones.

Until recently, it was considered desirable to get as close to the author's original text as possible, and this was especially true for Eckhardt's generation. But we no longer share this desire in cases where the manuscript transmission makes it methodologically impossible, and especially when the text or genre type is not served by this approach. Especially for legal, reference, and other texts intended for practical application, it is more important to recognize and deal with the many changes than to seek the original. In the case of the *Sachsenspiegel*, the earliest form carries no superiority over the later forms, for each individual version provides us with documentation on a specific time and place.

Therefore, for the purpose of historical, linguistic, art historical, and cultural studies, it is essential to choose a single seminal manuscript that is as complete as possible; represents a primary line of textual transmission based on the established stemma (Homeyer, *Rechtsbücher*, 5–6) and is thus representative of the *Sachsenspiegel* tradition; is datable with relative accuracy, and shows evidence of actual use by contemporaries and a verifiable influence on the interpretation of customary law and the making of new laws. A number of manuscripts would fit these criteria, but of the groups discussed, the illuminated has the most to offer to the widest contemporary audience. It is according to these criteria that I have chosen to translate the Wolfenbüttel picture codex.

All the *codices picturati* are available in facsimile format, but the others lack the advantages of the Wolfenbüttel codex. The Heidelberg manuscript is a fragment and lacks the feudal law and the first book of the territorial law. The Oldenburg manuscript contains the most complete text, but fewer than half of the illustrations have been completed; some folios contain the outline drawings but many show only the blank columns. The Dresden manuscript also has a dependable, complete text lacking only a few, short sections. Unfortunately, it is very poorly preserved; it suffered badly from water damage that occurred during the fire-bombing of Dresden during World War II and will not be accessible until conservation work is complete. Its black-and-white facsimile is not useful to those who would study the illuminations although the text is easily legible. W, on the other hand, is a reliable copy of D, and both were illuminated by better artists than the other two manuscripts. Thus it is the Wolfenbüttel manuscript that offers the advantage of a relatively complete text (both territorial and feudal law) with continuous illuminations of both territorial law and feudal law in one single, well-preserved codex.

Contents and Description of the Manuscript

The Wolfenbüttel illuminated manuscript (ca. 1358–62) is a large codex of eighty-six parchment leaves measuring 35 × 27 cm. (13.75 × 10.62 in.). The folios were numbered with roman numerals in the eighteenth century and misnumberings corrected in 1819. The loss of gatherings in three different sections is not reflected in the folio numbering but is revealed by missing segments of text (see below). The text is written in an even gothic textura. Accompanying the text are 778 picture registers (Milde, *Facsimile W*, vol. 2, 12–25). The worn, discolored edges and torn corners of the leaves show wear from the hands of many who consulted it as reference, giving us a physical indication of its seminal status.

The manuscript contains the following: the Imperial Landpeace of Mainz ("Mainzer Reichslandfriede"), which was not in Eike's first version (fol. 1r–3v, double columns), the Lineage of the Lords ("Von der Herren Geburt") (fol. 3v–4r), a detailed table of contents (fol. 4v–8r), and the first and second prologues (fol. 9v). The territorial law is divided into books I, II and III (fol. 10r–58r) and the undivided feudal law is labeled book IV (fol. 59r–86v). The numbering system in my references follows the numbering in W.

Another advantage of basing the English translation on this particular manuscript is that the facsimile of W is available to those who wish to work with the original along with a translation. My translation serves to guide those unfamiliar with German legal history or with the extensive legal vocabulary of the medieval East Middle German text to an understanding of this particular yet representative text. For the specialist, of course, it is no substitute for the manuscript.

This Translation

The customary nature of the lawbook sets the parameters for a translation. The text is neither systematic nor exhaustive. In order to make sense out of it, we as readers always try to reconcile its inconsistencies and contradictions and endeavor to interpret and fill in where the text is not clear and explicit enough for us. Since I wish to avoid the temptation to provide unity where there is none, I have eschewed broad interpretations and modern technical legal vocabulary that would mislead rather than elucidate the medieval customs.

The overriding principle, therefore, has been to translate the manuscript text as literally as possible in order to render the content clearly while not sacrificing readability. Although I make reference to the manuscript illustrations at times, I do not interpret the pictures to clarify the text and translation. Some parts of the text are ambiguous, and many others simply take for granted information we lack today, but the translator's role is not to second guess what the scribe or the law intended or interpret for the readers and possibly mislead them, but to transmit genuine ambiguities.

When possible, I have attempted to convey the style and metaphor inherent in the original. For example, some of the imagery has been retained in statements that have parallels or corresponding phrasings in English. It is particularly tempting to render the phrasing of the rich collection of maxims and proverbs in the text. Where this is not possible, I discuss the original formulation in the notes.

A few deliberate, interpretative decisions were necessary, however. To make a passage read more coherently, I have at times added a term or phrase in square brackets. I have also added but left unmarked little formulaic connectors such as "this means," "consequently," and "for this reason" to link thoughts where I sensed the type of implied connections that medieval German rarely makes explicit. Long sentences have been broken up into smaller units to approximate English sentence patterns. To make some lengthy and complicated passages readable, I had to insert nouns specifying the subject or agent to replace the superabundance of pronouns, many of which have no clear antecedents. In statements where the antecedents are genuinely a question of interpretation, I supply the original and my interpretation.

Occasionally, interpretation in translation was forced upon me because of certain key abstract terms that can have slightly different meanings. For example, *richter* meaning "judge" occurs frequently, but it is often unclear which judge (that is, which level of jurisdiction) is meant. In these cases I have rarely attempted to be any more precise than the original and have translated *richter* simply as "judge." The term *kint* can also mislead because it normally refers to a male child even though it can also refer to a female. The text thus rarely makes clear whether a particular rule is applicable to female children as well. Other terms such as *herr* (lord or master) and *knecht* (servant, serf) can designate people with very different status depending on the context. *Knecht* in certain phrases can even refer to the princes of the empire (II 66). Often I translate these terms differently if a specific context warrants it. In cases where I did make a specific interpretive decision, I provide the original in a note and indicate why I have chosen that particular English term. Abstract terms and unfamiliar concepts appear in the glossary.

Because many *Sachsenspiegel* manuscripts exist, none of the editors has developed a systematic numbering system for comparing one manuscript or edition to another. Eckhardt's edition, containing more than one system, reveals the problems involved. Numbering inconsistencies also exist within the W manuscript between the chapter listings and the text itself. In some cases, the numbering in the table of contents does not correspond to the chapter numbers because the scribe seems to have occasionally omitted a chapter number or added an extra one where other manuscripts do not. One could simply rectify the discrepancies by renumbering the text, were it not for the fact that occasionally the chapter number has itself been moved to a different section of text. This means that a few topics listed under a particular chapter in the table of contents may be in a different chapter. In the translation of the table of contents, I note when a topic has been placed into a different chapter. Rather than reorganize the numbering and rearrange the text, I follow in this translation the numbering of W itself. Often, two chapters will have the same number. The second is marked with a "a" for citation purposes (cf. chapters 20 and 20a, etc.). The result is that the chapter numbering in W does not always correspond to that of the other manuscripts nor to the German *Sachsenspiegel* editions. As problematic as this may seem, it is relatively easy to compare the *Saxon Mirror* to other texts because the discrepancy in chapter numbering is rarely greater than one or two chapters when moving from the English to Eckhardt or Homeyer, for example.

Normally, references to any edition of the *Sachsenspiegel* are given according to the divisions of general territorial law (*Landrecht*) and feudal law (*Lehnrecht*). The usual citation method lists *Lndr* III 22, to indicate territorial law book III chapter 22, and *Lnr* 63 to refer to chapter 63 in the feudal law, which is not subdivided into books. Most editions give paragraph numbers as well, but since W has no paragraph numbering, I have not added any. To make referencing easier, I use the book numbering system in the manuscript, which also contains the territorial and feudal divisions. The books of the territorial law are numbered I, II, and III as in all editions; the feudal law is numbered book IV. In the text of the translation I include folio numbers in W in angle brackets as a guide to the manuscript itself or its facsimile.

As far as the translation is concerned, I accept the text as found in the manuscript. When a word or phrase has obviously been omitted, I do not add to the text from other manuscripts. However, large sections of text were lost when leaves were removed from the manuscript; these are listed in the table of contents and have been filled in from D. The lacunae filled in from D include the following chapters: I 71; II 1–11; III 25–39, 77–84; IV 48–65. This is permissible because W and D correspond so closely that even most page breaks occur at the same place. These supplements from D, with their own folio numbering, are printed in italic.

W has few of the textual appendages such as prologues, but because the *Sachsenspiegel* manuscript tradition has them, German scholars distinguish between them and have given them specific designations. These terms need not be translated literally, and I have not done so. However, I feel it is important to provide the German terms with my equivalents so that those who consult any German primary or secondary works will more easily understand the distinctions:

"Vorrede in Strophen"	(strophic preface)
"Vorrede in Reimpaaren"	(rhymed preface)
"Von der Herren Geburt"	(The lineage of the Lords)
"Prologus"	(first prologue)
"Textus Prologi"	(second prologue)

The strophic and the rhymed prefaces together are often referred to as "Praefatio rhythmica" (Eckhardt, *Lndr*, 38). Neither of these prefaces is found in W. The first is not even considered Eike's work, but the rhymed preface is attributed to him. W does, however, contain the "Lineage of the Lords"[55] and the first and second prologues. The two prologues are each only one paragraph long, but have been viewed as two separate pieces by scholars, so I follow their designations. The manuscript tradition contains an epilogue, as does W.

The notes accompanying each book are principally intended for readers who may be unfamiliar with the legal language and circumstances in

Saxony at the time W was written. I imagine readers will read parts and consult the *Saxon Mirror* from time to time rather than read it as a whole from cover to cover. The notes may therefore appear a bit repetitive, but they will aid those who use it as a resource. Also, Eike wrote for practicing judges and not university jurists, and thus he did not organize the material for the benefit of the uninformed reader. My cross-references in the notes will help those interested in specific judicial actions to find the other chapters and passages necessary to understand better the section they are reading. The notes also point out ambiguities or translation problems in the original passage and offer alternatives. Readers who know medieval German can use the citations from the original to verify terminology when comparing other texts. The glossary is intended to guide readers to the original German terms and phrases, but its primary purpose is to explain the meaning of terms and the function of pivotal members of the judiciary.

Citations of passages from the manuscript have been left essentially without punctuation. I changed the spelling only to spell out abbreviated and contracted forms and to change the letter *v* to *u*. Individual terms in the notes and glossary are also listed according to the original spelling, and a modern German term is given where useful.

Text of the Wolfenbüttel Manuscript

Imperial Landpeace of Mainz[1] ⟨fol. 1r⟩

The emperor promulgated this law in Mainz with the support of the princes.

We establish and decree[2] by the power of our imperial authority and in conjunction with the loyal men of the realm:[3] If a son expels his father by force from his castle or any other property, or attacks it by burning or robbing, or allies himself with his father's enemies securing the alliance by word of honor or oath when the aim is to damage the father's reputation or ruin him, and if his father convicts him [with an oath] on the relics before the judge and is helped by two oathhelpers[4] of indisputable integrity and full legal capacity,[5] then the son shall be stripped of all property held in fief and in free ownership, all movable property and all inheritance from father and mother forever so that neither the father nor a judge will ever be able to help him recover any rights to such property.[6] Any son who plots against his father's life or viciously attacks him, wounding or imprisoning him or laying him in any type of bonds that one would call imprisonment, and is convicted for it as previously stated,[7] forfeits his legal rights and privileges forever and may never regain them.[8] All those whom the father names as witnesses to the judge regarding any of the causes described previously will not be disqualified on grounds of feudal loyalty or for any other reason when they reveal the truth to the father. Whoever is not willing to do this will be ordered to do so by the judge unless he swears on the relics to the judge that he knows nothing of it. If the father's ministerials[9] or bondpeople aid and abet the son to commit any of these acts against the father as already described, and the father proves it against them with two others[10] by [swearing] an oath on the relics, they lose all legal rights and privileges forever and may never regain them. However, the father cannot take legal action against his ministerials or servile men for offenses carrying a penalty of complete loss of rights until he has first convicted his son. Should any other kinds of people aside from the father's ministerials and bondmen aid and abet the son against his father in any of these offenses previously described, and the father proves it as described, then the judge in whose jurisdiction the offenses were committed must impose imperial outlawry[11] on these people and not lift it unless they pay double compensation to the father [for] the ⟨fol. 1v,l⟩[12] loss they had helped cause him and to the judge his rightful [fine].[13] Should one of them hold a fief from the father, it reverts to him immediately if that person is convicted, and the father shall never again grant him the fief. Should the father do so anyway, then the feoffee must pledge or bring to the judge the equivalent from his allod or his fief. If he does not have either, then he must bring the judge silver equaling the value of the fief. With regard to all the cases described, each and every man enjoying full legal capacity, be he prince or noble freeman, may help the father prove his case if he knows the truth. A ministerial can also be a witness with others of his rank, a servile person with those of equal status, and a peasant[14] with fellow peasants. Also in this regard, each freeman may help a ministerial if he knows about it, and a ministerial may help anyone of a lower rank.[15] Those in lower rank cannot aid those in higher ones. Should it happen, however, that the father cannot demand his rights because of captivity, sickness, or other legal hindrance, then one of his kin will do it, and if the kinsman pursues the case [swearing] on the relics and explaining that legal hindrance prevents the father from appearing himself and states the reason, then, when he presses charges, the case shall be prosecuted with him as if the father were present.

This law is concerned with preventing anyone from taking revenge himself. ⟨fol. 1v,r⟩ We establish and decree that a person may not exact revenge for whatever damage he suffers before he brings his complaint to the judge and follows the legal process through to the end as is lawful unless the dispute has progressed to where he must defend his life and property with arms. Whosoever takes revenge in any other manner than here described shall repay twofold whatever harm he causes, and whatever damage he himself incurs shall be lost to him, and he will never be allowed to make any claims for compensation. However, if someone does bring charges as described above but is not given a hearing, then he must resort to declaring a feud[16] against his enemies. This he must do in daylight. From the day he declares the feud, he will not do the other party any injury either to person or property for four days so that he has three entire days of peace. The person thus challenged must likewise refrain from doing harm to the challenger's person and property for four days. And if this rule is broken by one party, then the other will go to his judge and bring charges against the malefactor. Thereupon the judge or his deputy shall summon him to court.

If the accused cannot clear himself on the relics with seven men having full legal capacity,[17] he is stripped of all legal rights and privileges forever so that he may never regain them.

Regarding tolls. ⟨fol. 2r,l⟩ We establish and decree that all [rights to collect] tolls on water or land established at the time of our father, Emperor Heinrich, are void unless someone holding a toll[18] can prove for certain with an oath on the relics that he has a legal right to it. We command that all tolls that have been raised higher than first set be reduced to that amount. Toll amounts shall remain as established by law. Whoever collects a toll greater than allowed by law or at a place other than the one established will be treated like a highway robber if it is proven against him lawfully before his judge or the realm. All those who collect tolls on water or land shall fulfill their duties by making repairs and improvements on roads and bridges. In addition, the tollkeepers shall accompany and protect to the best of their ability all the people from whom they collect tolls so that those people are not harmed within their district. If someone breaks this rule three times and is convicted with witnesses before the emperor according to law, the toll rights revert to the realm.

Regarding feuds. When two parties are feuding with each other, and one party or both has a protective escort, and one of them attacks the other's men and harms them, then if he is lawfully convicted, he will be sentenced as a highway robber.[19]

Concerning the roads. We establish and decree that people shall travel on the proper highways, and no one may eject another from a proper road by force. ⟨fol. 2r,r⟩

Concerning towns and castles. We establish and decree that if a lord wishes to build additions to his town or castle, he may do this only with his own property [i.e., wealth] or with the property of his men[20] and not with the property of country people.[21] And whoever collects a tax for [the construction] will be treated like a highway robber.

Concerning coinage. We establish and decree all minting rights from the time of our father Emperor Heinrich void unless a person in possession of one can prove to the realm that he has legal right to it. If anyone stamps someone's coin with a false mark, he will be treated like a counterfeiter along with the person who ordered the stamping. We command that everyone store his old coins according to established regulations and prohibit all counterfeiting. If a person breaks the peace against another after the two parties had sworn the peace with a handshake,[22] and the plaintiff proves it with an oath on the relics with two additional men having full legal capacity before the judge who had witnessed the peace agreement, the judge will then place the person who broke the peace in royal outlawry. The judge must never allow the malefactor to recover his legal rights without the plaintiff's permission, otherwise the judge forfeits his hand for it. But if the breach of peace was homicide, then a kinsman of the deceased will bring charges for the deed and prosecute the perpetrator as described earlier. And if he is convicted with an oath, he will never be released from outlawry except through death. ⟨fol. 2v,l⟩ And he shall have no legal rights or protection. However, if the person who agreed to the peace with a handshake does not admit truthfully that the peace was broken against the plaintiff, the judge will command him by the emperor's grace to aid the litigant in achieving justice[23] unless he swears on the relics that he knows nothing of it. If he fails to do this claiming vassal fealty or any other excuse, he forfeits his hand to the emperor.[24]

Concerning those who hold a judgeship.[25] We establish and decree by our grace that all our princes and all those who hold judicial authority from us judge justly according to the customs of the land and that they demand the same from those to whom they have delegated judicial authority in turn. Whoever does not comply will be sentenced severely, according to law, and whatever verdict against him is laid before us, we will not reduce; we will neither overlook nor spare anyone. We also command the princes to enforce the work of their enfeoffed judges with fines[26] so that they, too, judge lawfully and not reduce any penalty accompanying a verdict handed down to them. We establish and decree that no judge may place a person in royal outlawry except in public. Also, before a judge releases someone from royal outlawry, he must make certain that the plaintiff['s case] was tried according to the legal custom of the land. If the judge does not do so, then the emperor shall hear the case as is lawful. We establish and decree that each judge shall accept, collect, and not reduce the court fines due him when a person is released from outlawry so that people will want ⟨fol. 2v,r⟩ to avoid outlawry all the more. We also wish to maintain our right [to the fine]. We absolutely prohibit anyone to show favoritism. We establish and decree that the [practice of] people living outside the castle wall be discontinued.[27] We do not want them in our towns and do not want anyone else to allow them either. We forbid by our grace anyone to provide a protective escort for someone across the country[28] for payment unless he holds escort rights from the realm. We establish and decree that no one shall aid or give shelter to anyone in royal outlawry. Whoever does so and is lawfully convicted for it bears the same culpability as the outlaw and receives the same sentence.

But if the accused exonerates himself lawfully on the relics with seven men of full legal capacity saying he did not know the man was an outlaw, then he is not guilty. Should a person drive an outlaw away or attack him, no one may come to his aid. But if someone is proved to have protected an outlaw knowingly, he bears the same culpability and is sentenced like an outlaw. If an outlaw comes into a town, he may not be allowed to remain. And if someone does him evil, no one may hinder it. No one may give him anything, or provide him with anything to sell, or buy anything from him. One must avoid him in every way. If the community in a town knowingly agrees to allow him to remain there, then if the town has walls, the judge of the district will raze them. The landlord who gives him a lodging will be tried as an ⟨fol. 3r,l⟩ outlaw and his house destroyed. If the town is unwalled, then the judge shall burn it, and no one may hinder it. If the town opposes this, then the town and its people will forfeit their legal rights. If the judge cannot carry this out, the emperor shall be notified, and he will do it with force.

Concerning the imperial judge.[29] We establish a judge for our court. He must be a freeman and will remain in office at least one year if he performs well and justly. He will sit in court every day except Sunday and high feast days and hear all people who bring a complaint to him, and suits concerning all people except princes and other high [ranking] persons when the penalty is loss of life, legal rights, inheritance, fief, or other valuable thing. We reserve these cases for ourselves. He may not place anyone in outlawry nor release anyone from it; we will do that ourselves. He may not postpone anyone's case unless he has our special permission. The judge must swear on the relics that he will accept no goods from anyone in return for a judgment.[30] Further, he must not, for reason of love, pain, pleading, or fear judge otherwise than according to law, following the judgment given him and his best understanding without any kind of falsehood. The judge will collect all the court fines that he levies, all those resulting from cases argued before him and from the people released from outlawry. We give the judge this right so that he may be all the more willing a judge and not accept ⟨fol. 3r,r⟩ any other goods in return for a judgment. The judge shall have a court clerk who lists all those who are placed in outlawry, those who brought the charges that resulted in outlawry, and the reasons for outlawry; also the names of those who were released from outlawry, the reasons for their release, and the day they were released. Further, he will record the guarantors provided to the plaintiff, their names, where they are from, and the security offered the plaintiff according to the legal custom of the land. He will also write down the names of all who are charged as malefactors in the land, when and with whose help they cleared themselves,[31] and how they regained their legal capacity and were released from outlawry. And he will erase their names. He shall also record all the judgments regarding the important cases that have come before us so that we may consistently determine the same judgments for similar cases;[32] he will also include the places where the verdicts are collected. That same court clerk will collect all documents from suits brought to court and shall have no additional assignment. He must swear on the relics that he will fulfill his office by doing and writing only what is lawful to the best of his understanding and not [deviate from the law] for reason of love, pain or bribery. We have established this because it seems worthwhile and good for all who live in our realm and specifically for those ⟨fol. 3v,l⟩ messengers we cannot ourselves reach rapidly because of our manifold duties.[33] The court clerk shall be a layman [so that] if he acts unlawfully, he may be sentenced to capital punishment.

Regarding ecclesiastical issues. We decree that people in towns and villages throughout our realm follow the law and the commands of the bishops, archpriests,[34] and lay priests, and that no one oppose them with force.

Regarding the advocates[35] of ecclesiastical institutions. We establish and decree lawfully and explicitly that the magistrates of ecclesiastical houses counsel their houses. Within their districts, they shall protect them according to what pleases God and preserves our goodwill. Each advocate shall have a care to support the ecclesiastical establishments within his district so that none of them brings a complaint against him. If an advocate does not do this, and a complaint is brought before us, we shall judge him so strictly that we shall in no way spare him. We forbid by our grace anyone to cause damage by means of robbery, arson, or seizure to the property of an ecclesiastical house in the advocate's jurisdiction either through fault of the advocate or in order to injure him. If anyone commits these acts nevertheless, in order to harm the advocate, then, if the malefactor is convicted lawfully, he must be outlawed and may not redeem himself unless he pays threefold restitution; two parts shall go to the house and the third to the advocate. We ⟨fol. 3v,r⟩ forbid anyone to make a seizure without the judge's permission. Whoever does so anyway shall be sentenced as a robber.

Concerning anyone who buys stolen property. We establish and decree that whoever buys robbed or stolen property knowingly, or shelters a robber who is not an outlaw, feeds him in his house, and then is convicted with witnesses[36] [for sheltering him] according to law, must make twofold restitution immediately to the person from whom the goods were taken if the items were robbed or stolen. And if he is lawfully convicted[37] for doing this a second time, then if it is robbed goods, he is sentenced as a robber; if it is stolen goods, then he must be sentenced as a thief.

The Lineage of the Lords[38]

Now hear about the lineage of the lords in the land of Saxony. The princes of Anhalt, Brandenburg, Orlamünde, and the margraves of Meissen and those of Brehne are all Swabians. The Swabians among the free lords are the Hakeborn, Gneiz, and Mücheln. Among the *Schöffen* of the realm are the [families] of Dröbel, Elsdorf, Heinrich Judas the advocate, Albrecht of Spandau,[39] Alberich and Konrad of Schneidlingen, Schrapen squire[40] of Gersleben, Anno of Jerdingsdorf, Herman von Mehringen, the children of Heidolf of Winningen, and the [family] of Seedorf. These are all Swabians. The landgraves of Thuringia are all Franconians. The lords of Regenstein, ⟨fol. 4r,l⟩ Blankenburg, the burgraves of Wettin, the Klöden, Krosick, and Kottbus are all Franconians. The lords of Brunswick, Lüneburg, Poppenburg, Osterburg, and Altenhausen are Swabians. And the lords of Werningerode, Arnstein, Biesenrode, Emersleben, the burgraves of Giebichenstein, the episcopal advocate of Halberstadt, the lords of Suselitz, Lichtenberg, and Dobin are all of Swabian birth. The dukes of Limburg and their clan are all Saxons by birth. So are all the free lords and *Schöffen* resident in Saxony and known to me in my lifetime with the exception of those named earlier. All bishops enfeoffed by the realm with a banner estate[41] in Saxony and having the military shield[42] from it are all called Saxons no matter what land they came from. These men may certainly determine judgments and contribute in a majority decision[43] and may also serve as spokesman in both feudal and territorial law before the realm for any person when the penalty does not include life or hand, but not under any other circumstances under territorial and feudal law.[44]

The Saxon Mirror
Table of Contents

Book I

1. This topic is found in I 45 of the text.
2. This is found in I 49 of the text.

Book II

3. W lacks II 1–12 because the manuscript is missing several folios.
4. These topics are found in II 13.
5. From this point on, the chapter numbering in the text, up to and including II 20, is one chapter ahead of the table of contents.
6. This topic is contained in II 20a of the text.

7. This topic is found in II 30.
8. This topic is found in II 37.

Book III

9. This topic is found in II 51.

10. This paragraph is not in the W manuscript.
11. The text from III 26 up to and including III 39 is lacking in W.

12. This paragraph is not in D.

13. The W text resumes here, corresponding to the second paragraph of III 39.

14. The text is numbered one chapter ahead of the table of contents from the middle of III 39 up through III 53; they correspond again at III 53a. W Book III has no chapter 40.

15. This paragraph is found at the end of III 57.
16. W lacks III 77–84.

Book IV

17. The table of contents, like the text itself, skips from 89 to 100 and continues consistently. I have changed the numbering to 90, 91, and 92, respectively.

18. This topic is found in IV 14.
19. This topic is found in IV 22.
20. Chapter heading 25 was added as a correction in the margin above the left column in the manuscript but I have placed it in correct numerical order.
21. This topic is in IV 28.

22. The passages referred to here are missing from W.

23. The text inserts chapter number 41 at this point. What the table of contents labels as 41 becomes 42 in the text and so on. This discrepancy between text and table of contents continues until 50a where a section from D is inserted to replace the missing folios of W.

24. This topic is in IV 45.

25. The last part of this chapter is separate and numbered 50 in W. Chapters 50 to 70 are missing from W and have been supplied from D.

26. This passage, lacking in W, is numbered 50 in D. I have changed the numbering to 50a to indicate the discrepancy. After this the numbering in the translation coincides with the table of contents and the numbering in D.

27. This topic is lacking in D.

28. This topic is found in IV 63.

29. Chapter 73 is misnumbered 72 in the manuscript but I have changed it to 72a to distinguish the content from IV 72.

Manuscript Index to the Laws ⟨fol. 7r,l⟩
[Transcribed exactly as given in W.]

Inheritance: Book I: 5, 17, 27, 28, 30; Book II: 20, 21, 30, 43; Book III: 72, 81
Woman's personal belongings: Book I: 24, 28; Book III: 38
Witnesses: Book I: 6, 7, 8, 20, 25, 66, 60, 8, 70, 71; Book II: 6, 18, 22, 34, 69; Book III: 7, 10, 19, 21, 23,25, 28, 33, 37, 39, 41, 82, 89
Guardianship: Book I: 11, 23, 41; Book II: 30, 9
Morning gift: Book I: 20, 21, 24; Book III: 76
Rape: Book I: 37; Book III: 1, 46
Legal incapacity: Book I: 31, 48, 51, 64; Book III: 16, 46, 72
Royal outlawry: Book I: 38; Book III: 34
Trial by battle: Book I: 48, 49, 50, 63; Book II: 3; Book III: 29, 26
Tithes: Book I: 48; Book II: 54
Red-handed deed: Book I: 55, 46; Book II: 33, 34; Book III: 35, 88
Guaranty: Book I: 15, 16, 34; Book III: 3, 7, 14, 83
Hunting and injury to animals: Book II: 40, 61
Damage by animals: Book I: 47, 48, 54, 62; Book III: 49
Plowing someone else's land: Book II: 46; Book III: 20
Bondservants: Book III: 33, 42, 73
The King: Book III: 52, 54, 55, 57, 59, 60, 63, 64, 67
Transfer of movable property: Book I: 15; Book II: 60; Book III: 4 ⟨fol. 8r,r⟩
Prisoners: Book I: 69; Book II: 32; Book III: 32, 35, 41, 60; 2, 8, 12
The military shield is twice five shillings: 29
Minority: 3, 12
Fealty, royal outlawry, local outlawry, attainder must be proven with witnesses: feudal law
Illegitimacy
Robbery, theft
Removal of witnesses
Shorn champions
Minstrels, local outlawry, royal outlawry must be proven with witnesses: territorial law
Feudal law: 75; Book III: 13; Book II: 15
No one need compensate ancestors.
No one gives guaranty with another guaranty.

Plate 2. Folio 9v from book I (top to bottom): (1) the author, kneeling, with the Holy Spirit, Charlemagne, and Constantine; (2) sword of justice; (3) creation of Adam; (4) sin of Adam and Eve. Cod. Guelf. 3.1 Aug.2°, folio 9v, prologue. (Reproduced by permission of the Herzog August Bibliothek, Wolfenbüttel, Germany)

First prologue.[1] ⟨fol. 9v⟩ May the love of the Holy Spirit sharpen my mind[2] so that I may pronounce what is lawful and unlawful among the Saxons for the grace of God and the benefit of the world. I cannot accomplish this project alone. Therefore, I request the support of all law-abiding people who desire justice.[3] Should they encounter a juridical dispute that I have omitted from this book because of my limited knowledge, I request that they reach a just determination to their best knowledge and discretion.[4] No one should let himself be diverted from the law, not for love or jealousy, wrath or gain. God is Law itself; therefore, justice is dear to him.[5] Consequently, all those to whom God has given the task of judging shall strive to reach judgments in such a manner that God in His wrath and judgment may treat them mercifully.

Second Prologue.[6] God who is the beginning and the end of all worthwhile things created heaven and earth first, then formed man on earth and placed him in paradise. Man broke the commandment to the ruin of us all. That is why we all went astray like shepherdless sheep until the day He saved us with His martyrdom. But now that we have been converted, and God has summoned us, we keep His law and His commandments—the ones His prophets and pious spiritual people taught us, and also the ones the Christian kings, Constantine and Charlemagne, provided—in Saxony to the advancement of His law. ⟨fol. 10r⟩

Book I

1 God left behind on earth two swords for the protection of Christianity: To the pope he gave the spiritual sword, and to the emperor, the temporal one. Now the pope is also required to ride a white horse at a specified time, and on this occasion the emperor shall hold his stirrup so that the saddle will not slip.[7] The meaning is this: Any [entity] resisting the pope in a way that he cannot control by ecclesiastical jurisdiction needs to be compelled by the emperor and his use of secular law to obey the pope. So, too, shall the spiritual jurisdiction assist the secular power when necessary.[8]

2 Once he has come of age, every Christian is duty-bound to attend the ecclesiastical court three times a year in the bishopric where he resides. There are three levels of obligation.[9] Those belonging to the class eligible to be *Schöffen* shall attend the episcopal court;[10] the king's tenants attend the dean's court, and [the other] tenants, the archpriest's court.[11] Everyone also owes attendance at the secular court in the same manner. The *Schöffen* attend the count's court every eighteen weeks held under the king's legal jurisdiction.[12] Should a court be called into session because of a crime within a fortnight after the regular session, then the *Schöffen* are required to attend this hearing as well, so that the crime may be judged. With these actions they maintain their allodial land free of encumbrance before the judge.[13] The king's tenants are also duty-bound to attend the court of the *Schultheiss*[14] ⟨fol. 10v⟩ because of their heritable land. Whenever the local officer of the court (bailiff)[15] dies, another must be chosen from among this group. The tenants who have no hereditary interest in their land attend the court of the local district judge[16] every six weeks.[17] In addition, each advocate[18] must hold court and each village headman[19] must raise the hue and cry and make an indictment for each bloody wound inflicted by one person on another, for each sword drawn to inflict harm on another, for each person who fails to attend court when he is duty-bound to do so, and for each crime that is punishable with loss of hand or life if the complaint has not yet been made before the court. He may not bring a suit in any other way.

3 Origen foretold long ago that there would be six ages, each age calculated to last a thousand years, and in the seventh, the world is expected

to end. Now we know from the Holy Scriptures that the first age began with Adam. The second began with Noah, with Abraham the third, with Moses the fourth, with David the fifth, and with God's birth the sixth. We are now in the seventh age without certainty of its duration.[20] The orders of nobility[21] eligible to bear arms are organized in the same way. Within this hierarchy, the king belongs to the first order, the bishops, abbots, and abbesses to the second, the lay princes to the third since they became vassals[22] to the bishops; the free lords belong to the fourth, the *Schöffen* class and the vassals of the free lords to the fifth, and their vassals to the sixth order. Just as Christianity has no secure knowledge of the seventh age or how long it will last, it is likewise unclear whether the seventh order can participate in either the right to bear arms[23] or in feudal law. ⟨fol. 11r⟩ The lay princes extended the sixth order into the seventh when they became vassals of the bishops, which had not been the case earlier. Just as the hierarchy of shields extends to the seventh order, likewise blood relations also continue to the seventh degree. Now note how and where kinship begins and ends.[24] At the head are man and wife who have come together lawfully. The neck is the next generation of family members. They are the children born of the union and not outside of it. A child born of one of the couple, related by half-blood, cannot be considered part of the same degree. In fact, this child is removed into the next level of membership. If two brothers marry two sisters and the third brother an unrelated woman,[25] their children are all of equal degree of kinship, equally removed, equally close, so that each can assume the other's inheritance as long as they are of equal birth.[26] The children of legitimate brothers are located at the level where the arm connects to the shoulder. The same holds for children of sisters. These people are related in the very next level; that is, in the first degree of consanguinity. They are the children of brothers and sisters. The level of the elbow marks the second degree, the wrist the third, the first joint of the middle finger the fourth, the second joint the fifth, and the third joint the sixth. At the seventh level there is no joint; only a fingernail marks the degree and therefore the kinship ends with the nail members. Those persons between head and fingernail who stand at the same level of consanguinity share the inheritance[27] in equal parts. The heir who can be placed closest ⟨fol. 11v⟩ to [the head of] the clan lays first claim to the estate. Kin share legitimately in the estate up to the seventh degree although the pope permits marriage to a woman of one's own kin to the fifth degree only. This is permissible because the pope cannot promulgate any law that would weaken our land or feudal law. Neither tenancy nor hereditary property can devolve upon the feebleminded, dwarfs, or cripples.[28] The actual heirs and their next of kin are, however, responsible for their care.

4 A child born dumb, blind, or lacking hand or foot is a legitimate heir according to the territorial law but not according to feudal law. If he has been granted a fief[29] before this [disability] occurred, then he forfeits nothing. A leper cannot succeed to feudal tenancy or hereditary property, but if he was invested before the illness and becomes ill afterwards, then he does not forfeit it.

5 If a son marries a woman of equal birth during his father's lifetime, has sons by her and dies before his father has divided the inheritance, then the sons succeed to the grandfather's estate in their father's stead equally with their paternal uncles.[30] They all receive the portion due to males. It is not possible for the children of a daughter to partake equally in the inheritance from their grandfather or grandmother as their mother can. A daughter who lives in the [parent's] house without a dowry does not divide the mother's personal belongings[31] with the daughter who already possesses a dowry. However, she must divide with her sister whatever belongs to the estate. ⟨fol. 12r⟩ A woman can damage her reputation through unchaste conduct, but she does not thereby lose either her legal rights or her parental inheritance. A lay priest inherits the mother's personal belongings in equal portion to his sister, and the allod and heritable property in equal portion to his brother. No one can be called a priest who lacks the education of the clergy and who has not also been ordained as a priest before the mother's personal belongings devolve on him. But if a woman has only one brother, and he is a priest, then she and he share equally in both the mother's personal property and the inheritance. When a priest dies, one does not distinguish the mother's endowment because everything he leaves is considered one estate. The sister without trousseau does not share her mother's personal belongings with a priest who has a church or prebend.

6 Whatever property a man has at the time of his death is called his heritable estate.[32] Whoever inherits the property must pay the outstanding debts of the deceased up to the value of his movable goods. However, he is not responsible for theft, robbery, or gambling debts, just as he is not liable for debts for which the deceased either did not receive compensation or was not a guarantor. The heir must discharge the debt if, as the law provides, proof of the outstanding debt is brought forth by seventy-two men, all of whom are either of legitimate birth or of the *Schöffen* class. If the person knows of a debt, then proof with witnesses is not necessary as long as the creditor is willing to forego the witnesses and makes his claim because the

heir knows of the debt according to land and feudal law. The heir should acknowledge and discharge the debt or deny it with an oath. Debtors shall pay the heir what they owed the deceased person. The debts that the man [heir] himself has incurred may not be proven through compurgators.[33] He must admit or deny them. ⟨fol. 12v⟩

7 Whoever offers surety or a pledge is required to fulfill it, and whatever he promises, he must keep reliably. Should he wish to void it later, he can withdraw from the other party with an oath whatever had not been arranged in court. In contrast, whatever he carried out before the court can be proven against him by the party initiating the case with two men swearing on the relics, and the judge shall be the third.[34]

8 In cases where a person alienates or transfers his allodial land or when he tries to prosecute a man in a court [case] that requires forfeiture of the defendant's rights, life, or health[35] because of what that man had pledged in court or lost as a result of a court decision, then the judge must be a witness along with six others who hand down a judgment for him. In cases where the oath of seven is required, the oath of the bailiff is equal to that of two men when he is needed. The bailiff's compensation payment[36] is also double, as is his wergeld.[37] as determined by his birth at the time he is selected. An oath of reconciliation as well as an oath of truce that a person vows before the court, however, is witnessed by the judge and two men.[38] Should this oath occur outside a court, then he must bear witness with six other men to the man to whom he vowed reconciliation or truce.[39]

9 If one person pledges his allodial land to another person in court, and the recipient gives his silver or other property in return, and if the latter dies before the transfer is confirmed, then one must accord to the heir what one would accord the deceased as long as he had paid for it in full. One must treat movable property in the same way. Further, if a person pledges his property holdings to another with a promise to convey it in the presence of his lord, and when he has discharged this, and the other has paid him in part ⟨fol. 13r⟩ or entirety, then if the recipient who made the contract dies before he could be invested with the promised property, the transferor is responsible for transferring it to the heir to the fief[40] whether he is of equal birth or not. And if there is no successor to the fief, he is required to convey it to the legal heir, whoever he may be, just as he had been required originally to transfer it to the first person [the deceased], provided that he had been paid in full. Otherwise, he must pay to the successor to the fief the amount that had been paid to him. A lord[41] shall follow the same procedure when a man pays him for a piece of land which he must enfeoff him with or make avail-

able to him, and the man dies before the enfeoffment.[42] However, if the man who is supposed to transfer the land swears that he is obtaining the property for the tenancy of another person, and if he does so and declares to the recipient before witnesses that he may come and take possession, and if the recipient refuses without just cause, then if the lord hereafter refuses to bestow the property or dies, and the transferor can no longer procure it as before, he is then released from riding in to transfer possession, but not of relinquishing the property if the other is still able to acquire it.[43] Whoever places real property in another's possession should, before he transfers it, first represent him in his right of possession whenever he requires this warranty, as long as the property has not yet been conveyed. Should the court deny right of possession to the person holding the property or to the person to whom the property is to be transferred, then the property holder should return it to the person who had [originally] placed it in his possession. If the person transferring the property dies, then his son is not required to transfer it unless he himself had pledged it or given security to do so.

10 If a father gives his son clothing, a charger and riding horse, and a mail coat when he needs them and is able to use them, and the father has them to give, then afterwards, if the father dies, ⟨fol. 13v⟩ the son is not required to share them with his brothers, nor to turn them over to his father's lord, nor to his father's heir if he is not of equal birth to the father, just as if he had never received any separate settlement from his father.

11 A father who also retains guardianship of his children after the death of their mother must, when the children separate from him, return and transfer their mother's entire property to them unless it was lost through misfortune for which he was not responsible. The wife should do the same for the father's children if the father dies, and so should every man who is the guardian of children.

12 When brothers or other people own property jointly and they improve it either through expenditure or through their own labor, the gain belongs to them jointly. The same holds for losses. But whatever a man gains from his wife [in marriage], he does not share with his brothers. If a man gambles away his property, or squanders it through debauchery, or wastes it on gifts or expenses to which his brothers or those with whom he stands in joint ownership have not agreed, then the resulting losses are his alone and not those of his brothers or peers with whom he owns property jointly.

13 It is possible for a father or a mother to give one of the sons or one of the daughters the rightful share of inheritance from his or her own

property whether the offspring continue to share in the household expenses or not.[44] If, after the death of the father or after the death of the mother, they claim their part of the inheritance, either the brother from his brothers or the married sister from her unendowed sisters, they must with an oath return for partitioning all the property that they had been given if it was movable goods with the exception of a dowry. But if the property is of a type that one must prove, ⟨fol. 14r⟩ then it cannot be forsworn. If, however, they have renounced their share of the inheritance, then they shall remain without it unless they rescind with an oath on the relics; but should they have sworn to abandon [their claim] in court, then it is easier to bring a judgment against them with witnesses than for them to be acquitted. In such cases the village headman is witness concerning the peasants within his jurisdiction in place of the judge.

14 Only according to feudal law may the lord bestow a father's fief to no more than one son. It is not consistent with general territorial law that one son alone retain it without compensating his brothers for the portion legally due them. It is equally unacceptable according to territorial law for the father to dispose of his fief to his son and transfer it to him immediately so that he may possess it already at the time of the father's death and, in addition, receive equal shares of another landholding with his brothers. Even if the brothers cannot deny him according to feudal law, it still does not hold for territorial law. And if they bring a suit against him according to territorial law, they easily force him to divide the inheritance justly with a court decision.

15 Whoever gives his movable goods to another in loan, pledge or in safe-keeping either for a specified or unspecified period,[45] and if afterwards the other person, or his heir after his death, contests [the agreement], the lender who transferred the property is closer to winning with his oath and that of two oathhelpers than the property holder is to proving his [case] using witnesses or his heritable property, or even if he has a guarantor for it.[46] When a man accuses another of possessing something that he does not have, he can clear himself with a cleansing oath,[47] but whatever can be proven, he must answer for without an oath.

16 No one ⟨fol. 14v⟩ can acquire any legal status other than that with which he was born.[48] Should he deny his legal rank and rights before a court of law and claim for himself a different legal status that he cannot substantiate, he loses both. The exception is the bondman who has been freed. He attains the legal status of a free tenant.

17 An offspring who is free and legitimate retains the legal rank of the

father, but if the father or the mother is a servant,[49] the child has the legal status of its birth. If a man dies without issue, his father succeeds to his estate. If he has no father, then his mother succeeds with more justification than his brother. The son and not the daughter inherits from father and mother, sister and brother. But when an inheritance is divided among more distant family members such as brothers and sisters, then all who can count themselves at the same level inherit equally, whether man or woman.[50] The Saxons call these people common heirs.[51] However, the offspring of a son or daughter precedes the father or mother and sister or brother [of the deceased] in sequence of inheritance for the following reason: Nothing may break the direct line of descent[52] as long as such members are alive. Whoever is not equal in birth to the decedent may not succeed to the inheritance. A Swabian[53] cannot inherit from the woman's side since the women in their tribe[54] have all been disinherited because of the transgression of their [female] ancestors.[55]

18 The Saxons uphold three types of laws in contradiction of King Charlemagne's will.[56] The first is the Swabian law resulting from the Swabians' enmity towards women.[57] The second concerns any action that a man does not establish in a court of law. Even if the act is well known, he may clear himself with a cleansing oath, and no one can press charges against him with compurgators. The third asserts that there is no ⟨fol. 15r⟩ judgment passed before the king's court in Saxony that cannot be challenged, no matter how consistent it is with the law. If a Saxon wishes to appeal, then he appeals to his right hand[58] and to the majority of men. He then contests the judgment [and does battle] together with six others against another seven men.[59] The party with the majority of victors wins the case. Furthermore, all Saxons retain their old law as long as it does not conflict with the law of Christianity or with correct faith.

19 A Swabian definitely succeeds to military equipment[60] and inheritance even beyond the seventh degree of consanguinity just as far as he can calculate the deceased man's relationship to him on the agnatic side,[61] and as long as he can prove with compurgators either that one of his ancestors had at one time demanded or taken the military equipment from [that man's] ancestor in a court of law, or that that man's ancestor had demanded military equipment legally from his ancestor. The Swabians contest a judgment among their own group on Swabian territory[62] and appeal to a court in old Swabia[63] which they must name and to the majority of men in a regular court session at the highest venue designated for holding the regular court.[64] Swabian law is not different from Saxon law except for the way eligibility of heirs is calculated and the way a judgment is appealed.[65]

20 Now hear[66] what each man of knightly birth is permitted to give his wife as a morning gift.[67] In the morning when he goes to table with her before breakfast, he may without prior oath or agreement of the heirs give her a servant boy or girl who is not yet of age,[68] also a house and enclosed garden,[69] and grazing stock. In a case where a lady[70] does not own the land on which the building stands, she must, when her husband dies, vacate the premises and remove the building within six weeks after the thirtieth[71] in such a manner that she does not damage the ground.[72] But if she offers ⟨fol. 15v⟩ to sell the building to the landowner based on the appraisal of neighbors, and he does not agree, then she may certainly dig as long as she levels the ground again. If she remains with the children or heirs of her husband for a longer or shorter term unseparated from her property, then when she separates herself from them, she retains the same rights to the property that existed when the husband died. In contrast, a widow who, after her husband's death, remains with her children in the children's property that does not belong to her and is not separated from that property, and if her son takes a wife while she is still alive, and later her son dies, then the son's wife has more right to her own husband's morning gift, the woman's share of the divisible food supplies,[73] her personal belongings, including her dowry, from her husband's property than his mother as long as she can prove with witnesses her husband's and her own uncontested ownership.[74] But if the son dies in the mother's property, then the mother has stronger claim to the property with oathhelpers than her son's widow. The wife retains her morning gift by swearing on the relics, but her claim of rightful possession can be proven only with compurgators. Accordingly, if she dies before her husband, then her niece[75] has more right to the woman's belongings after her death than does the husband's mother. The mother is guest in her son's property just as the son is in the mother's. All those who are not of knightly birth may give their wives as morning gift nothing more than the best horse or [head of] livestock they own.

21 A woman can certainly substantiate her morning gift by swearing on the relics without witnesses. One must also give a lady possession of allodial land during her lifetime with the pledge of the heirs no matter how young they may be. This must be accomplished in the judicial district in which the land is located in any site in which the court is held under the king's judicial authority. ⟨fol. 16r⟩ No one may deprive a lady of a life estate,[76] not an heir born after the agreement nor anyone else who rightfully succeeds to the inheritance unless she forfeits it by her own doing. She may forfeit the land if she cuts down fruit trees, or expels people from the property who were born to it, or relinquishes control over it in some way. If

she cannot reverse the situation by the next regularly scheduled court date when complaints are brought, then she can well lose her right to it. When a man is legally separated from his wife, she still retains right of use to that portion of his proprietary land that he had turned over to her in life estate.

22 The heir may assuredly visit the widow at the property before the thirtieth in order to prevent the loss of whatever falls to him. The woman shall arrange the funeral and the thirtieth with his advice. He shall have no other power over the property until the thirtieth. First it is necessary to pay the household servants their earned wages from the estate as they deserve, up to the day their master died. They should be retained in service until the thirtieth so that they can find another situation, but if the successor desires, they may serve full time and receive full pay. Should they receive too much pay, they do not need to return it. If anyone denies their wages of a year or even a half-year, they must claim their pay by swearing on the relics. Anyone who had been in the deceased person's service without pay should remind the successor of this arrangement to claim his reward.[77] If a hired man dies before he has earned the entire wage promised, a person is required to pay his heir only the wages for the work actually completed at the time of his death. ⟨fol. 16v⟩ Second, the lady must divide among the heirs all stored food supplies still remaining on the grounds after the thirtieth in every building owned by her husband or wherever he had stored them. Likewise, the lady shall hand over all the military equipment he owned [and used] until he died: her husband's sword, his best charger or riding horse with saddle, his best coat of mail and tent,[78] and also the field gear, which consists of an army cot, a pillow, linen sheet, tablecloth, two washbasins, and a towel. This, in general, constitutes the military equipment and must be given over by right although people include several items that do not belong. The wife need not supply the articles she does not have as long as she dares to swear that she does not possess them. This is to be done separately for each and every such item. However, if it can be proven, no man or woman can cleanse himself with an oath. When two or three men are born to one set of arms and armor, the oldest first inherits the sword separately, and then they divide the remaining items equally among them.

23 Where the sons are under age, the eldest agnatic relation of equal birth[79] takes the entire military outfit himself and becomes the guardian of the children until they come of age. At that time he must give it to them along with all their property, unless he can demonstrate that he used it for their benefit or prove that its accidental loss, theft, or damage is not a result of his own negligence. Even after a child comes of age according to feudal

law, his legal guardian shall continue to oversee his property ⟨fol. 17r⟩ as needed and represent the ward according to his status in his obligations to his lord while the ward himself is unable to act or make judgments because of ineptitude, feebleness of mind, or weakness of body.[80] However, the guardian shall give annual account of the property to his ward's heir, whoever he may be, and provide assurance that he has not been unjustly squandering the property since the child's maturity, for it often happens that the child's guardian is one person and the heir another. But when the guardian is also the heir, he is not accountable to anyone regarding the child's property, nor does he need to give surety. He is also the legal guardian of the widow until she marries, if the man is her equal in birth.[81]

24 After delivering the military equipment, a woman[82] takes possession of her morning gift. This includes all workhorses, cattle, goats, and swine that are herded by a herdsman, and the house with its enclosed yard. Fattened hogs belong to the partitionable food supplies,[83] as do all the stored foodstuffs in each of her husband's outbuildings. She also takes possession of her personal belongings, including her dowry. These include all the sheep and geese; chests with concave lids; all thread, quilts, beds, pillows, linen sheets, tablecloths, towels, bath sheets; washbasins; iron lamps; linen and women's clothing; rings and bracelets; chaplets;[84] psalters, and all [devotional] books related to the service of God that women are wont to read.[85] Also [included are] cushioned chairs, chests, rugs, curtains, wall hangings, and all ribbons belonging to the woman's trousseau. There are additional small articles that belong in this category ⟨fol. 17v⟩ that I cannot list exhaustively, such as brushes, scissors, and mirrors. Excluded from this list are fabric not yet cut for women's clothing and uncrafted gold and silver because they are inappropriate. Other existing items not listed here belong to the estate. Whatever property of the deceased had been pawned during his life may be redeemed by the rightful heir if he so wishes.

25 A lay priest divides [property] with his brother but not a monk. If an underage child is made a monk, he may, while still underage, leave the monastery and retain his rights in both land and feudal law. In contrast, if a man in his majority enters a monastery, he has separated himself from land and feudal law. His fiefs are released because he has forfeited noble status,[86] for which there are witnesses among either the monks whom he has joined, or seven of his equals in status who have seen him in the order. In this case he has forfeited his status even if he renounces within the year, an option allowed by the rules of the gray monks.[87] But if he joined the monastery without his wife's consent, and she demands in an ecclesiastical court that

he return from the monastic life, then he retains his rights in general territorial law, but not the feudal holding which he has relinquished. This is possible because a man may renounce his noble status of military shields without his wife's approval.

26 If a child dies, or if one places an underage child in a monastery [as an oblate],[88] then the person who has possession of his movable property should transfer it to the person who would inherit it after the child's death unless the property was depleted with the heir's agreement.

27 Every woman passes on property in two directions: Her closest female relative on her mother's side receives her dowry and other personal belongings. These items devolve upon her because of the cognate kinship.[89] The estate passes to the woman's next of kin, who may be a woman or man. ⟨fol. 18r⟩ Each man of knightly birth also transmits heritable property in two directions. The estate devolves upon the closest relative of equal birth, whoever that may be, and the military equipment goes to the closest relative on the agnate side. Whoever lacks knightly birth and membership in the noble orders of arms-bearing men passes on heritable property but no military outfit when he dies.

28 When someone dies and an heir is lacking for any one of the [three] items—the estate, the military equipment, or the woman's personal belongings including her trousseau—then it should be placed in the custody of the judge or bailiff after the thirtieth[90] if he requests it. The judge should hold these effects undisturbed and wait for a year and a day[91] to see if someone lays rightful claim to them. After this time, the judge may appropriate them for his personal use unless the heir has been imprisoned, has departed in the service of the king, or is outside the country in the service of God. In that case, he must store the effects and wait until the heir returns because he cannot forfeit the inheritance during this time. These [rules] pertain to movable goods.

29 A Saxon's claim to allodial property or a hide of land[92] does not become invalid until thirty years plus a year and a day have passed and not any sooner. The realm[93] and the Swabian never lose claim to their inheritance so long as they can prove it with witnesses.

30 Each immigrant man inherits in the land of Saxony according to territorial law, and not according to the man's personal law, whether he is Bavarian, Swabian or Franconian.[94]

31 Husband and wife have no separate property for their livelihood.[95] If the wife dies while her husband is still living, she passes on to her closest kin the woman's personal belongings, but no movable property and no allodial land if she owns any.

32 No woman may make an irrevocable disposition of her property without her husband's consent.[96] ⟨fol. 18v⟩ When a man takes a wife, he accepts into his rightful possession all her property in lawful guardianship. As a result, no woman may give her husband allodial or movable property as a gift. This [provision] ensures that she cannot deprive her rightful heir after her death because the husband can claim no other possessory right[97] to his wife's property than what he received at the beginning of the marriage. No woman can retain in ownership that portion of property set aside as her life estate, nor can her heir do so after her death when it can be proven with witnesses that it had been assigned for her lifelong use. If she asserts her ownership, then she forfeits both the allod and the life estate.

33 Now hear about the pregnant woman who reveals her condition after her husband's death at either the burial or on the thirtieth. If the child is born alive, and the woman has the oath of four men who heard the child and of two women who attended her in her labor, the child retains the father's inheritance. And if it dies thereafter, it passes the inheritance on to the mother if she is of equal birth and forfeits all claim to the father's tenured holding because it lived after the father's death. This is the way fiefs revert to the lord even when the child is presented and considered to be robust enough to survive. Yet if it is brought to the church publicly, whoever sees it and hears it can certainly witness that it lived.

34 A person can dispose of his heritable property without permission of the judge with the agreement of all heirs as long as he retains half a hide of land and a yard[98] large enough to turn around a cart. He is to fulfill his legal duty to the judge based on this landholding. ⟨fol. 19r⟩ When a man transfers his allodial property, and it is returned to him in fief, this gift offers the lord no gain unless he retains it unoccupied in his possession for a year and a day.[99] After this time, he can invest the original owner with it and still retain it with confidence because neither the original owner nor his heirs can claim it. However, if the judge decides incorrectly that the man cannot alienate his allod, then when the king comes to Saxony,[100] the land can be transferred before him, as the man should have done originally before the judge. This way one has witnesses proving that the judge had wrongly prohibited the transaction.

35 Any hoard buried in the earth deeper than the plough cuts belongs to the royal domain. No one may dig silver on another's property without permission of the owner. If the owner gives permission, then the person digging has the responsibility to protect it.

36 When a woman takes a husband and gives birth to a child prematurely, when it normally would not survive,[101] one can contest its legal

status because it is born too early. Should she give birth post-term after the husband's death, one can also contest its rights because it is born too late.

37 Whoever violates a man's wife openly, or rapes a woman or a girl, will never have legitimate children by her even if he marries her.

38 Paid champions and their children,[102] minstrels, all who are born illegitimate, and all convicted robbers and thieves who are to make restitution or have done so and were convicted of their crime are all without legal rights.[103] Any person who has been in royal outlawry[104] for a year and a day [permanently] loses his legal rights and forfeits his allod and his fief by court decision.[105] The fief reverts to the lord's free disposal and the allod to the ⟨fol. 19v⟩ royal domain. If the heirs do not claim it from the royal domain within a year and a day with their oath, they forfeit it together with the outlaw unless legitimate exigency prevents them from appearing. In that case, they must prove the hindrance according to law.[106] The allod of a ministerial[107] cannot be placed in the royal domain, nor can it be removed from the lord's control if he forfeits his legal rights. A man without legal capacity cannot have legitimate children afterwards.[108] If a person is outlawed by the realm for a year and a day, and if after that year his rights and legal protection are withdrawn [permanently],[109] his outlawry can be commuted only to the extent that no one can take his life. He cannot, however, be reinstated into the law[110] unless he fights a joust before the emperor's retinue and prevails over a foreign king.[111] He can regain his rights in this way, but not the property that was confiscated from him.

39 People who have lost their legal rights and privileges[112] because of robbery or theft cannot, when accused by someone elsewhere, clear themselves with an oath. They have three choices: They may carry the glowing iron, thrust their arm up to the elbow into boiling water, or fight against a champion.

40 Whoever is convicted for betrayal or desertion from military service to the realm is stripped of his public rights[113] and his feudal rights, but not his life.

41 If a girl or a widow brings a complaint according to general territorial law against her guardian that he is misappropriating allodial or feudal land or life estate from her, and if he is summoned to court for this and fails by the third summons to appear and fulfill his legal obligation, then he must be declared a delinquent guardian. This means that he is barred by legal decision from any guardianship.[114] Afterwards let ⟨fol. 20r⟩ the judge be the woman's guardian and let her have, on behalf of the court, full power over the property which she previously did not control.

42 Before a man attains majority, and after exceeding it, he may have a guardian if he needs one and may dispense with one if he so wishes. If the guardian is not immediately available, he should be brought to the next court session scheduled to hear a case. A man attains majority at the completion of his twenty-first year. He needs a guardian [before reaching majority] and after exceeding it after the age of sixty-one. He does not reduce thereby either his compensation tariff or his wergeld. In case of a man whose age is not known, one can be sure he is of age if he has hair on his face, under both armpits, and down below. When a minor comes of age, he then must be guardian for his wife, and beyond that he should do so for others if he wishes and should also be combat guardian[115] right away once he is of age because if he has the legal capacity to represent himself, then he must also represent his charges.

43 In a complaint of rape, if it does not go to trial by combat, the judge must assign the woman a guardian and likewise in all crimes in which the perpetrator is caught red-handed[116] if the lawful guardian is not immediately available. If, however, the case goes to combat, then her guardian must be one of her agnatic male relations of equal birth.

44 If a girl or widow makes a complaint regarding her guardian according to general territorial law that he is taking her property, then with this complaint she establishes the court as guardian. The same applies when her husband has transferred allodial property to her in permanent ownership[117] or for her lifelong use. ⟨fol. 20v⟩

45 A man who is not of equal birth to his wife is nevertheless her guardian. Once she enters his bed, she becomes his peer, enters into his legal status, and is subject to it.[118] But if he dies, then she is released from his legal status and regains her rights according to her birth. For this reason her guardian must be her closest agnatic relation of equal birth and not a member of her husband's family. A woman may not alienate her property nor sell her proprietary land, nor transfer land held in life estate without her husband's approval because he shares right of possession with her. A girl or an unmarried woman may sell land she owns without permission of her guardian unless he is heir to it. However, girls and married women must have guardians to bring a suit because one cannot prosecute them with witnesses for what they say or do in a court of law.

46 When women[119] must swear an oath, they shall do it themselves and not their guardian. The woman's legal guardian shall swear security for her and accept and execute it.

47 A guardian appointed by the court must also swear and secure the

receipt of property for her and afterward may not suffer repercussions because of it as long as he speaks the truth when he is asked by the court about it. The reason is that his guardianship holds only for the duration of the court hearing. The judge needs to appoint a guardian separately for each court case.

48 All those who are born out of wedlock or have forfeited their rights by their own doing cannot have a guardian either for bringing charges or for a trial by combat. The handicapped can also bring complaint or defend without a guardian unless the ⟨fol. 21r⟩ case goes to combat. In that case any agnatic relation of equal birth who is willing should be the guardian. If the handicapped person cannot produce his legal guardian when challenged to combat and dares to swear an oath on it, he can obtain as guardian whoever is willing to act in his behalf or whomever he can pay to do so, even if one can ascertain the identity of his legal guardian. If he defends himself with a champion, then the plaintiff can also pursue his case with a champion, even if he originally did not bring the complaint through one, and this shall not be held against him in the case.

49 One can defend a deceased person in this same way if someone brings charges against him. A person can also defend himself with a champion in the same way. However, a person cannot use a champion to prosecute someone who has never been in conflict with the law.

50 If a wounded man challenges the person who wounded him to a judgment by combat and is not able to complete the duel for weakness of body and has no guardian who is willing to fight in his stead, one shall postpone the date [of the duel] until he is able to fight for himself. Further, if someone wounds or kills another and brings him bound before the court and wants to prosecute him for violating the peace[120] but does not complete the procedure, then he shall be indicted by the court for the injustice he did to that person. Even if a man is a minstrel or illegitimate of birth, he is nevertheless not the legal equal of a robber or a thief, so it is not possible to bring a case against him using a champion.

51 A person with diminished legal capacity is, in no way barred from all rights because someone with limited legal capacity can undeniably take a lawful wife and have children by her who are his equals in birth ⟨fol. 21v⟩ unless the children are distinguished from them through servile status.[121] A man and a woman, both of legitimate birth, do not succeed to the inheritance of an illegitimately born man. It is said that no child is illegitimate with respect to its mother, but this is not so. A woman can give birth to children who are of legitimate, noble, servile, or illegitimate status. If she is

of servile status, she can be freed, if she is a concubine,[122] then she can marry and bear legitimate children within the marriage at any time. Whoever is unblemished in his legal and social status in his family going back to his four immediate predecessors — that is, his two grandfathers and two grandmothers, and father and mother — cannot be questioned in his rights of birth unless he has forfeited them by his own actions. When someone eligible to be a *Schöffe* challenges someone of equal rank to a trial by combat, he needs to know accurately his four ancestors and his family estate[123] and must name them; otherwise the defendant can by rights refuse him the duel. If one person challenges another to combat by grabbing him,[124] and the other rightfully refuses, then the challenger must release him and make compensation.

52 No one may alienate his allodial land nor his unfree peasants without the agreement of the heirs and without a formal hearing of the regular court. However, the lords may exchange among each other people in their service outside the court if the exchange can be proven and witnessed. If anyone alienates property unlawfully without agreement of the heirs, then they can take possession by order of the court as if the person who had alienated the property without approval were dead, because he had no permission to do as he did. A man may transfer all movable property without consent of the heirs as long as he can climb on a horse by himself, with sword buckled on and shield in hand, using a wooden block or stone an ell[125] high without help from anyone except the person who holds the horse and stirrup for him. But if he ⟨fol. 22r⟩ cannot execute this, he may not give away movable property nor transfer nor lend it in order to deprive the person who has claim to it upon his death. If he has taken property from someone into his own possession, the original possessor cannot bring suit for conveyance of ownership; he can claim only the rights he had before it was taken from him. When someone gives away or pledges his property during illness or at a time when he is not permitted, no one can bring a case against the wife or the household for it because they may not contest the man's act of transfer, whether it be done according to law or not. If one person gives another something unlawfully, the law permits him to demand that it be returned by the person to whom it was given.

53 The woman is not responsible for her husband's property except for that which was in her possession at the time of his death. For each of the following listed offenses, a court fine must be paid to the judge: failure to appear when the hue and cry is raised; failure to make a complaint according to the law; or challenging a man to combat who has lawfully refused

before the court; or failure to appear in court at the appointed time or to appear at all; speaking or acting unlawfully during the court session; or refusal to pay on time a debt determined by the court. And for every liability that is awarded compensation by a court ruling, a court fine must be paid to the judge. In addition, the judge frequently collects a court fine for contumacy in court, even when neither the plaintiff nor the defendant receives restitution. If someone does not pay his court fine and the compensation amount by the due date, the bailiff shall distrain his property and pawn or sell it immediately in order to pay the debt. However, the bailiff shall not seize anything that ⟨fol. 22v⟩ was not authorized in the ruling. No one shall pay a court fine twice unless he violates the peace and also brings anathema upon himself with a single deed.[126] He must pay the court fine to both the ecclesiastical and the secular court, and must also pay a compensation to the person he injured.

54 No one who is required to pay rents need tolerate seizure by his lord exceeding the value of his yearly dues. Whoever does not pay his dues on the fixed days must pay double on the following day and so on each day thereafter as long as he fails to pay, providing the lord pursues the collection according to the proper procedures by seeking him out at home to demand payment. This is done because the man is not required to pay the duty outside of his dwelling. The lord or his representative can demand payment of dues more easily than the man can contest them. The same holds for the tithe that is due on the land in his use.[127] If the man claims he has paid the rent, and if his claim is contested, he must prove it with two others who saw and heard[128] that he had paid. The lord may certainly make seizure on his own property without the judge's permission for rent which had been promised him from the property. No tenant may dig a stone or lime pit without the permission of the lord to whom he owes duty. Nor may he cut wood or clear land for farming on property on which he pays rent unless it is his own heritable land.

55 There is no secular court without an elected [judge].[129] For this reason, no appointed man may be judge, nor anyone else, unless he has [also] been elected or invested with the office of judge. If, however, after a criminal act—either a theft or a robbery—the perpetrator is caught red-handed, then a local judge[130] can assuredly be elected ⟨fol. 23r⟩ from at least three villages to preside over a violent crime when the invested judge is not at hand.[131]

56 The local judgeship cannot by law be invested or transferred by inheritance as a fief because the villagers have the right to elect the local

judge freely for each violent act or for an agreed-upon period of time. Should the lord give the office in fief anyway, then he must fulfill his legal duty toward his man and his children according to feudal law unless the villagers overrule them both with their own lawful election.

57 And if the thief or robber is not brought to trial on that very day or the following night, then the local judge no longer has jurisdiction over the case. This pertains to the local judge who was elected to preside over a violent act the same day on which the perpetrator was caught red-handed. But if someone is elected to the office for a long period, the count or margrave should invest him with it. He presides over public assemblies and criminal cases older than one night.

58 Whenever the count comes to the local judge's court session, the judge shall defer to the comital jurisdiction. The same applies to the count's court when the king enters his territory, since they are both present. This holds for every judge when the king is present unless a charge is brought against the king.

59 The judge presides over all formal complaints, suits, and criminal proceedings within his jurisdiction wherever he is, except when someone brings a complaint regarding allodial property or accuses someone belonging to the *Schöffen* class of a criminal offense. In these instances the judge may pursue the case only in the legally stipulated venue and under the king's legal authority.[132] No one may hold a court under the king's jurisdiction without having first been invested with the king's delegated judicial authority. Once a person has received authority from the king, ⟨fol. 23v⟩ he need not receive it again if the king dies. Only one royal jurisdiction is allowed per advocacy.[133] Whoever presides in court under the king's jurisdiction without having been invested with its power must lose his tongue in punishment. A count who sits in court under the king's authority cannot hold regular sessions without his appointed *Schultheiss*, who is above him by law.[134] For this reason he must first ask his *Schultheiss* for the initial rulings: whether it is time for the court session, and after that, whether he should prohibit any disruptions and all commotion. Once this is affirmed for him, anyone can bring forth a complaint with a spokesman about any disagreements whatsoever.[135]

60 A man may bring a complaint and answer for himself without a spokesman if he is willing to be responsible for any disadvantage or loss that may occur. If he speaks incorrectly, he cannot correct such mistakes as is assuredly possible when he has a speaker whose plea he does not have to accept. The judge shall assign as speaker the person who was first asked to

do so and none other unless he is released of the duty by law. No one may refuse to act as spokesman in the judicial district in which he lives, owns property, or demands his rights except when the complaint is made against his family relation, his lord, or man, and the penalty is loss of life, health, or legal status. Should two men request the same spokesman at the same time, then the judge decides to which of the two he will be assigned. If they also bring a case at the same time, the judge decides whom he will hear first unless one can prove with witnesses that he began the case earlier. A stutterer can correct himself should he misspeak. If he places someone at a disadvantage[136] for whom he is spokesman, then he ⟨fol. 24r⟩ must correct [the damage] by means of another spokesman. Any man uncompromised in his legal standing may act as speaker in the territory of Saxony according to territorial law with the exception of a priest. A person who has no inheritable property must offer security for the court fine and compensation payment when he becomes liable to pay, but not before. Wherever a man demands justice, there he must answer to the law and foster it.[137]

61 No plaintiff need offer security before the date of the hearing is decided. If a person has no guarantors and no inheritable property in the district,[138] he shall be detained and held in custody[139] if he brings charges for a violent crime or if a charge is made against him. Whoever a man chooses as spokesman must speak for him in all complaints brought against him and, in addition, in all cases he himself brings to court as long as that spokesman is not removed by court order or as long as neither severs the relationship.

62 A man may not force another to pursue a claim he did not initiate himself before the judge. A man may remain silent about damages incurred as long as he wishes. But if he raises the hue and cry, he must follow through and press charges according to the law because the hue and cry is the beginning of a court case. Whoever draws his sword to harm another man forfeits his sword to the judge.[140] The fine for raising the hue and cry without cause is three shillings when one does not carry through with the charges according to law. However, if the plaintiff pursues the case legally without trial by combat, and if the accused clears himself with an oath of innocence, then the plaintiff goes without damages unless he had challenged the other to trial by combat. And if he does not know the name of the perpetrator, then he should bring charges against him without a name. ⟨fol. 24v⟩ A man who has offered proof with witnesses shall fulfill it within six weeks, or immediately if he so desires. If one must bring proof of allodial ownership, it must be executed right away or at the next scheduled court

session. The judge must always ask the man whether he accepts the plea of the spokesman, and must ask for a ruling after each of the two parties has spoken once.[141] If he asks on his own accord and not according to the law, then he does not hinder or aid either party. Decisions requested first must be decided first.[142] The plaintiff and the person against whom the charges have been made may each consult up to three times after each statement until the time the court official summons them.[143] A law court may be held in all places where the judge presides over a judgment. A man may not speak publicly in court when he has an advocate. However, when the judge asks him if he accepts his spokesman's plea, he may certainly speak to say yes or no, or he may ask for a consultation.

63 Whoever wants to challenge his peer to trial by combat[144] must ask the judge for permission to seize the offender he sees there in order to stand trial.[145] If the judge rules that he may do so, then he will ask where he should seize him so that it may help him to his rights. The following ruling is then given: he may seize him by the neck opening with propriety.[146] Once he has seized and released him with permission, then he must make known to the accused why he seized him. He may do so immediately, if he so wishes, or hold consultation regarding it. Then he must bring formal charges that the offender ⟨fol. 25r⟩ has violated the peace against him either on the king's road or in the village [and describe] the manner in which he acted against him. This is the way he must bring charges. If he then also accuses the man of wounding him and using force against him and can prove it, then he must exhibit the wound or, if it has healed, the scar. Then he may bring further charges that the accused has robbed his goods and taken so much that it is not unjustified to challenge him to trial by battle. It is necessary to bring suit at the same time for these three criminal charges. If one withholds one of them, he has lost his combat. He shall state the following: "I myself saw this person and raised the hue and cry. If he admits this, then I accept it, and if he does not, then I shall prosecute him with all the rights that the people within this jurisdiction accord me or the *Schöffen* deem when the court convenes under the king's jurisdiction." After that the accused shall request security, and it shall be granted. However, the plaintiff may correct his charges before the security is granted. Once the security is given, the defendant offers his proof of innocence, which consists of a cleansing oath and a legal duel if the accuser challenged him to a rightful settlement and if it is so, as I suppose, that the accuser is able to fight in spite of his injury. Any man may refuse a challenge from someone of lesser birth, but if the challenger is of higher birth, then the lesser-born man may not

refuse him. A man may refuse a duel if he is challenged after the noon hour unless the proceedings began earlier. The judge must also ⟨fol. 25v⟩ supply the defendant with a sword and shield should he need them. A man may refuse a duel with family members if they are related to each other by swearing with six others on the relics that they are so closely related that they may not lawfully do battle. The judge shall designate two deputies, one to each person who will fight, in order to ensure that they arm themselves according to proper custom. They may wear as much linen and leather as they wish; head and feet are bare in front; only thin gloves are worn on the hands. [They may have] an unsheathed sword in their hand and one or two on their belt, according to preference; in the other hand [is] a round shield of wood or leather only, with the exception of the boss, which can be of iron. A coat without sleeves is worn over the armor. Order shall be maintained in the enclosed combat ring on pain of death[147] so that no one may interfere with their duel. To each fighter the judge shall assign a deputy to carry his pole. These men shall not hamper the fighters in any way. But if one of the combatants falls, the deputy shall place the pole between them, or if one is wounded or asks for the pole. He may not do this of his own accord but only when he receives permission from the judge. After the combat ring is made secure, the fighters shall request to enter it for judgment, and the judge shall give them permission to do so. Next they break the tip of the scabbard once they have permission from the judge. Both should step fully armed before the judge and swear—the one that the accusation made against the defendant has been truthfully ⟨fol. 26r⟩ made, and the other that he is not guilty—so that God may stand by them in combat. When the opponents first face each other, it is necessary to align them so that neither is at a disadvantage by having the sun in his eyes.[148] If the defendant is convicted, then he shall be sentenced, but if he prevails, he shall go free with a court fine and a compensation payment. The plaintiff enters the circle first. If the other tarries too long, the judge must send the bailiff with two *Schöffen* to the house in which he is arming himself to summon him. This shall be done a second and a third time. If he does not come at the third summons, the plaintiff stands up and offers to fight. He swings two blows and makes one thrust into the wind. With that act, he convicts the defendant for the charges as he had spoken them. The judge shall then sentence him as if he had been convicted by the combat.

64 One should bring a dead man to judgment in the same way if he was killed in the act of robbery, or theft, or similar deed. But if someone can convict the dead man with the oath of seven witnesses, then he does not

have to offer to fight against him. But if a relative of the dead person, whoever that may be, offers to represent him in combat then he disqualifies any proof by means of compurgation. In this case the plaintiff cannot bring the deceased to justice without a trial by combat, unless he already has been outlawed.[149] This is also the procedure for bringing to court a person who has been seized and challenged to combat, has sworn and given security that he would appear before the court, and then does not come at the appointed time, as already stated above. Whoever ransoms life or hand forfeited by court sentence remains without any legal rights or privileges. ⟨fol. 26v⟩

65 If a person guarantees that he will bring a man to court because of a crime and then is unable to do so, he must pay the accused man's wergeld.[150] This event does not damage the legal rights of the person who had made the guaranty. The wergeld is to be paid within twelve weeks from the time it is awarded. One may pay [money] debts to whom they are owed before the day they are due provided that one makes payment in a place from which the receiver can transport it without obstruction. But he should obtain proof through witnesses, if he needs it, from two men who observe that the debtor repaid or offered payment with silver or with pennies[151] that were in common use there, and also that the other person refused unlawfully to accept it.

66 A person caught red-handed should be brought before the court just as he was when captured, and the accuser shall convict him with six others. One does the same with a convicted man if one proves with witnesses the deed for which he was outlawed. However, no one may pronounce a sentence of capital punishment on anyone as a result of either limited outlawry or complete outlawry if he had not been outlawed by name.[152] If a person makes accusation before the court against someone who is absent, he shall be summoned to the next court session.

67 If a person presses charges against someone for a criminal offense, the accused shall be summoned three times, each of a fortnight, but if one brings charges against a man of *Schöffen* rank, he shall be summoned three times as well, but each of a six-week period, under the king's jurisdiction and to the official court location. Whoever does not appear at the third scheduled hearing shall be placed in limited outlawry. On no other grounds shall anyone ⟨fol. 27r⟩ outlaw a man except for crimes that are punishable by loss of life or hand.

68 However, when one person bludgeons another so that the wounded spots swell, or beats another black-and-blue without breaking the skin, and if the injured person brings charges to the judge, or to the bailiff,

or to the village headman and villagers and proves it right away as a fresh crime,[153] and if the accused does not appear by the time of the regular court session to defend himself or to make restitution according to law, then he shall be outlawed. A man can challenge another to combat with black-and-blue injuries lacking lacerations, or with scars, or with the words leading to a challenge. A man can even kill or permanently disable another without breaking the skin, be it by beating, shoving or punching, throwing, or in many other ways.[154] In these cases, the perpetrator forfeits his life or his hand for it and draws limited outlawry upon himself. Regardless of the liability for which a man has been outlawed, if he is caught in limited outlawry and brought before the court, the penalty is death if he is convicted of the deed and of the outlawry. But if he releases himself from limited outlawry and comes before the court uncaptured, he can be restored to his rights as if he had never before been outlawed.

69 If a person captures a dead or wounded man and wants to prosecute him for breach of the peace either with or without a trial by combat, and if he does not prove it, then one shall render judgment over him according to peace law.[155]

70 If a man has brought a case regarding real property on three court sessions, then one shall install him in it and give him control over it. No one may then evict him unless a suitor brings a complaint against him according to law. ⟨fol. 27v⟩ A person can oppose the installation of this man in the property by means of an oath on the relics within the one-year time limit, but he must immediately answer for the property in three subsequent court sessions once the legal proceedings have begun. If a person brings suit to collect a debt against someone who does not have the legal responsibility of attending court, then a court order must be issued so that he may make recompense within a fortnight or plead his innocence according to the law. If he does not do so, one should distrain [property] for it and give that item to the plaintiff as security three times each for [a period of] a fortnight if the plaintiff desires it as security. And if he does not want it, it should be retained anyway undamaged for six weeks.[156] And if the accused does not refute the accusation in this time period, then he cannot refute it later unless a lawful excuse had prevented him. The attached property must then be pawned, or [it shall be] sold if it cannot be pawned in order to pay the debt. If any amount is left over, it should be returned to the debtor. But if the amount is not enough, then one should make another attachment and [continue] to do this until the plaintiff receives the [full] payment. If someone is brought before the court for a crime once the hue and cry has

been raised, and the accuser can prove the crime with the oath of six witnesses before a night passes, then the one who committed the crime shall be outlawed right away. But if the judge is outside of the court district when this occurs, then the accuser must make the accusation to the bailiff in lieu of the judge. If he proves with witnesses the charge on the first day when the judge returns to the district, then the perpetrator is outlawed as if the crime had occurred the same day.

71 When the elected local judge or the invested judge outlaws someone in the count's presence and proves [with an oath] the limited outlawry *⟨D, fol. 22r⟩*[157] *before the count, this immediately places him in the count's outlawry. Likewise, the count can impose the king's outlawry on a person in the same way.*

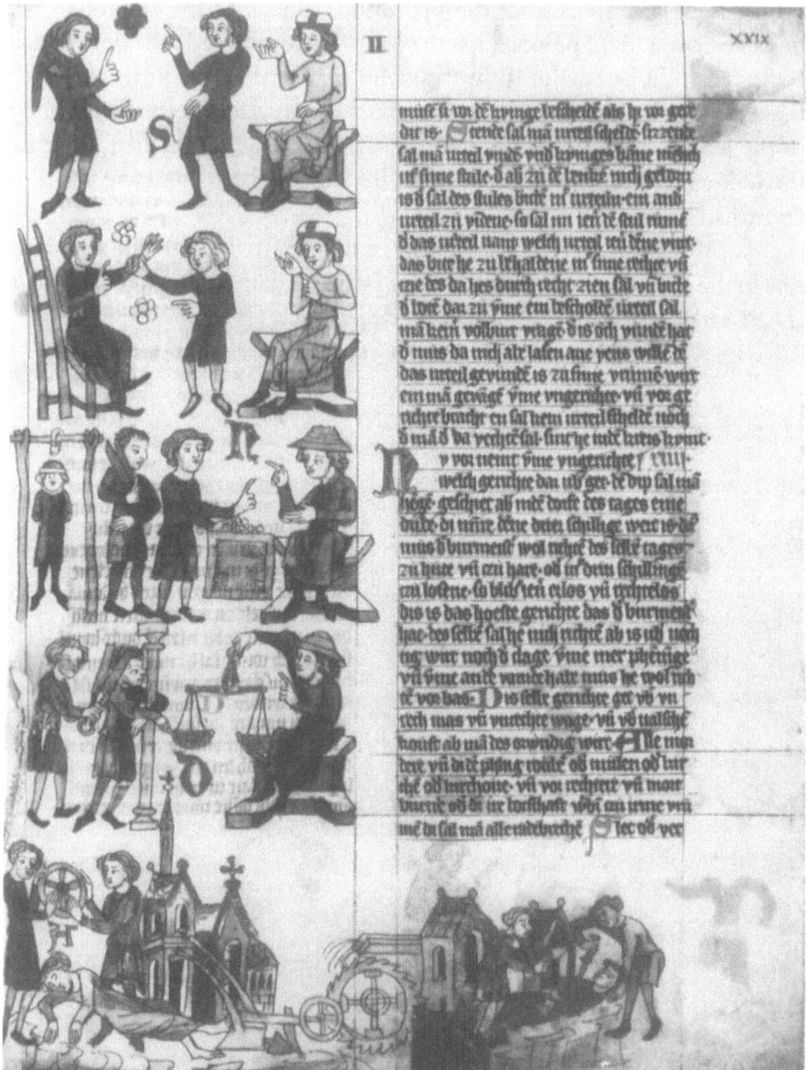

Plate 3. Folio 29r from book II. Top two registers: (1) appealing a judgment; (2) Handing down a judgment in a court of law. Registers 3—5, show punishments: (3) hanging; (4) shearing of hair; (5 left) breaking on the wheel, symbolized by the upheld wheel; (5 right) homicide. Cod. Guelf. 3.1 Aug.2°, folio 29r, II 13—14. (Reproduced by permission of the Herzog August Bibliothek, Wolfenbüttel, Germany)

Book II

⟨D fol. 22r⟩[1] 1 *Where princes or lords enter an alliance with an oath, they are acting against the realm unless they exclude the realm from it.*[2]

2 *If the count misses his regular court session, only the plaintiff is at a disadvantage. If he misses any hearings called because of violent crimes, the charges must be brought anew. If a person sues another who is present for allodial land or landholding in tenancy to which he has right of possession, the hearing shall be scheduled for the next court session if he says, "Sir, no hearing was set for me regarding this." Then if he asks for a postponement at the second presentation* [of the suit], *it shall be granted, but after that he must respond.*

3 *If a man, arriving unawares, is challenged to a trial by combat by another,*[3] *and he knows nothing about the case brought against him, he shall have* [time] *according to his birthright, if he requests it, in order to prepare himself once the combat is sworn and not before: The freemen of* Schöffen *class have six weeks; the ministerials have a fortnight, and so do other freemen. For any other type of suit that can be brought against a person, he shall plead immediately and deny or admit.*

4 *Whoever wishes to release himself from limited outlawry*[4] *shall be given immunity by the judge so that he may appear* [in court] *if he initiates* [the procedure] *himself. When he releases himself with an oath upon the relics, the judge shall cancel the outlawry with fingers and tongue in the same way that the outlawry was imposed.*[5] *If someone refuses* ⟨fol. 22v⟩ *unlawfully to do this, and he releases himself by swearing on the relics, he is no longer an outlaw. Consequently, he must be given safe conduct. He shall appoint a guarantor to ensure his appearance at the next three court sessions and to answer if someone brings a suit. Then, if no one brings a complaint at those three sessions, he shall be declared free of any charges. However, if someone releases himself from outlawry when the accuser is absent and pledges and establishes a bondsman that he will appear* [before the court] *and then does not come, the judge and not the plaintiff receives the pledge money because the judge outlaws the man again, as he must do by law.*

5 *Whoever has so much allodial land in the judicial district that its worth is greater than his wergeld need not set bail if he is charged with a criminal offense. A debt proven in court must be paid in a fortnight, a judge's fine in six weeks' time,*

and the compensation payment in a fortnight after the fine. But if the plaintiff is granted his compensation before the fine [is established], *that compensation shall be paid in six weeks time and the fine a fortnight later. A debt must be paid at the house of the creditor in daylight if he has a house in the* [judicial] *district; and if he does not, then it must be paid at the nearest judge's house.*

6 *A person who turns down his rightful indemnity payment in court does not receive any. All debts that are paid shall be proven by the debtor with two others who saw and heard* [the transaction]. *Whoever does not attend court sessions when he is obligated to do so must pay a fine unless he can challenge it according to law. Whatever transfer a person witnesses* ⟨fol. 23r⟩ *or whatever judgment he hears, he may challenge immediately, but not later.*

7 *There are four legally acceptable grounds for failure to appear before the law: imprisonment, illness, service to God outside the country, and service to the realm. If any one of these situations prevents a person* [from appearing], *it must be proven by that person's messenger. If this is done as required by law, he suffers no disadvantage and is given time until the very first regular court session after the hindrance is past. But if someone names a guarantor that he will come before the court and due cause prevents him, then the guarantor shall name the hindrance swearing on the relics, and no other messenger is necessary.*

8 *Whoever brings criminal charges against another when that person is absent, and then he does not pursue the suit once the accused comes forward, the accuser must then pay the court fine to the judge and a compensatory fine to the defendant, who is declared free of the charges.*[6] *But if the plaintiff does follow through with his case and loses, he suffers no disadvantage unless he had challenged the man to combat.*

9 *Also, if someone begins a plea, and it is determined that a hearing will be set, and he does not appear,* [the court] *will find against him. The judge shall also have a guarantor from the plaintiff and the defendant that they will appear for judgment.*[7] *The guarantors must ascertain that both parties' rights are upheld by the court. Whenever a case with a prisoner is postponed by a ruling until the following day, he shall be released on bail unless he was apprehended for a red-handed crime.*

10 *An outlaw may be apprehended during peace days,*[8] *but one may not* ⟨fol. 23v⟩ *make any determination about him unless it concerns a red-handed deed. In court, no one is required to give a surety higher than his wergeld unless it concerns a debt that he admits or that has already been determined against him in court. On peace days one may not swear anything but the peace* [to someone] *or against a man caught red-handed. Anyone who transgresses the peace on peace days is unprotected by the peace law. Likewise, the church and churchyard do not*

protect anyone for a deed committed there. The judge may certainly preside over any complaint on a peace day except a felony; the judge shall instruct the accused to come at the appropriate time to admit and make compensation, or to deny the complaint.

11 *A person who pledges with an oath regarding a debt and does not fulfill it by the proper time is convicted for the debt unless he is prevented by just cause, which he must prove. If the oath was pledged before the court, then the judge receives his fine, and the person to whom the pledge was made receives his compensation payment. If the man is ready to fulfill his oath at the appropriate time, but the other does not accept it, or he is absent from the place where it is to be fulfilled, then the oath-taker is free of his obligation and the debt for which he swore the oath as long as he has witnesses for it.*

12 *If a person who is owed money in silver or in pennies is not available at the appointed time to receive payment or does not accept it, he does not forfeit his money but does lose the due date of the payment. Further, if he had promised the debtor that he would ride there, he is released from that promise but not of the money nor the duty.* ⟨fol. 28r⟩[9] A court of law may not convene on peace days.

13 No one may determine a judgment regarding one's own lord, one's man, or one's own relative if it carries a death penalty or if it affects health or legal capacity. Members of the *Schöffen* class can determine judgments regarding any man. In contrast, no one may make a judgment regarding them that carries a death penalty or endangers heritable property and legal status; nor can anyone appeal their judgment unless he is of equal birth. Anyone may reach a judgment regarding another person or dispute the judgment of another person in the lower court provided he has full legal capacity,[10] and the type of case can be adjudicated outside of the king's authority.[11] To appeal a judgment, one must bring it before the next higher judge and finally before the king. In that event, the judge shall send along his deputies, who then hear the decision before the king. These envoys must be of the *Schöffen* class if this occurs in the jurisdiction of the count, but if it occurs in a march, then the envoys can be anyone who is unblemished in his legal capacity. The judge shall supply the needs of the deputies: he shall give them plenty of bread and beer and three meals at the appropriate times and a cup of wine. He shall provide two meals for the servants, five sheaves [of fodder][12] for each horse for a day and a night, and they shall be shod in front. There shall be six servants and eight horses.[13] As soon as they locate the king on Saxon territory, they should ride to the royal court and bring the judgment back within six weeks.[14] If the person who appealed the judgment does not prevail, he must pay the court fine to the judge and a compensation pay-

ment to the person whose judgment he appealed. ⟨fol. 28v⟩ He must also reimburse the judge for the expenses incurred with the envoys. No one may appeal a judgment in a count's court and take it to a margrave's court even if the count received the territory from the margrave. The reason for this rule is that the king does not invest judicial authority in the march. The law there is distinct [as well].[15] Consequently, one must take the appeal to the realm.[16] When a person is asked for a judgment and cannot reach one, and dares to swear[17] that he is unable to do so, then one may ask a second person, and a third, and a fourth. The final person [to be asked] receives a grace period equal to the time the defendant had had [before his court date]. A Saxon who challenges a judgment and appeals to his right hand and to the majority of the people[18] must fight with six of his peers against seven others.[19] The party with the most victors wins the decision. Each defeated man pays the court fine to the judge, and a compensation to his opponent. Dueling for a judgment shall only be done before the realm.[20] If a man is asked for a judgment and he reaches one to the best of his understanding according to his knowledge, and this judgment is incorrect, he suffers no disadvantage from it. If a person contests the consensus and supplies a different judgment which then has the support of the majority, his judgment holds. In that event, no one pays a court fine since no one has appealed the decision of another. To appeal a judgment, one says the following: "The judgment by this man is incorrect. I appeal it and bring it where I must according to law." Should a Swabian appeal the decision of a Saxon, or a Saxon that of a Swabian, then ⟨fol. 29r⟩ the determination must be made before the king as described above. Within the high court[21] one stands to appeal a judgment and sits to render a judgment, each on his own chair. Anyone who is not born to the benches shall ask for a ruling to take the chair in order to render a different judgment.[22] Thereupon the person who made the first ruling shall turn his chair over to him. After handing down his own ruling, he offers to strengthen it with an oath and to bring it where it belongs according to law;[23] he then requests an official deputy for this purpose. Once a judgment is challenged, one may not ask for consensus. The one who determined [the judgment] may not renounce it without the permission of the person in whose favor the decision fell. A man who is apprehended for a crime and brought before the court may not appeal a judgment. Likewise, a man who is supposed to undergo trial by combat may not challenge a judgment once he has entered the [dueling] circle.[24]

14 Now hear about criminal acts [and] the penalties that apply.[25] A thief shall be hanged. If one day a theft occurs in a village amounting to less

than three shillings in value, then the village headman shall try the case the same day. The theft carries the penalty of flogging and shorn hair.[26] The sentence can be redeemed with a fine of three shillings, but the thief suffers impaired legal capacity. This is the village headman's highest jurisdiction.[27] If the case is carried over to the day after the charges had been made, then he may no longer preside. He may also preside over greater amounts of money and other types of movable goods. The same penalty applies to the use of false measures and weights, and fraudulent vending in cases where someone has been able to win a conviction.

All murderers, those who take by force a plow or [something from] a mill or a church or churchyard,[28] as well as traitors and murderous arsonists, and all those who use their deputation[29] to their own advantage shall be broken on the wheel.[30] One who beats or abducts a man ⟨fol. 29v⟩, or robs, or commits arson (with the exception of murderous arson), or rapes a woman or girl and violates the peace shall be beheaded. So too must one behead anyone who is caught in adultery. If those who possess or protect articles acquired through theft or robbery, or those who aid the perpetrators are convicted, then they shall be sentenced to the same penalty as thieves and robbers. A Christian man or woman who is without faith and practices magic or mixes potions and is convicted must be burned on the pyre. A judge who does not sentence a person for a crime draws upon himself the same penalty that is applied to the perpetrator. In addition, no one is required to attend the court of a judge or support him as law requires as long as he himself refuses to carry out the law.

15 If a man slays another in self-defense and cannot remain with him in order to bring him before the court and be judged because he fears for his life, then he may come without the dead man. If he does this and admits the deed before anyone brings a charge, and offers to fulfill his legal duty, one may not condemn him to death.[31] The judgment should grant the highest court fine in pennies permissible within the customary range to the judge, and wergeld to the family of the deceased. The relatives are to be summoned to receive their money at the next court session, and at the second and the third. If they still do not appear, the slayer shall keep the wergeld until they bring an action to claim it, and he shall be given immunity. No one may bring a suit against him that requires a death sentence since he offered himself for justice before anyone brought charges. However, if one brings the slain man unburied to court to make a formal complaint against the slayer, he must prove his case against the dead man or answer for his own deed with his life. ⟨fol. 30r⟩

16 When a person brings the type of claim before the court that requires a pledge of surety, and he so pledges, and another comes making the same claim, then if the first person who had [already] pledged the surety cannot disprove the latter's claim according to law, he must then abandon his own claim and pay a penalty for failure of surety and a court fine to the judge.[32] The penalty for failure of surety is loss of the person's right hand, with which he has sworn, or half of his wergeld. If a man pledges guaranty to claim a military outfit or inheritance, or if a woman [does so] to claim a dowry or nothing but movable goods, then if the guaranty fails so that [the claim] is proved against them according to law, they must pay the court fine to the judge and forfeit the property with a fine.

17 Each man shall provide guaranty to his lord and his agnatic relation in cases of manslaughter or [assault resulting in] injury or permanent disability. If someone is convicted of wounding or permanently injuring another, his hand shall be cut off. If a man is convicted of a criminal act in trial by combat, it costs him his life. For every compensation fine, the tariff is levied according to each man's legal status determined by his birth unless he has forfeited it [through misdeed].[33] When the bailiff pays a court fine to the judge for failure to fulfill his legal duty, he suffers the penalty of the king's *malder*, that is, thirty-two lashes with a green oak rod two ells long.[34] A man is to be compensated when he suffers permanent injury to any one [of the following]: the mouth, nose, eyes, tongue, ears, his sexual organs, hands, or feet. One must pay him a compensation that is half of his established wergeld. Each finger and each toe carries its own specific tariff based on ⟨fol. 30v⟩ a tenth part of the person's wergeld according to his birth.[35] Regardless of how many injuries a man receives during a single violent act, he is to be indemnified once with half of his wergeld if he does not die. As many times as a person injures a disabled person in a different part of the body, that many times shall he compensate that person with half his wergeld individually for each injury.[36] Whenever one person strikes another without breaking the skin, or calls someone a liar, he must pay that person compensation according to his birth. If someone is injured by another in a body part that has already been redressed by the court, even if it is severed completely, he may sue for no higher compensation than his composition tariff.

18 When the father dies, the son is not liable for any crimes the father committed. The father can clear his son once if he is charged with a felony while he is still an unseparated member of his household[37] by swearing on the relics that the son is innocent of the deed. But if both the father and son

are indicted for the same deed, then he cannot clear his son unless he first clears himself with a cleansing oath.

19 In a case requiring sentencing, one may not determine an end-judgment until the defendant has first been convicted to the stage where one may sentence him.[38] Likewise, one may not reach an end-judgment where one must prove a property or a possession of goods unless the ruling to require evidence has first been made.

20 The father can assuredly detach his son with an inheritance in court using whatever property the son accepts, however small it may be. The lord can also clear one of his servile men when a judgment is handed down as long as he dares to swear on the relics that he has been his unfree servant since birth ⟨fol. 31r⟩ and that he is innocent of the charges brought against him.[39] That man then remains without legal rights or protection.

20a[40] Brothers and sisters inherit from their full brothers and sisters before half-brothers and half-sisters who were born either to the mother or to the father. Children of full brothers stand at an equal level with half-brothers in line of inheritance.[41] Each man shall receive his full wergeld and full indemnity tariff even if he is missing an appendage as long as he does not use his injury before the court to obtain a guardian or to be compensated.

21 Any man required to pay ground rent passes his buildings to his heir to the land held in leasehold unless he is a man of knightly birth who gave them to his wife as a morning gift.[42] If the land becomes available to the lord for investiture, then he takes the buildings together with the fief unless the man had a wife to whom he gave them as a morning gift. Likewise, a woman who has a life estate without allod or fief does not pass on the buildings she has on the property to her next of kin when she dies. The person to whom the land reverts also takes possession of the buildings because every fiefholder may improve his buildings or let them deteriorate on his holding against his lord's will. The lady may assuredly do the same on her life estate.[43] If a man has a son who is his feudal heir but not his heir according to territorial law, the son has more right to retain his father's buildings on the feudal land than the person who inherits from the father in territorial law. If a lord invests a man with property without taking inventory of the buildings on it, it becomes the fiefholder's along with the land just as it had been the lord's unless he had stipulated [that he would keep] the buildings for himself.

22 For that which a man must prove to a judge, ⟨fol. 31v⟩ he does not need the judge as witness if the penalty is not higher than the court fine. He

proves it with an oath with two others from among those who are required to attend court and determine judgments. But if the charge is higher, then instead of the judge, he must have the *Schultheiss* or the bailiff as witness above the judge. Whenever a man proves his case with the *Schultheiss* or the bailiff and with the *Schöffen*, the judge should also be witness regarding the truth of their evidence which he had heard but does not know about.[44] If the judge refuses to be witness, contrary to the law, the man's proof prevails nevertheless. If a layman in his majority enters [a monastery] and puts on monk's clothing and tonsures himself after that but does not do this before the law, then if he tries to deny it later, it can well be proven against him without a trial by seven peers of the oblate who entered the monastery, when the peers have seen him [living] this life, or in association with the brothers he joined. Whether he takes the vows or not,[45] he has nevertheless relinquished his status within the ranks of knighthood.[46] When seven men are needed to bear witness, twenty-one men shall be asked about the evidence.[47] If someone gives testimony about a man against whom evidence is directed, then for the sake of justice the witness must say upon oath what he knows about [the case] or counter [saying] that he knows nothing about it. Then if the presenter completes his proof about himself with the witness, he has no need for additional testimony. The other person must pay the court fine to the judge right away, and compensation to the one [who prevailed], just as he [the latter] should do for the former if he had failed to prove [the case] completely, because that situation would have meant that he used the witness in a fashion contrary to the law and to his own knowledge.[48] ⟨fol. 32r⟩

23 Any man who does not wish to be or cannot be without a wife may remarry even after the death of three, or four, or more wives. A woman in the same circumstances may remarry and may have legitimate children with her last husband the same as with her first. She passes on her estate and her legal rights to her children.

24 No one may expel a person from his property holding by court order, even if he came into it unlawfully, unless the claimant can dispossess him with a legitimate claim when he is present. Or he can summon him by court order on the scheduled court date. If he does not appear in court, then his right of possession is denied by law. It is possible for any person to forfeit his legitimate holding according to law if he sells, pledges, or transfers it, or he exceeds the [renewal] limitation period,[49] or if he is dispossessed by territorial law, or if he loses possession in any other way but without force. In these instances, he loses possessory right by law. For this

reason no one is permitted by law to challenge someone's right of possession with an oath when that person has possession unless it is judged against him while he is present or unless he is sued for it and summoned to his scheduled hearing.

25 When a man is accused of possessing property taken by robbery and still carries the marks of the crime on his person so that it can be proven against him, and the judge is summoned with hue and cry, the judge shall follow immediately and reach a judgment on the robber and his criminal accomplice concerning the robbery speedily on behalf of the plaintiff. After that he must place the plaintiff back into possession of the property as long as the defendant does not contest it lawfully. ⟨fol. 32v⟩ And in the event that the judge cannot achieve an end-judgment or cannot sentence the robber, the king should reach a judgment for him as soon as he arrives in Saxon territory as long as one has evidence for the accusation.[50]

26 Coins must be updated when a new lord accedes. A mintmaster who offers a counterfeit penny to make a purchase receives the death penalty. Anyone who is deficient in his legal capacity[51] resulting from a conviction for theft or robbery loses his hand if found with three and a half pence unless he can present a warrantor for them.[52] Anyone unencumbered in his rights carrying a shilling worth of counterfeit pence loses them but nothing else. But if he has more than that, he loses his hand unless he has a bondsman for them. If the mintmaster makes false coins and does not store them according to law, then during that period of time he may not accuse anyone of counterfeiting and cause that person to pay the fine for it. The minter shall store pennies in pound amounts, equal in weight and even in color.[53] No one may set up a market or a mint without the permission of the judge in whose jurisdiction it is located. Also the king must by law send his glove there to prove that it is his will. No one is permitted to mint coins that resemble other coins unless they carry a clear distinguishing symbol. Whenever coins are revoked [from circulation], one must allow their continued use for payment and for redeeming collateral for a fortnight. But if someone attempts to pay with these coins after this time limit, the mintmaster must break them and return them to the owner.

27 Anyone who evades a bridge toll or water toll must pay thirty shillings. Four pedestrians pay one penny, a horse and rider pay a half, one loaded cart four [pennies] to go up and back. These are the fees for conveyance across water. For bridges the toll is ⟨fol. 33r⟩ half that amount. Priests and knights and their retinue are not charged. Every person should be free of tolls if he travels or rides or walks where he needs no boat or

bridge. By law, he is free of an escort fee where he is willing to risk his goods or his life. However, the person to whom he does pay escort should provide protection from damage within his own locale or compensate him for such damage. An empty cart pays half the toll of a full load, and a half load yet half again.[54] Whoever takes a false path on a cultivated field must pay one penny for each wheel, a rider a half a penny, and that person shall repair the damage. If the crop is standing on the field, then one may seize [the intruders] for the damage. If they refuse, contrary to the law, then it can be proven against them by raising the hue and cry. They then must pay a fine of three shillings for causing the hue and cry to be raised, in addition to paying restitution for the damage.

28 The fine for someone who chops wood or cuts grass or fishes in another man's stream[55] is three shillings; he pays indemnity for the damage in order to satisfy justice.[56] But if he fishes in ponds that have been dug, or chops down wood that has been planted, or fruit-bearing trees, or breaks off the fruit, or chops down a boundary tree, or digs up stone boundary markers, he pays thirty shillings. If a person discovers him at the site, he may definitely seize the malefactor as security or take him into custody where he has done the damage without the judge's permission. Whoever steals cut grass or chopped wood in the night shall be sentenced to the noose.[57] But anyone who steals [these things] during the day is sentenced to flogging and shorn hair.[58] Water that flows in a current is available to everyone for boat travel and fishing. Fishermen may obviously also use the shore as far as a person ⟨fol. 33v⟩ can straddle from the boat to the right bank.

29 If someone finds another person's property floating toward him in the water, he shall return it to the owner when the owner claims it as is proper and reimburses the finder for his expenses, estimated the way law-abiding people do. The finder should also make the find public and hold it safe for six weeks. Should someone ask about it, he must acknowledge it. Should he deny the article when someone inquires, then it is stolen goods if found in his possession later. If this happens, then he must return the items anyway and, in addition, pay a court fine and punitive fine because he had kept them as if by theft. [In point of fact,] he has not committed a theft that would cost him his reputation, life, or health because he did not remove the items from the person's possession by theft or robbery.

30 If a person claims an inheritance for himself not by reason of family relationship but based on a pledge instead, it may not be considered legal unless it can be proven with witnesses that the pledge had been confirmed in a court of law. If someone is executed,[59] his closest relation[60] inherits his property.

31 When a person takes his own life, the property devolves upon his heirs. Any stolen property found with him should be taken into custody by the judge for a year and a day. If during this time no one makes a legitimate claim, the judge may use it himself. No one may forfeit another man's property through misdeed if he has it in his possession, even if he forfeits his life.

32 Whoever beats, seizes, or robs a man's servant[61] solely because of the lord's wrongdoing shall by law pay both of them a fine unless he dares to swear on the relics that he did it neither to insult nor to cause harm to the master. In that case he is exempted from one fine. I say "insult"[62] ⟨fol. 34r⟩ in the event that he beat him because of the master's wrongdoing. I say "harm" in the event that he beat the servant in order to prevent him from performing his work for the lord. [In the latter instance] the perpetrator shall make restitution to the master, just as the servant would have to do if he had left the lord's service, and also compensate the servant with a payment unless he clears himself on the relics of insulting and disgracing the master of the servant whom he had detained or beaten.[63] A person who takes a man prisoner must answer to each of his lords, and each of his relatives, and to his wife while that man is in his custody if he is accused of it.

33 A violation is red-handed when someone intercepts a man in the act of a violation, or in flight from the deed, or if he has in his possession robbed or stolen goods to which he carries the key himself.

34 Upon finding one's own robbed or stolen goods a day later[64] in the possession of a man who had bought the article publicly and kept it unhidden and has a witness for it, the person robbed cannot charge the possessor with a red-handed deed even though he finds stolen goods in his possession unless the latter had lost his rights previously. Only with permission of the judge may the claimant clearly seize his property by law to claim ownership.[65] But if the possessor of the article wishes to protect his goods lawfully before the hearing, he shall ask the claimant to return to court.[66] If the claimant refuses, then the possessor can raise the hue and cry and seize him like a thief, as if he were caught red-handed, because he has made himself guilty by fleeing. But if the claimant comes before the law willingly, then he shall take possession of his property according to law. However, if the possessor contests by claiming that he had had the item made, if it is clothing, or that he had raised it in his barn, if it is a horse or livestock, then the person who has the property in his possession has more right to it, as long as he can prove it with two ⟨fol. 34v⟩ of his neighbors, than the claimant who had brought the suit for recovery of the article. However, if the possessor says he bought it at the market and does not know from whom, then he is not guilty of theft [as long as] he proves [the location][67] and swears

his oath on it.[68] Nevertheless, he loses the money he paid for it, and the claimant regains the property stolen from him if he proves his ownership on the relics with two oath-helpers unblemished in their legal status who know it was taken from him by theft or robbery. But if the possessor says it was given to him or he bought it, then he must name the warrantor from whom he bought it and the place where he bought it. He must also swear that he asserts his ownership rightfully. [Once this is established,] the claimant can follow him for a fortnight wherever he goes except across navigable water.[69] If he is permitted this, as is lawful, then the warrantor can answer for the goods in his stead. But if the warranty fails, he must forfeit the item with a fine and compensation payment. If someone accuses him of theft or robbery because of the article, he can release himself with his cleansing oath according to law. Also, if the person who had initiated the action loses, he must give up the article with compensation payment and a court fine. A person may call upon several warrantors, one after the other, until he comes to the source: in the case of animals, the one who raised it in his stall, and in the case of clothing, the one who produced it. The person who began the suit by seizing the goods to declare ownership shall make his claim with two oath-helpers. Yet even if the surety fails the person on whom the property was found, he [nevertheless] retains the property in his custody until it is won from him in a court of law.[70] ⟨fol. 35r⟩

35 Should a person find something and then deny it when he is asked about it, the items are considered stolen. Whatever a man finds or seizes while pursuing thieves or robbers, he should make known to the villagers and at the church.[71] If the person to whom the article belongs comes within six weeks, he shall claim it with two oath-helpers and reimburse the expenses the person had incurred in the case of a horse or livestock. If the owner of the property is from another judicial district, then the one who retrieved it from the thieves retains one-third of it. But if no one comes to lay claim in six weeks, then the judge takes two-thirds, and the person holding the property one-third.

36 Each man shall make restitution for damage to people caused by his negligence whether the damage occurs from fire, or a well he had left without an enclosure to the height of the knees above the earth, or if he shoots or strikes a man or livestock while aiming at a bird.[72] For these things, the [negligent] person does not lose his life or health even if the injured person dies, because he must pay the wergeld.

37 Anyone who steals grain in the night earns the gallows; if he steals it during the day, he pays with his neck.[73] A traveler who feeds [his animal]

grain in the field and does not carry it away shall make reimbursement for the damage according to its value. No one is required to be responsible to his servant for more than the amount of his wages unless the servant becomes his guarantor.

38 If the master drives away a servant, he shall pay him his entire wages. If the servant leaves the master deliberately, he shall pay the lord the amount that the lord had promised him, ⟨fol. 35v⟩ and what was paid him, he shall repay doubly.

39 If a servant takes a lawful wife, or, if following a death, the guardianship of underage children devolves upon him, he may leave the lord's service. He retains all the wages due to him until that time. If he has received more than is due, he shall return it without penalty.

40 If someone's dog or breeding boar or ox or whatever kind of beast kills or injures a person or an animal, his owner shall make compensation for the harm according to the proper wergeld or value if he takes the beast into his care after the damage occurred. However, if he turns it out, refuses it shelter in house or barn, and gives it no food or water, then he is not responsible for the damage. In that case the injured party can initiate a legal action for the animal [as compensation] for the damage. Under no circumstances does the judge ever lose his court fine when an animal causes damage. Harm of whatever kind done by a man's horse or livestock while under the supervision of his servant or others of his household shall be paid by the person in whose care it was. If that person flees, and the horses or oxen and cart are found with evidence of the deed on them,[74] and it is proven with an oath, then the owner of the animal and cart must pay indemnity if he cannot clear himself. He must pay the value of the horse or other draft animal and the cart which has been taken into custody, or he must forfeit the animal, and the other person keeps it in compensation for the damages. If a man allows his hogs or geese, which can not be confiscated, to feed on his neighbor's grain or another's crops, and then that man sets his dogs on them, and they bite the animals, wounding or killing them, he pays no penalty.

41 When a judge cannot [collect] his fee by attaching a man's hereditary land because it has too little value, ⟨fol. 36r⟩ the bailiff shall seize it by placing a cross on the gate in accordance with the judgment of the *Schöffen*. If the owner does not pay it off within a year and a day, he shall be denied his right to it.[75] Afterward his heir may come before the court within a year and a day and lay claim to his inheritance by swearing on the relics as the law provides. And he shall pay the fee that the judge has been accorded during

the hearing of the case which he can prove with two others. The judge may not fix the amount higher than three court fines or one wergeld.

42 Whenever one person accuses another of taking from him a landholding that each of the two claim to have received in fief, each receiving it from a different lord,[76] each of the two shall bring his warrantor to the hearing. The person with warranty prevails and keeps the property. The person whose warrantor fails, loses his possession of the property as long as they both began their claim without possession and have both been enfeoffed with the holding less than one year.[77] But if one of them has held uncontested right of possession to the property for a year and a day, then even if his warrantor fails to appear at the hearing and fulfill his warranty, the landholder can no longer lose the land nor his right of possession because he can respond on his own behalf to the claimant or his warrantor unless just cause prevents him, which he must then prove. However, the princes[78] can provide warranty to a person with an official, sealed document in such a way that they send with it a subordinate born into the household who shall represent the property in their stead.[79] The letter shall be delivered to the person against whom the complaint is being made as proof of the claim, if he still needs it. If, however, both claim the disputed property from a single lord, then they must go before him for judgment in six weeks time, and the judge shall send two court deputies along ⟨fol. 36v⟩ to hear who prevails and who loses there. The loser pays the judge's fee and a compensation fine.

43 When a person claims for himself a holding in fief,[80] and another says he holds it in free heritable ownership,[81] and if they both demand it with equal guaranty, then the person who holds the land in free ownership is in a better position to keep it, with the witness of two *Schöffen*, than the other in fief. A person's land inherited in freehold constitutes a stronger case for retention than another's heritable property acquired through purchase or as a gift.

44 A man who has occupied real property for a year and a day without legal dispute has right of possession to it. But while a person lawfully sues for possession of a property that another holds, the occupant will never be given right of possession as long as he maintains control of the property by force during the legal dispute, and the legitimate charges can be proven with witnesses. In contrast, whoever holds real estate that devolved upon him through death or was given or bestowed on him in fief, and he himself took it from no one, then he need return to no one what he takes from the property, even if it is withdrawn from him [later], as long as he has denied

no one his rights regarding it. A person claiming for himself an allod from his fief or his mother's or niece's life estate must prove free ownership[82] with witness of six freemen of the *Schöffen* class or his claim is dismissed.

45 If a person is present in a court of law when charges are brought against him, and he flees the proceedings, he is convicted. If he is accused of a felony, he is immediately placed in limited outlawry.

46 A person who unwittingly plows another's field or a field another lent him loses, if he is charged while plowing there, all his effort since the other keeps it. But the person who lent the land to him shall compensate his loss. Whoever sows a field under dispute loses his efforts and his seed. Whatever crop he sows in a field in this way [i.e., mistakenly] he keeps when it is not under dispute. He pays his rents to the person ⟨fol. 37r⟩ who holds the land. Whoever plows again the sown field of another shall make restitution for the loss to satisfy legal custom and pay him his fine.[83]

47 Whoever drives his livestock onto another's field of grain or grass shall make restitution to satisfy justice and pay a fine of three shillings. But if the owner is not present where the livestock does the damage, and if the animals are seized as collateral, he shall make restitution as long as it is proven immediately according to the consensus of the peasants. Each owner then pays six pence compensation for each animal. But if the animals are of the kind that cannot be herded–for example geese, frightened horses, or breeding boars–then the landholder shall bring two men there and prove the damage to them, then follow the animals to their owner's house and make his complaint to him. The owner then must make restitution for the animals as if they had been seized.

48 A person who drives livestock to a different section of the common grazing land[84] is fined six pence if he is seized. Whoever drives the animals across uncleared land leaves it without penalty, unless it is an enclosed meadow. If a herdsman loses any animals under his supervision, he must pay compensation. If a man leaves his grain standing once all others have taken theirs in, and it is eaten or trodden on, no one compensates him. The same holds for the tithe payment if the collector does not take it when the renter lets it stand in the field and proves it to his fellow peasants.[85] Each animal shall be taxed where it is sheltered at night when it produces its young. The crops are taxed in the field, the livestock in the village in each man's house where the young ⟨fol. 37v⟩ are born. One pays a tenth from each kind of animal except chickens. Each yard, farmstead, and separate house tithes with one chicken on St. Martin's day. When a person pays his proper tenth on the field, he shall hand over the tenth shock, each one equal

in quality to the others, or the tenth sheaf.[86] Whenever a man is ready to take in his grain, he must announce it to the tithe collector when he is in the village or in the fields, and if the collector does not collect the ten percent, the tenant divides it himself in such a way that he swears an oath establishing when it was done, if an oath is requested, and proves it with two fellow peasants and leaves the grain on the field. Thus he incurs no loss if it spoils or is lost afterward. Sometimes a specified shock is tithed from the arable land and a lamb from the sheep herd that returns to the yard. Where a grain tithe is being paid, the cord with which the sheaf is bound shall be one ell long between the two knots when the cord is measured for winter grain. Whoever pays the tenth following lawful custom has paid fully. The collector may take his tenth in all kinds of animals and bees as well if he wants to wait from year to year until he is entitled to it from the tenant's house.[87] But if he is not willing to wait, then he shall be paid yearly the amount he is entitled to. For each foal and mule he receives 1 penny, and for a calf, and donkey, and goat, and sheep, and piglet, a halfpenny if there are five or fewer of them. If there are six or more [animals], the collector takes one. The sixth is redeemed for twopence, the seventh for one and a half,[88] the eighth for one, the ninth for a half. ⟨fol. 38r⟩ However, the owner of the livestock shall first remove from them two from the six and three from the nine before the collector chooses. The tithe is levied on geese the same way but paid in halfpennies.[89]

49 No one may let his gutters extend into another man's yard. Each person shall enclose his portion of the yard. If anyone fails to do so, and damage occurs as a result, he shall make restitution. He remains without a fine if the damage is his.

50 If a person sets up a border tree or border stone, he shall have the holder of the adjoining property accompany him.[90] Whoever plants a hedge[91] shall keep the branches growing [inward] toward his yard.

51 The oven, cesspit, and pigsty shall be three feet distant from the fence. Each man shall maintain his oven walls so that the sparks do not fly into another's yard and cause harm. A cesspit adjacent to another man's yard must be enclosed.[92]

52 If the hops becomes attached to the fence, the person who has the roots on his side shall go up to the fence, grab the hops, and pull it toward him. Whatever comes off is his; whatever remains on the other side is his neighbor's. A person's tree should not have any branches hanging over the fence to his neighbor's detriment.

53 If a man builds on another's property for which he pays rent, he

must remove [the building] when he leaves it, or his heirs must do so after his death, except for the fence in front and back, the house, and the manure pile. These the lord shall pay for according to the estimate of the peasants. If the lord does not do so, then the owner shall remove them all.[93]

54 A person may not leave any livestock enclosed that can follow a herdsman except for sows that are suckling piglets. These sows should be ⟨fol. 38v⟩ protected so that they do no harm. No one may employ his own herdsman since that will reduce the wages of the village herdsman. If, however, a person has three hides of land or more in freehold or in tenancy, then he may assuredly hire his own shepherd. Where the herdsman's wages are based on the number of hides and not on livestock, no one may withhold wages from him. This rule ensures that the village will not be left without a herdsman. If the herdsman fails to return to the village any animal entrusted to him, he must make restitution. He must also pay indemnity whenever any animals are lost to wolves or robbers, and he remains uncaptured and fails to raise the hue and cry that would bring him witnesses for the loss. If one animal lames another, or if it kicks or bites another in the presence of the herdsman, and someone presses charges against him, he must name the animal that caused the injury and swear an oath. Thereupon the owner of the culprit must care for the wounded animal until it is well enough to go back to pasture. But if the animal dies, he must pay compensation in the amount of the [animal's] wergeld.[94] If someone accuses the herdsman of failing to return an animal to the village, then the herdsman can clear himself of the charge if he dares to swear a cleansing oath. In contrast, if someone misses his animal, and goes to the herdsman, and accuses him with two men as witnesses,[95] then the herdsman cannot cleanse himself with an oath because he must compensate for the livestock. But if the herdsman claims that the animal was not part of the herd, then he has a stronger proof with two men who claim that it was herded outside the herdsman's supervision. In this case the herdsman is not responsible for [the loss].

55 Whatever the village headman achieves for the improvement of the village with the agreement of the majority of the peasants may not be challenged by the minority.

56 Where villages adjacent to water have a dike ⟨fol. 39r⟩ that protects them from flooding, each village shall reinforce its section of the dike against a flood. But if the flooding occurs and breaks the dam, and the hue and cry is raised to summon to the dike the residents living inside, then any person who does not help repair the dike forfeits by law whatever heritable

land he owns inside it. Whatever land the water washes away is lost to the owner, but if it breaks a new wash, he does not lose his land.[96] If a land bar or island builds up in a river, it belongs to the closer bank, and if it is in the middle, it belongs to both banks. The river bed is dealt with in the same way when it dries.[97]

57 Even though real property may be held by more than one man in such a way that one received it from the other, whatever the one person does on the land, he shall make good to the person who has primary enfeoffment and to no one else.[98]

58 If the man has no heir in fief,[99] then after his death his heir according to general territorial law shall collect the rents produced on the fief.[100] Now hear when payments are due:[101] on St. Bartholomew's day (August 24) all types of rents and dues are paid.[102] On St. Walpurgis day (May 1) the lamb tenth is due; on the Feast of the Assumption of the Virgin (August 15) the goose tenth is due.[103] On St. John's day (June 24) all kinds of meat tithes that are redeemed yearly with cash are paid to the collector. When the person does not redeem it, it is due when the animal's young are born.[104] All other grain tithes are due on St. Margaret's day (July 13), but what was shocked earlier was already due on that day. On St. Urban's day (May 25) vineyards and orchards are due. A man's crop that he prepared with the plow is due when the harrow goes over it, and the garden [produce] once it is sown and raked. Payments from mills, ⟨fol. 39v⟩ tolls, mints, and vineyards are due on the day specified for each. If a child reaches his majority before the day a particular payment is due, he should collect it, but if he attains maturity after the legal payment day, then he loses the revenue from the property. I speak of this for the following reason: If a lord or one of his household cultivates a garden, or orchard, or vineyard, and if he supplies meals for the workers until St. Urban's day, and the ward has not yet reached maturity, the lord reaps the yields. Hence, if the lord has sown the child's fields before he comes of age, then the lord keeps the crop but not the stubble nor the vine stakes since they stand in the ground and are tied to the stock. In addition, he may not allow the child's woods to be chopped down nor the grass to be mown once the ward comes of age; but if he comes of age beforehand, the lord has lost his efforts because the child does not compensate him for it.[105] Following this pattern, the lord compensates neither the child nor his heirs when he takes what devolves upon him.[106]

59 If an owner wants to expel from his land a leaseholder who was not born to [the land], he shall inform him at Candlemas (February 2). A man who wants to quit the property shall do the same. If the owner's tenant dies,

his heir steps into his place and pays on the land as his predecessor did. If the lessor also dies, the tenant then pays the rent originally pledged to the lessor to the person on whom the property devolves. The tenant needs no other proof than his plow.

The king's highway shall be wide enough that one cart can leave room for another: an empty cart shall make way for a full one, and the one with a smaller load for the more heavily laden one. Riders yield to carts, and pedestrians to riders. If, however, they are on a narrow road, ⟨fol. 40r⟩ or on a bridge, and if someone is being pursued on horseback or on foot, then the cart should stop so the pursuer can pass. The cart that reaches a bridge first, crosses it first, whether it is empty or full. The person who arrives at the mill first, mills first.[107]

60 A person may lend or give in security a horse, or clothing, or any other type of movable goods in whatever way he transfers it out of his possession according to his decision. Then if the one holding the item sells it, or pawns or loses it gambling, or if it is stolen or robbed from him, the owner who lent or transferred it can demand it from no one except the person he has passed it to. If the owner dies of natural or unnatural causes, the property holder may lay lawful claim to it against the heir or the judge if he is entitled to it.

61 Once God created man, he gave him dominion over fish, birds, and all wild animals. We have proof of this from God that no one can forfeit his life or health because of these things. However, three places in Saxony ensure peace to animals–except to bears, wolves, and foxes–by the king's authority.[108] These areas are called game preserves.[109] One is in the heath of "Koine," the second the "Harz," and the third is the "Magetheide."[110] Anyone who takes game must pay the king's fine, which is six shillings.[111] Anyone riding through the game preserve shall ride with unstrung bow or crossbow, his quiver closed, his racers and trackers on leash, and hounds coupled.[112] If someone is hunting game outside the forest, and the hounds follow it into the preserve, he may follow them provided that he does not sound [his hunting horn] nor incite[113] the dogs, and does nothing wrong there. When he takes the game, he must call his hounds off. No one may ⟨fol. 40v⟩ trample crops while hunting or chasing, nor may one [go through a field] once the grain gets its head.

62 A person who keeps a mean dog, or a tame wolf, or a deer, or a bear, or monkey shall make compensation for any harm the animal may cause. If he tries to transfer it after the damage has been done, he is nevertheless liable unless he can prove with two witnesses that he kept the animal

only until the time it did the damage. If a man beats a dog or bear to death while it is trying to do him harm, he pays no penalty if he dares to swear on the relics that he acted in self-defense.

63 If a person wants to keep wild animals outside of the preserve, he shall keep them in an enclosure in his custody. No woman may be a pleader, nor may she bring a suit without a guardian. Calefurnia forfeited this [right] for all [women] when she misbehaved before the emperor in a fit of rage because her demands could not proceed without a spokesman.[114] Of course, any man can be a pleader and a witness, and bring suit and defend himself except in the district in which he is outlawed or if he is in royal outlawry. But he may not do so in a religious court if he is outlawed by royal authority.

64 A woman or girl bringing charges for rape shall do so with hue and cry for the red-handed deed and for rape, which she must prove.[115] In the same way, a person bringing a captive with stolen or robbed goods before the law shall make formal accusation with the hue and cry for a red-handed deed, which he confirms with the people. Likewise, when a person brings a dead man to court and accuses that man of perpetrating a crime against him, he shall bring charges with the hue and cry for a red-handed deed that is evident. In a case where a man has been robbed, and he knows where his goods have been taken, and if he wants the judge to accompany him there, he too should raise the hue and cry to press charges for the red-handed deed he wants to prove. Where the red-handed condition does not obtain, one may not raise the hue and cry if one wants to avoid disadvantage.[116] ⟨fol. 41r⟩

65 No underage child can do anything that would exact the death penalty. If he kills or injures a man, his guardian shall pay compensation in the amount of that person's wergeld if it is proven against him. Whatever damage the child causes shall be compensated from the child's property by the guardian according to his estimation. If a man beats a child to death, he shall pay his full wergeld.[117] If a man reprimands a child, or pulls his hair, or beats him with a broom for his misdeed, he does not pay a penalty if he dares to swear on the relics that he beat him only for the misconduct.

66 Now hear about the old peace ordinance that the imperial power confirmed in Saxony with the agreement of the respected servants of the land.[118] Every day and at all times, priests and religious, girls and women, and Jews shall enjoy immunity[119] of their person and property. The same holds for churches and churchyards, each village within its fosse and fence, plows, mills, and the king's highway, [and everything] on water and in fields. Everything that enters [these places] shall have constant immunity.

Holy days and certain peace days[120] have been instituted each week as peace days for all people. These consist of four days: Thursday, Friday, Saturday, and Sunday. Thursday is the day to consecrate the holy oil with which we are all anointed to Christianity at baptism. On Thursday God dipped [bread] into the chalice with his disciples.[121] That was when our law was instituted. Also on Thursday, God granted heaven to humankind and re-opened the path for us that had been barred. It was on a Friday that God made man and was martyred by man. On Saturday he rested once he had created heaven and earth and all that is in it. It was also a Saturday when he rested in the grave after his martyrdom. In addition, ⟨fol. 41v⟩ priests who are the teachers of Christianity are consecrated on Saturdays. It was on a Sunday that we were reconciled with God for Adam.[122] The very first day that existed was a Sunday, and that will also be the last when we arise from the dead and make our way to grace in body and spirit; [that is,] those who had earned it before God. Because of these things, these four days are peace days common to all people except those who are apprehended red-handed for a crime or have been outlawed by imperial jurisdiction or by their local district.

67 A person charged with a crime cannot bring more than thirty men to court. When he appears, they may not carry weapons except a sword.

68 If a man's horse tires while he is traveling, he may definitely cut grain for it, cutting as far as he can reach standing with one foot on the road. However, he may not take any away.

69 If a person kills or wounds a lawbreaker, he shall not be fined as long as he can prove with the oath of six oathhelpers that he wounded the man in flight or in the act of committing the violation.

70 No one may eject a person from a property in his possession unless it has been granted to him in a legal decision.

71 A violation of the peace shall be judged as explained earlier.[123] No one may carry a weapon other than a sword during a sworn peace[124] except in the service of the realm and to tournaments. All those who carry weapons in other places shall be tried[125] because they are placed in imperial outlawry if they are caught with them. No one may carry a sword in castles, towns, or villages except all those people who have a domicile or shelter there. Of course, one may carry weapons when responding to the hue and cry. By law, all those who have attained majority to the extent that they are able to wield a sword must respond to it unless they are prevented by due cause. Priests, women, sacristans, and stockherders are exempted. If the men follow the

hue and cry to a castle,[126] they shall continue for three days, each with his own provisions, within the ⟨fol. 42r⟩ judicial district while the person who raised the hue and cry walks or rides ahead. But if he is wounded so that he cannot go, then the people must still follow the hue and cry, which is their duty as long as they have the violator in view. Even if the offender immediately flees into another district, the pursuers can capture him in the open field and lead him back if the local people do not come. If, however, he flees to a town or castle, they shall renew the hue and cry and gather together the village headman, and the peasants, and the reliable servants[127] who are available at the time and summon them to a proper legal hearing. He shall be surrendered to the court if the red-handed crime is proven against him with the oath of seven witnesses [stating] that they pursued him while he carried evidence of the deed from their own district to this place. They shall then set bond for the man's wergeld in case they do not judge him according to law, so that they may then take him back and fulfill justice thereby.

73[128] If lawbreakers are harbored in a castle contrary to law, then when the judge is summoned there by means of the hue and cry, and the inhabitants and the malefactors are summoned down according to law in such a way that it can be heard from the castle, but the inhabitants do not hand [them] over for judgment,[129] then the castle and all its inhabitants are placed in outlawry and the case is tried. If, however, they allow the judge's six deputies and the plaintiff to enter so that they may seek the perpetrators and the robbed goods, then the castle [inhabitants] shall not be outlawed. If the castle is accused of the robbery, [claiming] that it occurred and originated from there, then the lord of the castle or one of the citizens must clear it with a cleansing oath on the relics. Anyone who is himself accused of the crime cannot clear the castle unless he has already cleared himself. However, if someone wants to prosecute the castle with trial by combat, the lord of the castle or the citizens must defend their innocence against their social equals. Otherwise they shall be outlawed and tried. If one person makes a complaint against another [claiming] that he attacked him with force from the castle, ⟨fol. 42v⟩ then the lord of the castle shall bring him forward so that he can make restitution or clear the castle of the charges. If he does not do this, he must defend himself personally against [the charges]. If a man brings charges against a castle saying that he was robbed by an inhabitant but does not know who the perpetrator was, the lord of the castle must answer for it before the court within six weeks of the day the charges were made in order to exonerate the castle with his oath or pay restitution for damages to satisfy legal custom, but without fine if he is not guilty of aiding or abetting.[130] Whenever people ride from a castle, cause harm, and do not return within three days and nights, and, in addition, the robbed goods are not found either in or near the castle, then the castle is innocent. But if the robber returns to the castle, and the stolen goods appear there or close by, then the castle is responsible for the crime.

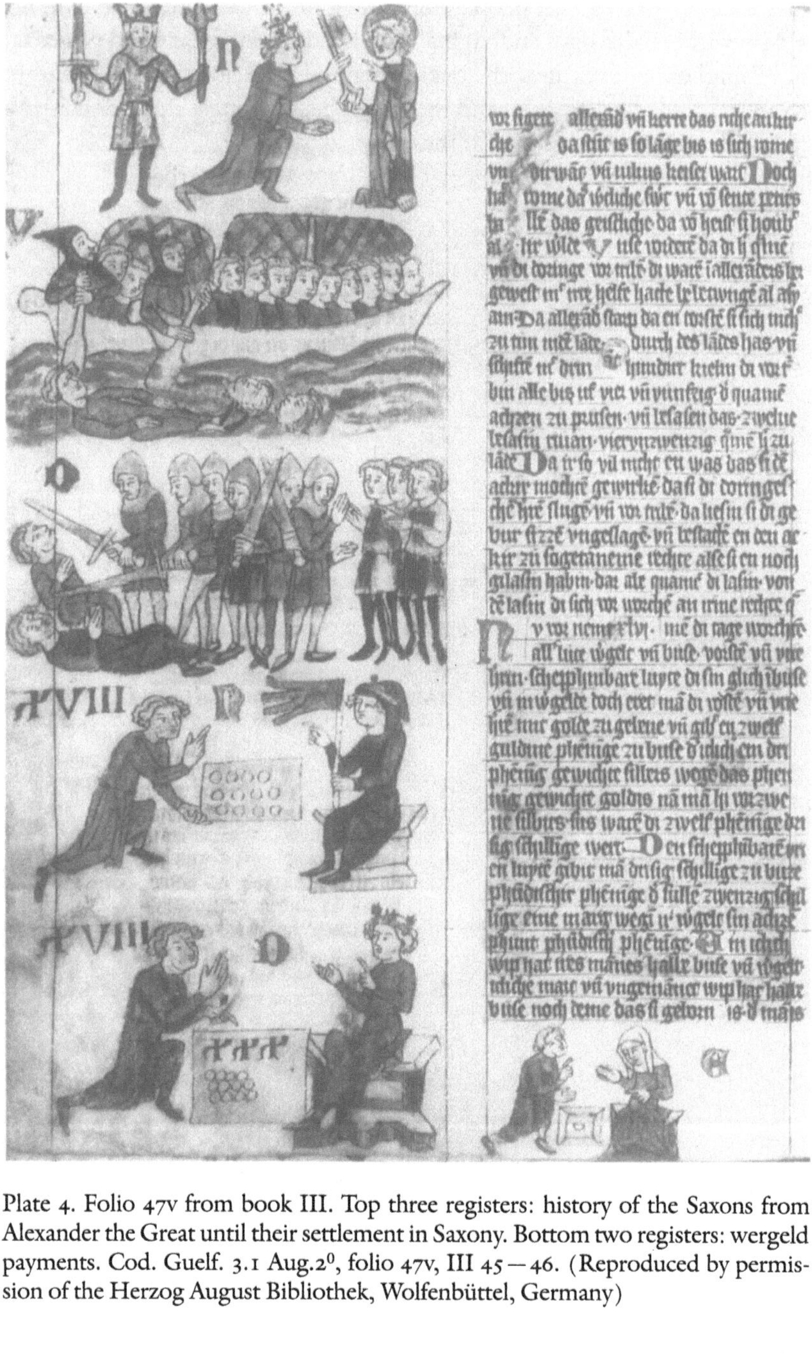

Plate 4. Folio 47v from book III. Top three registers: history of the Saxons from Alexander the Great until their settlement in Saxony. Bottom two registers: wergeld payments. Cod. Guelf. 3.1 Aug.2⁰, folio 47v, III 45–46. (Reproduced by permission of the Herzog August Bibliothek, Wolfenbüttel, Germany)

Book III

1 No one shall raze a village building by reason of any type of crime unless a girl or woman has been raped in it or brought into it after the rape.[1] It shall be condemned or cleared legally. Once a judgment has been laid down,[2] then even if a person comes forward to clear [the building], he receives no compensation for it, because he did not clear it before the court reached its judgment. All living creatures present at the rape shall be beheaded.[3] All those responding to the hue and cry [shall] seize the victim and the attacker. They suffer no penalty for bringing the accused to court even if he is not convicted.[4]

2 Regarding priests, tonsured according to their rule, and Jews: when they carry arms in transgression of the law, they shall be compensated as laymen if they are attacked because those who are included in the king's peace are not permitted to bear arms.[5] ⟨fol. 43r⟩

3 A woman with child may not be given a sentence more severe than flogging and the cutting of her hair. Neither shall fools nor the feeble-minded be sentenced to punishment. If they cause harm to someone, their guardian shall pay compensation.

4 If a person demands back what he has transferred or sold and denies the sale or the gift, then the person holding the property can certainly keep it with the oath of two others who saw [the transaction]. However, with this type of proof, a man cannot obtain another as warrantor when a second person begins a legal suit for ownership by grasping the property[6] because the plaintiff (now possessor) proves himself with his cleansing oath. A person who admits to a sale shall warrant that he indeed sold it, because he who admits a sale but refuses the surety is a thief or a thief's accomplice unless he eliminated the need by having witnesses present when he sold the item.

5 Any property one lends or transfers publicly, and is able to prove with two oathhelpers, cannot be grounds for an accusation of theft or robbery. He shall be summoned three times in intervals of a fortnight to defend his property if he intends to do so. If he does not do this, the claimant is granted rights to it. The person in possession shall notify the owner regarding the [hearing] date with a notice[7] in house and yard if

he wants to avoid a penalty. If a property that has been transferred for safekeeping is stolen, robbed, or burned—or in the case of an animal, if it dies—the one holding the property does not suffer the consequences provided he swears a [cleansing oath] that he is blameless. But whatever one person lends or pawns to another shall be compensated according to its value or returned undamaged. If livestock or a horse dies while held in pledge without fault of the person who has custody, and if he proves it and swears an oath, he ⟨fol. 43v⟩ does not pay compensation. However, he has lost the money he paid out unless their agreement stipulated otherwise.

6 If a servant loses his master's property at dice, or pawns it, or sells it, the master may certainly demand its return as provided by law when he claims it. But if he squanders his own property in whatever way, he loses it of his own accord, and the master may not demand its return since he is not required to pay even if he has agreed to compensation. However, if the servant's horse or other property is stolen or robbed while in the service of the master and without fault of the servant, the master must replace it. However, the servant must render an account to the lord for it if he brings charges.

7 A Jew need not be a Christian man's guarantor unless he is willing to be accountable in the Christian man's stead. If a Jew kills a Christian, or if he commits a crime against him and is seized in the act, he shall be tried the same as a Christian. In addition, if a Christian kills a Jew, he is to be sentenced for violating the king's peace against him. A Jew named Josephus earned this protection from Emperor Vespasian when he cured his son Titus of gout.[8] If a Jew buys or accepts chalices, books[9] or priest's clothing in pawn for which he has no warrantor, and if it is found in his possession, he shall be tried as a thief. Whatever other items he buys openly in daylight and not behind closed doors that he can prove with two others, he retains the money he paid for it or lent upon his oath even if it has been stolen. Should his warrantor fail him, however, he loses his money.

8 It is said that castles and princes need no peace[10] that can be broken because castles have fortifications, and princes ⟨fol. 44r⟩ travel with armed defenders. But that is not so. Anyone who pledges peace to the princes and is bound in loyalty to it will be tried and sentenced if he violates it.[11]

9 A person who gives surety that he will bring a man to court and is unable to compel his appearance must pay compensation according to the level of the charges if they are proven against the defendant. But if the judgment requires capital punishment, the guarantor must pay the defendant's wergeld. That money goes to the plaintiff and not to the judge,

although the judge receives his court fine as well. A person may compensate in the same way for a breach of the peace that one person pledged for another; but if someone violates the peace he swore himself, it is a capital offense. In contrast, if a person becomes a guarantor to bring a man to court, but then the man comes without his bondsman and offers to fulfill the law and can attest to it with witnesses, the bondsman is released from responsibility. Whenever someone pledges surety to return a captive, the guarantor himself and not the captive must prove that he has been delivered back in fulfillment of the pledge. A person who forcibly removes from court a man charged with a crime suffers the same penalty as the accused if he is caught. But if he escapes, he is outlawed right away provided that the hue and cry is raised for the fresh deed and it can be proven with an oath.

10 When a man is supposed to bring the person accused of a crime to court on a specified day,[12] and if the accused dies during this interval, and the guarantor brings the body, he is then released [from liability]. However, if a man is being sued for a debt that has not yet been decided against him, and he dies during this time, he need not be exhibited as long as the bondsman can prove his death with two oathhelpers. His heir shall answer for the debt. If a horse or livestock that one customarily exhibits in court dies, then the bondsman shall display the hide and be released [from liability].

11 If any person designates a guarantor for a pledge and dies before he can fulfill that pledge, then his heir ⟨fol. 44v⟩ or his bondsman can fulfill it in place of the deceased man at the promised time; otherwise the guarantor is required to pay the debt because the oath had already been vowed.

12 When one person brings a claim against another, and that second person brings suit against the first one, then the first plaintiff does not have to answer the claim of the second until the second plaintiff has been cleared of liability in the first suit.[13] If several people press charges against a man, he does not have to respond to the others before he is cleared of the first charge. If the case continues to the next day, he may not give surety except for his wergeld even if the charges are numerous.

13 If a man is charged with a crime in court when he is not present, and a date for the hearing is set, then if the plaintiff meets the defendant before that date, he may certainly detain him according to law based on his accusation until the accused provides surety that he will appear. [This procedure is allowed] because the judge provides protection for the plaintiff and not for the defendant who is summoned into his presence.

14 Whenever a man does not accept his spokesman's statements, he

shall for the duration not be damaged by the spokesman's speech. A person charged with a crime should first ask for surety because until that is pledged, the plaintiff can correct his formal charges but not thereafter.

15 If two people claim the same property after the thirtieth,[14] the occupant needs to answer to no one unless the parties reach an amicable agreement, or one of them defeats the claim of the other by law in court.

16 Anyone who refuses to transfer military equipment, or dowry, or heritable property after the thirtieth must pay a punitive fine and a court fine if a formal complaint is brought to court. If two men claim one property, and the judge demands it as provided by law, it must be surrendered to the judge, who shall have control of it until the parties reach a determination according to law. The man who had surrendered the property to the judge is then free. Whoever lays claim to military equipment in this manner must belong to the agnate ⟨fol. 45r⟩ side of the family. People deficient in their legal capacity may not have an advocate. No one need answer to outlaws of the realm or to those in local outlawry within the judicial district that outlawed them.[15]

17 A man can certainly free himself of outlawry anywhere within the judicial district that outlawed him. Just as any person may bring a suit anywhere, one can free himself anywhere. He shall, however, assign a guarantor that he will appear. If he has no guarantor, then the judge shall keep him in custody until he fulfills his legal duty.

18 When a person claims in court that he has released himself from outlawry but does not complete his proof with the judge, or in his stead, with the *Schultheiss* or the bailiff and with two men, then the plaintiff needs no additional witnesses to prove the outlawry. A person who is outlawed in the superior court, however, needs two *Schöffen* as well as the judge as witnesses in order to free himself.

19 Freemen and imperial ministerials[16] can certainly be witnesses before the realm and determine a judgment. By these means, each performs his service[17] to the realm according to his legal status. However, ministerials of the realm may not reach a judgment concerning a person of the *Schöffen* class or be witness for him when it may damage life, reputation,[18] or health.

20 Whoever plows unwittingly another man's land pays no penalty. But if someone plows land that he claims for himself, and the court decides against him, he must make compensation for it. The owner may, without permission from the judge, also accept a surety on his land from the person who plows it so that he will stand to justice. No one can forfeit his life or health by plowing unless it occurs in such a way that the land has already

been denied that person by means of a legal judgment, and peace has been established on it.[19]

21 If two men claim the same property with equal rights to it and ⟨fol. 45v⟩ with equal evidence, it shall be divided between them. The decision regarding the proof shall be made by the inhabitants of the village. Whoever has the majority [support] for the proof keeps the property. If the local inhabitants do not know who holds the property, then it can be decided with a trial by water,[20] or one of the two, either the claimant or the person against whom the claim is made, shall swear that he claims it by right and that it belongs to him. The judge shall appoint his deputies for this, and if the claimants both swear this, then the property shall be divided equally.

22 When a person borrows a horse or article of clothing from another for a specified time and is sued for it because he kept it longer, he shall return it immediately and pay compensation if he returns it in a worsened condition. A person may legally take possession of his own property where he sees that it is being withheld from him unlawfully.

23 Whoever gives shelter and food to a man in limited outlawry must pay the judge's fine. But if he does not know of the outlawry, he clears himself of the fine with a cleansing oath.

24 It is not possible to convict a person [in one district] on the basis of his outlawry in a different district.[21] A person who is outlawed in the highest jurisdiction is also outlawed in all the subordinate judicial districts within it. Conversely, anyone outlawed by the lowest court is not outlawed in the highest unless he is outlawed there according to proper procedure.[22] The judge of the lowest court cannot rule on the limited outlawry that the highest judge has imposed unless he is informed about it to the extent that he himself can witness it on behalf of the highest judge.

25 Whenever a judge dies, his successor in court shall be witness to what had transpired during the predecessor's judgeship even though he was not privy himself [to what preceded] as long as he is informed of the truth by the evidence of the *Schöffen*. No one need respond [to a charge] at a market or court of law outside of his own district unless he has a dwelling or property there. However, he must respond if he forfeits [that right] by committing a felony there or[23] ⟨D fol. 40r⟩ *is a guarantor there.*

26 *The king is the judge for all people.*[24] *A man of* Schöffen *class does not accept a challenge to a duel outside of his district. He is, however, responsible to the judicial district in which his ancestral holdings are located.*[25] *If he holds a* Schöffen *chair there, then he is a member of the judiciary and must fulfill his judicial functions in that district. A person who has no chair must attend the*

highest court of the district in which he resides. The Schöffen *chair is passed on from father to oldest son, and if he has no son, then to the oldest and closest male relative of equal birth.*

27 *Should a man unwittingly marry a woman whom he may not* [legally] *marry and have children by her, and if they are legally divorced later, it affects neither the rights of the children born before the divorce*[26] *nor the one* [the mother] *may yet be carrying.*

28 *If one person claims that another is deficient in legal capacity because of birth or occupation,*[27] *he must prove it with the oath of six others who are unblemished in their legal capacity. However, a man can more easily substantiate his legal rights and privileges*[28] *with witnesses than another can disprove it. But if someone claims that a person has lost his rights because of theft or robbery, the judge can prove it with six others.*

29 *No one of* Schöffen *class needs to prove his ancestral estate*[29] *nor name his four ancestors unless he is challenging one of his equals to a trial by combat. A person may certainly lay claim to his ancestral estate with an oath if it is not in his possession.*

30 *In a case where two men must divide one inheritance, the older shall divide the goods, and the younger shall choose his portion. Whoever answers charges himself must do without a spokesman. As long as a person withholds an answer lawfully and with the agreement of the court, he has not yet pled. The judge shall be judge equally for all people; he shall neither determine a judgment nor challenge one.*

31 *If one person owes another* [something] ⟨D fol. 40v⟩ *or has something of his, and the lender dies, the borrower must account for the item to the heirs.*[30] *But if the borrower dies, his heirs do not answer in his stead unless they are in possession of the item under dispute.*

32 *Whoever accosts, wounds, or beats someone without killing or* [permanently] *injuring the victim does not answer to the heir if the injured person dies after a year has passed unless he had pressed charges against the attacker before he died. Any person claiming to be a freeman when another claims him as his bondservant, asserting that he had entered into this service freely, can certainly be found guiltless unless the bondage agreement had been made before a court of law. But if the master claims the man was born to him in bondage, then he can prove it with two of his own bondservants.*

33 *If, however, a second lord also claims the same man as his bondservant, then the first claimant can make his claim with six of his relatives or other respected people. But if the person whose freedom is in question can prove his freedom with six oathhelpers who are his relations, three from the father's and three from the*

mother's side, he maintains his freedom and voids the others' claims. Whoever has possession of a man[31] *can bring him to trial with witnesses more easily than another who lacks possession.*[32] *Anyone who gives himself into servitude before a court of law may be challenged lawfully by his heir and given his freedom again.*[33] *If the lord retains the man in his possession until his death, then the belongings of the deceased bondman and the children born after* [he entered serfdom] *also belong to the lord.*[34] *Should a person quit* [the service of] *one lord and acknowledge another, then if he is called before the court and his new lord fails to appear to confirm his rightful service, then the master who claims him wins his case with two oathhelpers from his family, if he has them. If he lacks kin, he can prove his case with two of his bondmen born on his land.*[35] *Once his case is proven, he shall take legal possession [of the bondman] with a blow to the neck if he wishes. The person from whom the claimant wins compensation or wergeld* ⟨D fol. 41r⟩ *is also the one who pays the judge's fine if the judge levies one.*

34 *Each man has his legal rights before the king and shall make his plea before the king in any city according to his own rights and not those of his accuser. He must answer all charges that are brought against him except when he is challenged to a trial by combat. He may legally refuse challenges except in the land of his birth. If someone lays claims to his allodial property, he need not respond except in the district in which it is located. The king shall not judge regarding allodial land according to the man's law, but only according to the law of the territory in which it is located. When a judge places a person in limited outlawry and also places him in the king's outlawry, then if that person is to release himself from it, he must follow the king's court for six weeks, and the king shall give him safe conduct.*[36] *He shall pledge to come before the judge who had placed him in the king's outlawry and offer to fulfill his legal duty there within a fortnight of arriving in the land. He shall bring with him the king's letter and seal as proof that he is released from the king's outlawry. If anyone who is placed in the king's outlawry without a previous limited outlawry is to release himself, he must follow the court for six weeks and is then free. However, anyone who releases himself from outlawry but does not fulfill his legal obligation and is convicted for it, is placed in the superior outlawry as if he had been in outlawry for a year and a day.*[37]

35 *A person caught red-handed with stolen or robbed goods cannot call on a guarantor if someone challenges him to a trial by combat.*

36 *If one man challenges another to a trial by combat in a court of law, and the court rules to postpone the complaint until the next day, then peaceful conduct is imposed on both parties.*[38] *And if this peace pledge is broken,* ⟨D fol. 41v⟩ *the offender must pay compensation before any lawful combat [can be held]. But if the offender is caught in flagrante, he is judged according to law.*

37 *A person who offers himself to the court as witness before he is called shall be excluded from giving evidence. A man does no wrong if he brings in his neighbor's livestock with his own and drives it out again in the morning as long as he does not deny it and removes none of them. A man who cuts another person's ripened grain in the belief that it belongs to him or to his master does no wrong if he does not remove the grain. He shall be paid for his trouble.*

38 *A person who has not had right of possession to [a property] for the minimum of a year and a day must answer immediately in court if a claim is brought against him. No pregnant woman may be expelled from her husband's property when he dies until she has given birth. No woman inherits the food supplies or her morning gift during her husband's lifetime; she takes them after his death.*[39] *If a man's wife dies, then the niece who inherits the woman's personal property shall take from it what is necessary to make his bed as it was during her lifetime, to place a tablecloth on the table, a cushion on the bench, and a pillow on the chair.*

39 *Anyone who comes to court to collect a debt from a man who cannot pay and cannot find a guarantor shall be given the man himself as a servant in place of the money. He shall keep the debtor as part of his household, providing him with food and work. If he wants to tie the man, he may do so, but he may not torment him in any other way. If he lets the debtor free, or if the debtor escapes, he is not free of his debt until he has repaid it. And* ⟨D fol. 42r⟩ *as long as the debtor cannot pay, he remains*[40] ⟨fol. 46r⟩ the creditor's collateral for his money. Whenever a suit is brought against a person, and the judge calls him to answer the complaint, and he does not make a plea or clear himself saying that he need not respond, then he is judged liable to pay the judge's fine. This is repeated a second and a third time, and if he still does not answer the complaint, then he is determined to be guilty. But if the penalty costs life or health, the plaintiff must prove him guilty with the oath of six others.[41]

41[42] Whoever is owed money shall wait until the sun goes down in his own house or the closest judge's house where the money is transferred. If the person who is to pay pennies or silver offers security for it,[43] he is still not free [of the debt] unless their agreement allowed for this. One may pay silver using deputies. No one should hand over [money] to a deputy unless that deputy was appointed to the task in court by the person to whom the money is to be paid. The debtor shall pay the kind of pennies or silver that was pledged, but if that was not stipulated, then one shall pay with silver coinage that is common currency in that judicial district at that time.

42 The oath of a captive made while he is in prison is not legally binding. But if one allows him to ride free upon his word of honor, he must

by rights return and fulfill his promise. If he pays or is freed without payment, then whatever oath of truce[44] he swears or pledges he must fulfill, but no other pledge. If a man vows or pledges something in good faith in order to save his life or health, and if he then cannot execute it, his legal rights shall not be diminished thereby. Whenever a person captures another with guile, and if he releases the captive on his word of honor or has him swear or pledge in good faith a second thing, then the captive need not fulfill it if he can ⟨fol. 46v⟩ prove that he had been forced to pledge in bad faith by his captor. When a person demands payment in court, and the other party asks the reason for the debt, the claimant shall explain whether it is based on his receipt of a pledge or inheritance from the supposed debtor.

43 God created man in his own likeness and saved man, each and every one, with his martyrdom. The poor man as well as the rich one was dear to him. Therefore, do not be amazed that this book speaks so little about legal custom concerning unfree people because it is so multifarious that no one can cover it exhaustively.[45] There are different laws for the unfree persons subordinate to each bishop, abbot, and abbess. I cannot report on it because when laws were first established, there was no unfree person.[46] All people were free when our ancestors came here to this land. My mind cannot comprehend that one person could belong to another. Nor do we have any proof of this. Numerous people certainly are missing the truth when they claim that servitude[47] began with Cain, who slew his brother. Cain's kin were destroyed when the waters flooded the earth. Others maintain that bondage commenced with Shem, Noah's son. Noah blessed two sons but mentions no servile status of the third. Ham held Africa, Shem remained in Asia, and Japhet, our forefather, settled Europe; thus no one belonged to the other. It is also said that servitude comes from Ishmael. The Holy Scripture calls Ishmael son of a servant woman, but in no other way does it mention any type of servitude. Claims are also made that bondage originated with Esau. Jacob was blessed by his father who made him lord over his brothers, but he neither cursed Esau nor mentioned unfree status. In addition, we even stipulate ⟨fol. 47r⟩ in our own law that no one may place himself into bondage when his heir clearly opposes it.[48] How then could Noah or Isaac place another person into bondage if no one may even place himself into servitude? Moreover, we have additional evidence: God rested the seventh day, gave us law, and sent us his Spirit; he commanded that we keep the seventh month and the seventh year, which is called the year of redemption.[49] All who were captives and those who had fallen into servitude are to be freed and restored to the same rights they had

when they were taken if they wish to be released and freed from bondage. After seven times seven years comes the fiftieth year, called year of the jubilee.[50] At this time each and every person is to be freed whether he desires it or not. God also gave us proof based on a penny with which he was tempted when he said, "Render unto Caesar the things that are Caesar's and to God the things that are God's."[51] We thereby know from God's words that man has God's image and shall belong to God, and anyone other than God who promises him something acts against God.[52] The genuine truth, however, is that bondage resulted from coercion, imprisonment, and unlawful exercise of force, which has become unjust custom since ancient times, and now people take it to be right and good custom.[53]

44 If a person takes possession of something unlawfully with the result that it is proven against him according to law, he must relinquish the object with a fine. But whatever he takes into custody with agreement of the owner, such that the owner lent it to him, and if he does not repay it or return it by the date agreed upon, he is not fined unless he had pledged it in court.

45 Babylon was the birthplace of the empire that ruled over all the world. Cyrus destroyed that realm and transformed it into the Persian empire, which survived until Darius the Last. ⟨fol. 47v⟩ Alexander the Great conquered him and transferred the empire to Greece. The empire flourished there until it succumbed to Rome, and Julius Caesar became emperor. To this day Rome controls the temporal sword and, on behalf of St. Peter, the spiritual one also. Hence it is called the capital of the entire world. Our forefathers had been in Alexander's army, and when our forefathers came here, they routed the Thuringians. Alexander had conquered all of Asia with their help. Once Alexander died, they no longer dared to establish themselves in the land because of the people's anger.[54] They set out with three hundred ships. All but fifty-four were wrecked; of these, eighteen went to Prussia and settled there, twelve took the island of Rügen,[55] and twenty-four came here to this land. Since there were not enough Saxons to work the land after they had defeated and scattered the Thuringian lords, they spared the peasants and lent them land so that they would cultivate the fields [for the Saxons] according to the rights they still have. The *lasin* come from this group, and the *lasin* who forfeited their rights became the day laborers.[56]

46 Now hear about the wergeld and compensation penalties for all people.[57] The princes, and free lords, and the class eligible to be *Schöffen* are all equal in the amount of their penalty and their wergeld. However, one

honors the princes and free lords by giving them gold; they are given twelve golden pennies in damages, each of which weighs three silver pennies. Earlier the weight of the gold penny equaled the weight of two silver pennies, thus making the three pennies equal to the value of thirty shillings. To members of the *Schöffen* class one pays thirty shillings of full-weight pennies in compensation; of these pennies, twenty shillings shall weigh one mark. Their wergeld is eighteen pounds of full-weight pennies. Each woman receives half of her husband's wergeld and fines. To each girl and unmarried woman is due half the fines allowed for her birth status.[58] The husband is also guardian of his wife from the time she is wedded to him. In addition, the wife acquires the legal status of her husband at the time she enters his bed.[59] After the husband's death, she is released from the husband's legal status. Those called sharecroppers and rent-paying tenants who attend the *Schultheiss*'s court are awarded fifteen shillings in fines and ten pounds in wergeld. When a bailiff is needed, one is chosen from among them who holds less than three hides of land. The judge and *Schöffen* shall select him. Other freemen, called free tenants, who come and go as outsiders[60] and have no heritable land in the district are also granted fifteen shillings in compensation. Their wergeld is ten pounds. Two woolen gloves and a pitchfork make up the compensation fine paid to a day laborer, and his wergeld is a rick of wheat made from twelve rails all spaced one fathom apart.[61] Each rail shall have twelve nails going up, and they shall be spaced as far apart as a man's height to the shoulder so that one can measure from nail to nail. Each nail shall have twelve bags, and each bag twelve shillings. The children of priests and those illegitimately born receive in compensation as full a cartload of hay as two yearling oxen can pull. Minstrels and all those who have given themselves into bondage[62] are awarded the shadow of a man. Champions and their children receive in compensation the reflection of a shield against the sun.[63] Those who have forfeited their rights through theft, or robbery, or in some other way receive two brooms and a pair of scissors in fines.[64] The indemnity fine awarded to illegitimate people is of little use but is nevertheless stipulated so that the judge's fee may be collected subsequently.

47 People with diminished legal capacity have no wergeld. However, if anyone robs, injures, or slays one of these people, or if someone rapes a woman with reduced legal capacity and violates the peace against her, he shall be judged according to the peace law. It is possible to receive the death penalty for having intercourse with an itinerant woman[65] or one's lover ⟨fol. 48v⟩ against her will.[66]

48 A man may not press charges against more than one person for a single wound, but he may charge several people for aiding and abetting the perpetrator. When someone takes something belonging to another by force or by mistake, he shall return it with a compensation fine or swear that he is not able to return it. [If he cannot return it,] he shall reimburse the owner according to the terms the owner demands unless the debtor reduces the estimated value with his oath. Singing birds, hunting falcons, greyhounds, chasing hounds, and trackers are replaced in kind with animals that are equally good when one swears this on the relics. When someone kills the kind of animal we normally eat that belongs to another, either intentionally or not, he must make restitution in the amount of the fixed wergeld.[67] If he wounds it, he reimburses the owner with half [the tariff] without a fine, and in addition, the owner also keeps his animal.[68]

49 However, whoever willfully kills or lames the kind of animal that is not eaten, he must [pay] the full money tariff and punitive damages; if he injures it in the eye, he pays half [the tariff]. But if a man is responsible for the unintentional death or injury of an animal and confirms it with an oath, he pays restitution without a fine as discussed earlier.[69]

50 When a person's dog goes into the fields, he shall be kept on a leash so that he does no one any harm, but if it does do damage, that person whom the dog follows out into the fields shall make restitution, or if he himself is not able to pay, then his master shall do so.

51 If a German is sentenced to lose life or hand because of a crime, then whether he ransoms himself from the sentence or not, he need not pay either a court fine or a punitive fine.

52 Now hear about the wergeld of birds and animals. A chicken is compensated with a half-penny, as is a duck; a goose with one penny; a broody hen or goose ⟨fol. 49r⟩ during their hatching period and a call duck[70] with three pennies. The same compensation payment applies for a piglet and a kid while they are still suckling. For a cat and a lamb four pennies shall be paid; six for a calf, one shilling for a foal during its suckling stage, and the same for the guard dog. The tariff for the dog called sheepdog is three shillings; for a horse, a yearling pig, and a cow it is four shillings; for a draft ox and a grazing horse eight shillings; and for a workhorse able to do a full day's work, the tariff is twelve shillings. Younger animals are valued according to their age. The tariff for a riding horse with which a man serves his lord is one pound. No tariff has been set for a knight's horse, charger, saddle horse, small horse, or for fattened pigs. Instead, one shall return them and all movable goods or make restitution according to the appraisal

of the owner unless the person paying the compensation is able to reduce it with his oath.

53 Germans elect the king by law. After he is anointed by the bishops appointed to the task and is installed on the throne in Aachen, he carries the name and power of king.[71] After the pope anoints him, he wields power over the empire and has the name of emperor. The king is elected for the purpose of judging land in free ownership, fiefs, and each man's life (i.e., capital crimes). However, the emperor, cannot be present in all territories and cannot judge all crimes at all times.[72] He, therefore, invests the imperial princes with the banner estate.[73] In turn, the princes invest the counts with their jurisdiction, and each count invests his *Schultheiss* with his office. At the fourth level [removed from king], there shall be no jurisdiction conferred[74] to judge crimes carrying a sentence of death or mutilation beyond the office of *Schultheiss* because the count cannot preside over a regular court of law without him.[75] ⟨fol. 49v⟩ Should someone bring a suit against the count, he must defend himself before the *Schultheiss* because the *Schultheiss* is judge over his duties,[76] as the count palatine is judge over the emperor and the burgrave over the margrave.[77]

53a[78] Saxony, Bavaria, Franconia, and Swabia had all been kingdoms. After the Romans conquered them, their names were changed and they were called dukedoms. Nevertheless, the Romans retained the princes as their men, and their banner estates under that name.[79] Later the emperors discontinued both the offices of the crown vassals and their banner fiefs. Each and every judge collects his court fine within his jurisdiction but no indemnity payment because the judge cannot be judge and plaintiff at the same time. Consequently, no one but the plaintiff may receive a compensation payment. That is why people say that the princes have no indemnity payment, but that is not so. One may not divide a legal jurisdiction, nor may the invested person divide a fief completely to the extent that an irrevocable feudal succession is set up so that the peasants must accept it unless it is a separate county that is part of a banner estate. But such land cannot be left vacant either. Likewise, the king cannot leave a territory vacant but must confer it within a year and a day.[80]

54[81] A fief with legal jurisdiction can only be given to a person who is of the *Schöffen* class, has pledged his fealty to the king according to the law of freemen, and by his homage, has committed himself to be a witness whenever he is called upon.[82] When the king is elected, he shall pledge allegiance to the realm, swear that he will reinforce justice, thwart injustice, ⟨fol. 50r⟩ and defend the law of the realm to his best ability and knowledge. After that he need never swear another oath unless the pope should bring charges that he wavers in the true faith. Consequently he is witness for all matters when called upon in homage to the realm. And he shall make his pledge instead of an oath as one pledges a truce. A cripple, a leper, or someone excommunicated by the pope cannot be elected king. The king shall be of free and legitimate birth, which means that he retains his legal rights and privileges. At the time of his election, the king assumes Franconian law regardless of his birth for the following reason: just as a Franconian cannot forfeit his life unless he is caught red-handed or unless his Franconian rights have been revoked by the court, likewise no one may bring charges against the king for a capital offense unless a judgment had first divested him of the realm.[83]

55 None but the king may judge the imperial princes at the level of life and health. As for the *Schöffen* class, if they are convicted and sentenced to capital punishment, then only the bailiff may execute them.[84]

56 When the bailiff is chosen by the judge and the *Schöffen*, he shall pledge loyalty to the king according to the law of freemen. Then the judge shall take him by the hand and seat him opposite to himself on a chair with a cushion on it, ⟨fol. 50v⟩ place the relics in his lap, and establish immunity as provided by law.[85] The bailiff now possesses the authority to attach, and arrest, and seize each and every man and his property when given a court order following a judgment. If he commits a crime, he can forfeit his life and property just like any other man. He may not carry a sword or any weapon. If anyone opposes his enforcement of the law, he must summon the entire community with the hue and cry to perform what is required by law if he can. If he cannot carry out the law, he must bring his complaint before the judge. He has the authority to allow every tenth man who is about to be condemned to ransom his life with a money payment. And where a man or woman dies without an heir, the harvested grain[86] is his, as are the man's everyday clothes. When a person transfers a freehold, and peace has been agreed to, the bailiff shall receive three shillings from it. He can excuse any man except the village headman from court duty in each village if that person has no suit pending against him.

57 Neither the pope nor anyone else can place a ban on the emperor after he is anointed except for three causes: if he wavers in the faith, repudiates his legal wife, or destroys churches. Among the imperial electors, the first is the Bishop of Mainz, the second is the Bishop of Trier, and the third is the Bishop of Cologne. ⟨fol. 51r⟩ Among the lay princes, the first of the electors is the Count Palatine of the Rhine, who is the imperial steward; the

second is the marshal, Duke of Saxony; the third is the chamberlain, Margrave of Brandenburg. The King of Bohemia, who is the imperial butler, has no vote because he is not German.[87] After that the princes of the realm, lay and religious, all vote. Those named in the first electoral group may not elect according to their own desire but rather shall choose by name the person elected by all the princes.

58 The imperial princes of the realm shall have as lord no layperson other than the king. A banner fief that makes a man a crown vassal is only valid when it is conferred by the king. Whatever a second man receives before the king does not make him first holder of the estate because another had already been invested with it before him. Therefore, the estate cannot elevate him to a crown vassal.[88]

59 When bishops, or abbots, or abbesses who are members of the military shields are elected, they should be invested with the fief first and the spiritual office thereafter. Once they have been invested, they can carry out feudal law, but not before. In cases where bishops, abbots, and abbesses are not elected within six weeks, the investiture reverts to the emperor, who then has free choice to invest a person who is upright in his actions.

60 The emperor invests all ecclesiastical princes with the scepter, and all lay princes with the banner.[89] ⟨fol. 51v⟩ And he may not leave a banner estate vacant for more than a year and a day.[90] As the king travels from region to region within the realm, tolls and mints are under his authority. And wherever he goes, the law court is also his since he can certainly judge all the suits that have not yet formally begun and not yet concluded. When the king first arrives in a territory, all prisoners shall be relinquished to his authority to satisfy justice.[91] They shall be brought before him to be convicted or set free lawfully. [This shall be done] as quickly as the prisoners can be summoned after the king or his envoy has called them to judgment as the law provides and served summons either to the man himself, or to the farmstead, or to the house where the prisoners are or were held. If the captors refuse to bring them before the court after they have been rightfully commanded to do so, and the king's messenger has evidence for this, [the court] summarily outlaws all those who captured them as well as the castles and people who held them against the law.[92]

61 The count shall preside over his court every eighteen weeks at the legal venue where the *Schultheiss*, and *Schöffen*, and bailiff are all present except on the fixed peace days. To be a *Schultheiss* one must be a freeman and native of the judicial district of the court. The bailiff shall own at least one-

half hide of hereditary land. All members of the judiciary shall attend court from sunrise until midday while the judge presides.

62 There are five locations in Saxony called [imperial] palaces where the king holds imperial court.[93] The first is Grone; the second is Werla, which has been transferred to Goslar; the third is Wallhausen; ⟨fol. 52r⟩ the fourth is Allstedt; and Merseburg is the fifth.[94] Saxony also contains seven banner estates: the Duchy and the Palatine County of Saxony, March of Brandenburg, Landgravate of Thuringia, March of Meissen, March of Lusatia, and the County of Aschersleben.[95] Saxony also encompasses two archdioceses and fifteen dioceses.[96] The Magdeburger archdiocese contains the dioceses of Naumburg, Merseburg, Meissen, Brandenburg, and Havelberg. The Archbishop of Mainz has four subordinates in the land of Saxony: the bishops of Halberstadt, Hildesheim, Verden, and Paderborn. The bishops of Osnabrück, Minden, and Münster are subject to the Archbishop of Cologne. The Archdiocese of Bremen includes Lübeck, Schwerin, and Ratzeburg.

63 King Constantine gave Pope Silvester a secular court fine of sixty shillings in addition to the ecclesiastical court [fine] so that he may compel all those who are not willing to serve God with their lives to do so with their property.[97] This arrangement enables secular and ecclesiastical jurisdiction to work hand in hand. Thus if a person resists the one, he can be compelled by the other to obey and fulfill his lawful duty. Anathema damages the soul yet causes no loss of life and diminishes no one's rights ⟨fol. 52v⟩ in territorial law or feudal law unless the king's outlawry also follows. Limited outlawry can cost a man his life if he is caught in it, but not his legal capacity while he is still an outlaw.

64 When the king calls for service to the realm or summons a royal court by decree and has it proclaimed to the princes with his official letter and seal six weeks before it is to take place, then the princes are required to attend wherever the king is residing in German territory. If they do not appear, they must pay a fine. The imperial princes holding a banner fief pay one hundred pounds; all others pay a fine of ten pounds when there is no punitive fine exacted for a felony. Each nobleman pays a fine of ten pounds to the duke. Within the duchy there are several regions such as Holstein, Stormarn, and Hadeln, that have their own laws, so I will say nothing about their scale of fines. A person pays sixty shillings to the count and to the advocate[98] who presides over a superior court when he possesses the king's judicial authority.[99] No one but the king may invest royal judicial

authority. The king may not legally refuse to invest his judicial authority in a person who has been invested with the judgeship. If a count invests someone with part of his county, or an advocate a portion of his advocacy, that action is unlawful. The person thus invested does not have the jurisdiction of superior justice that would subject others to him. Judicial authority is invested without men.[100] The count palatine and landgrave preside over a superior court as does the count. ⟨fol. 53r⟩ A sixty-shilling court fine is paid to him. Each margrave whose judgeship rests on his own authority receives thirty shillings. The *Schultheiss* is paid eight shillings by the sharecroppers. The invested [person] without the king's judicial authority receives three shillings at most in court fines. The local judge receives six pence, or one shilling, or according to the determination of the peasants. The village headman may charge six pence as a court fine and occasionally three shillings for a sentence of corporal punishment. This sum goes to the village peasants' fund for drinks.

65 The margrave presides over the court every six weeks on his own judicial authority. Here each person may determine a judgment over another as long as he has full legal capacity. However, no one answers in legal combat to anyone who is not of equal legal rank. If a man becomes a vassal of his equal, it does not diminish his legal status or his rights in general territorial law, but it does reduce his status in the ranks of arms-bearing men.[101] No one may set up a market within a mile of another. No one may erect a castle or fortify a town with either thick boards or walls, or build a hill, or island, or towers within a village without the consent of the judge of the district. However, his permission is not required to dig as deep as a man can pile up earth with a spade without raising a mound.

66 In addition, the judge's permission is not necessary in order to erect [a building] with three stories of wood or stone such that one is below ground[102] and the other two above and with a door in the lowest level ⟨fol. 53v⟩ knee high above the ground. One may also secure a yard with hedges,[103] or with a stockade, or with walls high enough that a man can reach the top when sitting on a horse. However, no crenelations or rampart are allowed. No one may rebuild a castle without permission of the judge once it has been razed by a court judgment following a crime. But if a castle has been razed by force, or if the lord allows it to become dilapidated intentionally or out of poverty, it may be rebuilt without the consent of the judge.

67 If someone seizes another's castle in violation of the law, and the lord of the castle brings suit for justice, and the aggressor holds the castle

with force while the plaintiff who has right of possession refrains from use of force, no one may make a complaint lawfully against the castle which would cause it to be razed.

68 The judge shall first strike three blows with an axe at a castle or a building that has been condemned by court decision. The peasants shall help with the hewing and ramming. Nothing shall be burned; no one shall remove any wood or stone from the site or anything that is in it unless it was placed there as robbed goods. If someone makes rightful claim to an item, he shall take it with him. The fosse and bulwark shall be leveled with spades. All those who attended the trial shall help, bringing their own meal if they are summoned to this work with the hue and cry. ⟨fol. 54r⟩

69 When a court hearing is held under royal judicial authority, no *Schöffen* or judge may wear a cap, hat, cowl, hood, or gloves. They shall have cloaks on their shoulders but shall carry no weapons. Without having broken their fast,[104] they shall hand down judgments concerning each and every man, be he German or Wend, free or unfree. No other person may render a judgment. A judgment is reached while seated. If one of their peers contests a judgment, he shall ask the bench [to be allowed] to make a different determination. Then the person who rendered the first judgment shall stand up, and the other shall sit in his place, and hand down a judgment that seems right to him, and present it where it belongs lawfully [to see] whether it is accepted or rejected for settlement as was previously described.[105]

70 When a court does not meet under the king's authority, every man who cannot be accused of legal incapacity may certainly determine a judgment regarding another, with the exception that a Wend may not hand down a judgment over a Saxon, nor a Saxon over a Wend.[106] However, if a Saxon or a Wend is caught red-handed and brought before the court with the hue and cry, then the Saxon is a witness against the Wend, and the Wend against the Saxon. And each one who has been thus captured must accept the judgment of the other.

71 Every man who has been charged may refuse to respond if the charges are not pronounced in the language of his birth if he swears that he does not understand German. Then once the charges are made in his own language, he must ⟨fol. 54v⟩ answer them, or his spokesman shall do it for him in such a way that the plaintiff and the judge understand him.[107] However, if he has brought a complaint or answered one or handed down a judgment in German in a court of law, and it can be proven, then he [must] answer the charges in German. When responding to charges before the

realm, he does not have to [use German] because there each person has rights according to his birth. A free and legitimate son retains his father's status within the order of military shields[108] and inherits his estate as well as the mother's as long as he is her equal or higher in birth.

72 Should a free woman of the *Schöffen* class marry a tenant or a sharecropper[109] and have children by him, these children are not her equals in wergeld and compensation amounts because they have the father's legal status and not the mother's. For this reason, they do not inherit from the mother's estate nor from the estate of any family member on the mother's side. Until the time of Bishop Wichmann of Magdeburg,[110] the ministerials[111] were subject to the same law, namely, that the son retained the father's legal status, and the daughter retained that of her mother. The children belonged where [the parents] belonged. If they were servants, then there was no need to exchange them.[112]

73 It has been right and proper since law began that a free woman does not produce servile children. Since the time of Bishop Wichman a law has been in effect that sons and daughters of a German mother belong to whomever she belongs to, whether the father is a German or a Wend. The child of a Wend woman belongs to the father if he is a Wend. ⟨fol. 55r⟩ But if he is German, then he belongs to the mother. It is said that all Wend women are free since their children belong to the Wend father, but this is not so because they pay a wedding tax[113] to their lord each time they marry. If the woman leaves her husband, as Wend law permits, she must pay her lord the fee[114] that amounts to three shillings and even more elsewhere according to the custom of the region.

74 If a woman is lawfully divorced from her husband, she nevertheless retains the life estate he gave her from his proprietary holding and her buildings on that land. She may not, however, raze the buildings or move them elsewhere; otherwise she loses the buildings and her morning gift. She retains the woman's personal belongings and her portion of the food stores. The property she brought into the marriage[115] shall be returned to her possession, or that portion of her husband's property that had been promised her when they first came together.[116]

75 A woman's legal life estate is on allodial land because no one may confiscate it during her lifetime. However, [this is not the case] with a fiefholding because it can be canceled in several ways. A fiefholding is her fief in reversion during her husband's life, and after his death it becomes her legal fiefholding.[117] Neither man nor woman has a longer tenancy in fief than his [or her] life. Only the man passes it on as inheritance, not the woman.[118]

76 If the husband dies, and the wife continues to live in the husband's property unseparated from the children for a longer or shorter period of time, then when they separate from her, the lady ⟨fol. 55v⟩ takes her morning gift, the woman's personal belongings, and her portion of the food supplies from the whole of the existing property as she had the right to do when her husband died. But if the woman marries, and the husband joins her and the children in the undivided property, and the woman dies, then the husband retains the woman's right to the movable property but not to the buildings or the woman's personal belongings. If a man marries a widow who owns land, or possesses a fief, or life estate, or land with tithes attached, then whatever he gains from his working the land with a plow is determined in the following way. If his wife dies before he sows, then he shall complete the work of sowing and harvesting and pay tithes or rents on the land to the heir. If, however, the wife dies after the seed is sown, and once the harrow has gone over the fields, then the harvest belongs to the husband, and he is not required to pay dues or rents on it as long as no [previous] rent had been owed on her property. Dues and rent owed to the woman's property that were due to be paid her go to the husband's earnings, just as they would go to the heir if she had not married, as long as she died after the day rents are legally due.

77 If a man leases his sown land for dues or rent for a specified number of years stipulating that it be sown upon its return and dies during this time, the leaseholder shall sow the land and relinquish it to the heir because the lessor cannot lease the land for a period longer than his lifetime. The heirs shall pay appropriate taxes or rents from the harvest to whom it is due, just as it would normally be paid to the person who lent the land because[119] ⟨D fol. 52r⟩ *it was not the lessor's plow that worked it when he died.*[120]

78 *The king and every judge preside over capital crimes and serious felonies, the property of each of his men*[121] *and kin, and does not act disloyally thereby. In turn, the man may on behalf of his king and judge certainly oppose any injustice and help resist it in all ways possible. Even where his kin or his lord is concerned, he does not act disloyally. The man may certainly pursue his lord, the lord his man, the kinsman, his kinsman and should help bring him to justice for a felony if he is called with hue and cry to a red-handed deed. In this case, too, he maintains his allegiance. The man may certainly pursue his lord, the lord his man, and the kinsman his kinsman right to his castle when he is called with hue and cry because of a crime, and may certainly help raze the castle if it is not legally exculpated. This, too, a person does without breach of loyalty.*

Each person shall help defend cities, castles, lands, and the lives of his lord, his relations, his men, and his friends against lords, relations, or men who seek them out with force; he shall certainly fight for them without breach of fealty as long as he takes nothing of theirs. Should a man wound his lord or kill him in self-defense, or the lord do so to his man, he is guilty of no disloyalty if self-defense is proven before the law. ⟨D fol. 52v⟩

Each person has the responsibility to help his traveling companion, his guest, his innkeeper where he resides, and anyone who seeks asylum from him to resist the unlawful force of others, and is not disloyal when he does so. If the man attacks the lord, or the lord the man, without having brought an accusation before his men as provided by law, this is a breach of fidelity. However, if the attacker's purpose is not to damage the person, and if the attacker himself incurs damage on his own or from those accompanying him, or if he is an unwitting accomplice in an attack, then he must make restitution for the damage to satisfy justice but is not guilty of disloyalty.

79 *If a person who is not a captain is on a military campaign and riders attack him along with his men, and the attackers injure his lord, or his men, or his kin, or whomever but without his advice or support, then if he swears this on the relics, he suffers no fine or shame.*[122]

80 *When peasants clear land of wild roots* [and lay out] *a village, the lord of the village may give them the right of inheritance even though they were not born to it.*[123] *However, he may not give them a privilege, nor may they themselves establish a privilege that would restrict the right of the territorial judge or enable them to reduce or increase his court fine. No outsider is required to answer in the village according to the particular laws of that village, but he must answer according to the general law of the territory unless he brings a suit to claim inheritance of land or property or a debt.* ⟨D fol. 53 r⟩ *The place where a person brings a complaint is the place where he must also respond to complaints when they are brought against him except for a trial by combat.*

81 *If a sharecropper dies without an heir and leaves three hides or less, it belongs to the office of* Schultheiss. *If thirty or fewer hides are left without heirs, they go to the office of the count. But if more than thirty hides have no heir, they revert to the king. If the king or another lord frees his ministerial or his bondman, the freedman obtains the rights of a free tenant.*[124] *If, however, a* Schöffen [family] *dies out in a county, the king can certainly free an imperial ministerial by decree and make him a* Schöffe *so that people can receive justice, and a superior court can be held.*[125] *The king shall also give these people enough imperial land in freehold—that is, three hides of land or more to each—so that they may remain* Schöffen. *The land must be situated within the county where the count has available land because the allodial land belonging to the deceased* Schöffe *had*

become available. A ministerial inherits and passes on an inheritance just as free people do according to general territorial law except that he neither receives nor passes on inheritance outside of his lord's authority.

82 *A person who loses his rights in a court of law in one place forfeits them everywhere else if one has proof of this from the court. No one is required to bring his court record to another jurisdiction. Rather, the judge before whom his loss of rights is asserted will* ⟨D fol. 53v⟩ *send two of his messengers to the judge who presides where the man had forfeited his rights so that the envoys may hear whether it can be proven. The messengers will then witness it. If a person gives a property to another lord and gives the recipient possession when he himself does not have right of possession, and if the recipient is installed in the property by a court decision, then the person who actually has right of possession can oppose the court's installation and expel the recipient if he makes his case at the next scheduled court session, because a man is not required to vacate his possession unless a suit is brought against him and he is summoned. Then if he is given possession and instated in the property by court decision, no one can expel him without a judgment.*

83 *Whatever a person gives to a man or a woman must remain in that person's possession for three days.*[126] *Whatever they are awarded in a suit, or whatever they inherit, they do not need to keep in their possession. Whoever leases or transfers a piece of land to another shall be his warrantor for a year and a day. Anyone who sells allodial land or movable property shall remain its warrantor as long as he lives. The property shall remain his right of possession, to defend or lose, as long as he represents it because the recipient may attest only to the transfer.*

84 *If anyone takes control of another's property by force so that the possessor dies, the aggressor loses all possessory right to the land even if such right would have normally fallen to him upon the death of the property holder. If a man kills his lord, he forfeits*[127] ⟨fol. 56r⟩ life, reputation, and the property he received from him. The lord forfeits the same if he kills his man because then the overlord cannot install the perpetrator's children in the estate. Likewise, if a man kills his father, his brother, his kinsman, or someone belonging to the allod or fief for which he is awaiting, he voids his grant in expectancy[128] totally unless he committed the deed in self-defense, and the deceased is convicted for it, or if the perpetrator acted without knowing, so that it happened unintentionally.

85 In a case where several people have pledged to pay a wergeld or other payment, they are all liable as long as the full amount remains unpaid. No single person should pay the entire amount, but each should contribute just as much as is proper and as much as is forced upon him by court order, by the person to whom it was promised, or by the person who had prom-

ised to make the payment [in the debtor's stead] and has done so.[129] Further, if several people pledge to pay a debt for a person, and many people receive this pledge, then once the outstanding payments are made to the creditors, or a mutual agreement is reached, then all have carried out their pledge in full. Whoever makes a guarantee such that he will pay it himself, or his bondsman for him, then if he is able to pay it, he has released his guarantor [of responsibility]. On the other hand, whoever becomes a bondsman for another and pledges to pay a fixed sum must then fulfill it himself with witnesses to prove that he paid it or someone did so ⟨fol. 56v⟩ on his behalf.

86 Any person who plows, or digs, or encloses the village commons can be accused and charged before the village headman and must pay a fine of three shillings. But if he refuses to fulfill the village headman's ruling and is then charged before the highest judge,[130] he must pay the judge's fine and a penalty of thirty shillings to the peasants and vacate the commons. One peasant community[131] indemnifies another in the same way with three shillings and payment of damages when someone brings a complaint against them to the community according to law. If they then refuse to fulfill their legal obligation and are brought before the highest judge, their village headman must pay the judge's fine, pay the thirty-shilling penalty to the peasants, and make good the damages for them.

87 Whenever a layperson makes a complaint against another in ecclesiastical court for a kind of deed that should be judged in a secular court and causes the defendant harm because of it, then if the defendant brings charges against him according to territorial law for the harm done him, the person who brought the first complaint shall pay the judge's fine and penalty, and make restitution for the damage. Country people shall treat each other in the same way if they live in the same district or village, and the one presses charges within a city jurisdiction or in another jurisdiction not his own unless he is denied justice in court.

88 A judge denies justice[132] if he does not hear a case or does not preside over the regularly scheduled court session. A man also circumvents the law[133] ⟨fol. 57r⟩ when he is accused and is outlawed or does not pay a debt owed, especially when he cannot be forced by court order to comply by means of seizure. In this case, the plaintiff should pursue his suit in all places where he can achieve justice. For those cases that need to be proven in a court of law, the judge shall, based on his oath of loyalty to the king, be responsible along with the *Schöffen* and all the members of the judiciary based on their oath.

89 Whenever someone brings an outlaw before the law, except when caught red-handed, and demands his sentencing, and the prisoner denies the outlawry, his outlawry must be proven with witnesses before the hearing with the judge and the members of the judiciary proceeds. The plaintiff may not be a witness if the court can establish the facts without him. Once the man is indicted, the plaintiff should be the first to swear that the man is indeed guilty of the deed for which he was outlawed. Next, the plaintiff's witness must swear that his oath is true and not false. The same holds for a plaintiff and his witnesses who swear regarding someone not outlawed but caught red-handed in connection with a crime after the defendant has been convicted and sentenced. Regardless of what kind of proof a person needs to establish either for the court or against it, be it for property or right of possession, his witnesses shall first provide the testimony up to the oath, and he shall perform the oath himself.

90[134] If one person removes another's sword, clothing, basin, or shaving knife from the bath house when these articles are very like his own according to the agreement of several people; ⟨fol. 57v⟩ or carries away a full or empty sack from the mill or takes a saddle, bridle, or spurs; or beds, pillows, sheets, or other articles—whatever they may be, when he thinks they belong to him and leaves his own items there, then if he keeps any such items openly in the conviction that they are his, and if he places his oath upon it, the other person [who finds the items missing] may still lay legal claim to them by grabbing them in order to initiate a suit for their return.[135] If the man is charged with theft or robbery, he can clear himself with an oath on the relics as long as he has witnesses that he had kept the items openly.

91 If a man is murdered in a field and no one knows who did it, the man who then buries him in the field or in the village with the knowledge of the neighbors does no wrong. If a man's relative or friend is killed, he may bury him even if he well knows who the perpetrator is unless he brought the suit with the dead man to court. In this case he may not bury the man without the judge's permission while the case is being pled. If a man falls, or is injured, or is so badly beaten that he cannot get to the village by himself, then whoever carries him back incurs no difficulties if the injured person dies while in his care.[136] The heirs of the deceased shall reimburse him for the expenses if the articles the deceased was carrying do not cover them.

[92][137] Should a person give shelter to a number of people, and then if one of them slays another without cause in his hostel or just outside, or whatever crime ⟨fol. 58r⟩ one of them perpetrates on the other, the host is not liable, nor are the peasants liable if they are not able to detain the

malefactor and swear it on the relics. This type of case shall be brought to the local court. The judge cannot force anyone, whether he has a guardian or not, except the plaintiff to a trial by combat or to [perform] more than his cleansing oath as long as each person swears according to his rights. He may not impose on the district any prohibitions, the housing of people, nor duty, nor any other requirement without the agreement of the community. ⟨fol. 59r⟩

Plate 5. Folio 59r from book IV. From top to bottom: (1) the seven orders of military shields; (2) those not under feudal law; (3) fiefholders without knightly status; (4) enfeoffment of someone who lacks knightly status; and (5) enfeoffment of priests and women. Cod. Guelf. 3.1 Aug.2⁰, folio 59r, IV 1–2. (Reproduced by permission of the Herzog August Bibliothek, Wolfenbüttel, Germany)

Book IV

1 Anyone who wants to know about feudal law should follow the instruction of this book. First of all, we state that the orders of knighthood[1] begin with the king and end in the seventh order because the lay princes demoted the sixth order down to the seventh when they became the bishops' men.[2] This situation had not existed previously. The following groups are excluded from feudal law: priests, merchants, villagers, women, all who are encumbered in their rights or born illegitimate, as well as all those who cannot trace their knightly status to their father and grandfather. Nevertheless, if a lord invests [such] a person with a fief, then the invested persons have feudal rights based on the land even though this land does not devolve upon their children, and the fiefholders themselves lack the right to have the relationship renewed by any [successor of the original] lord.[3] Fiefholders lacking knightly status can be excluded from giving testimony and determining a judgment in a feudal court. However, the lord who gave them feudal law must accept their testimony and judgment and may not use it against others. If two men claim an estate equally and offer witnesses, and one of the claimants is without knightly status, then the claim of the person possessing knightly status precedes, and the other is dismissed.

2 A man not born to knightly status may not refuse to enfeoff someone with property who also lacks knightly status, and may not refuse to have it renewed by any lord even if the new lord lacks knightly status.[4] When a man of knightly class is enfeoffed by an ecclesiastic, a woman, or someone lacking knightly status, he does not have the right to have the fief renewed by the lord's successor. ⟨fol. 59v⟩ Should it happen, however, that a priest or woman receives imperial property by election and acquires knightly status as well, he or she may lend the property [in subfief] and also have it renewed by another lord.[5] In contrast, investiture of a castle, an ecclesiastical fief, and all investitures not requiring military service may be conferred by a priest or a woman even if that person does not possess knightly status. And that fief can also be renewed with another [i.e., succeeding] lord.

3 The man shall do his lord homage as is his duty and swear that he

will remain as loyal and faithful according to law as every man must toward his lord as long as he desires to remain his man and keep his property. Until he has done this, he may not be a witness for anyone in a feudal court. Also, he shall honor his lord with words and deeds when he is with him, allow his lord to proceed before him, and stand in his lord's presence.

4 The man is obligated to perform military service for the empire[6] within all the German-speaking areas subject to the Roman Empire.[7] The call for service is proclaimed [to each] six weeks before departure and announced [in each place] so that two of the lord's men hear. All those who are invested on the east side of the river Saale shall serve in Poland. Each man must serve six weeks at his own expense. Six weeks prior to the campaign and six weeks after, he shall have imperial immunity and a rest period,[8] meaning that none of his lords may call him to feudal court ⟨fol. 60r⟩ or command him to imperial military service.

However, whenever the Germans elect a king, and he travels to Rome for the consecration, the six foremost princes among the electors must accompany him.[9] These princes are the bishops of Mainz, Trier, and Cologne, the Count Palatine of the Rhine, the Duke of Saxony, and the Margrave of Brandenburg. Their attendance confirms for the pope the proper election of the king. In addition, every man invested with imperial property shall make the journey with his lord or redeem the trip with the tenth pound he receives annually from the fief. This service[10] shall be decreed one year, six weeks, and three days before the assembly and ends for the Germans once the king is consecrated. The man must also serve his lord by determining judgments in feudal court in the mornings, but not on feast and peace days. Whatever begins in the morning, excluding peace days and holy days, that requires a judgment can certainly be completed after the noon hour, even during peace days but not on feast days. If a person lends his horse or another item he owns, or if he loses something of his while in service to his lord, then he is not required to serve his lord or fulfill his feudal duty as long as he is not compensated. ⟨fol. 60v⟩ Should the lord refuse his man his rights when that man brings a suit against him before his men, then the man shall not serve him or fulfill his feudal duty for the duration.

5 A lord may invest two men with a single property in such a way that the first obtains right of possession,[11] and the second the reversion if[12] the holder in possession dies without an heir in fief. No grant of a fief in reversion is binding on the lord's successor.[13] If the holder in possession grants the fief [in subfief], he breaks the enfeoffment in reversion unless he

recovers possession and then dies [without an heir]. Whoever has a fief with right of possession can prove it when necessary with the lord's men who know that it is his fief. A person having a fief in reversion can prove it with those who saw and heard that he has indeed been enfeoffed with it while he is awaiting possession.

6 The father passes on to the son his right of possession along with the property so that the son does not need to be invested in his father's property. When a man has no son, right of possession to his property reverts to the lord unless the lord has previously invested it as a fief in reversion, and the enfeoffed man claims it within a year and a day according to law.

7 If a lord bestows on his man the first property that becomes vacant, be it small or large, and if afterward he also enfeoffs another with a specified fief in reversion, then the person awaiting the first available property cannot void the other's reversion for the specified property when the person in possession of that property dies.[14] ⟨fol. 61r⟩ The fiefholder with reversion must prove his right to the designated property based on the law of reversion before the lord and against the man claiming his first available property only if the lord recognizes both enfeoffments. A man can confirm his property with the lord's acknowledgment against another lord who has no proof, but not against the claims of his fellow vassal.[15] Whenever a lord bestows a property on his man, the lord does not lose right of possession with respect to his overlord even if the overlord does not recognize it because the man received it directly from his lord [and not from the overlord].

8 Should two men claim one property when neither has possession, then both must state the date of their enfeoffment. The one who can prove the earlier enfeoffment gains possession by right. Whenever a lord [offers to] bestow property on his man once it reverts after his fiefholder's death and has not made any other decision regarding it, the man shall have the first property that becomes available, be it free or enfeoffed [in subfief]. Whatever uninvested property the man has been bestowed, he must accept with witnesses when he is enfeoffed because he still lacks right of possession. The man must claim the first property that becomes vacant even if it is less or more than what he was granted until he receives his fief in full. If the man spurns the fief that reverted to the lord and does not claim it within a year and a day, then the property reverts to the lord's discretion ⟨fol. 61v⟩ unless the man clears himself with a cleansing oath, swearing that he did not know the property had become available. In a suit regarding a fief, the two parties may not be witnesses as long as the property remains undivided between them.[16] When two parties are invested with a fief, and they lend a

portion of the property in fief to a man, then neither one may revoke the land from the man or transfer the property to the lord without the [approval of] the other and damage the joint fiefholder by these means while the property remains undivided between them. The lord can by court order definitely command the men who hold a [single] property from him jointly to designate one of them within six weeks so that the lord shall know whose service he will call on. If they do not do this, they shall be fined and their holding revoked if the lord sues them under feudal law.[17]

9 Anyone who is the lord's man may act as spokesman[18] and also determine judgments in feudal court even if he holds no property from the lord. As a litigant, he cannot appeal the judgment of the lord's men unless he establishes the lord's invested man as guarantor that the litigant shall prove his case or accept the judgment lawfully. If a man appeals a judgment three times, and the decision is made against him because he did not appeal on the correct grounds that would aid him, he may not appeal it again unless he corrects the error he had made in the previous three appeals. Some people say that no one may bestow a fief in reversion ⟨fol. 62r⟩ without the request of the person who holds the property in his possession, but that is not so

10 because the man proves his enfeoffment with witnesses when necessary and not the request.[19] A lord can enfeoff a man with the first available [rent of] one pound or two, [and] that person has a legal right to it once the property is invested and named.[20] When a lord invests his man in the holding immediately after enfeoffing him, the man then has immediate right of possession to the property that had been the lord's before he invested the man with it. But if the lord refuses to invest the man in the property once he enfeoffs him, then [the man occupies] it without investiture wherever it is available to him.[21] But if the lord designated a village or place in which he enfeoffed the man with property, then the man may not travel to another place. If he took possession of the property without investiture and holds it for a year and a day without legal objection from his lord, then after that time the lord may not remove him from it. When a man does not have property in his possession and has not been invested with it, he may not have his tenancy in it renewed by the lord's successor and may not pass it on to his son.

11 In a case where a property is taken from someone by force and the injured person responds with proper charges, the property devolves on the son, and the tenancy may be renewed by the lord's successor. Hence, if he pursues the proper remedy, he loses only possession. Should the lord invest

his man with an entire village, vineyard, rents, a judgeship,[22] or similar thing in part or entirety that he has available in [any] location, the fief follows the man and devolves on his son, even if he has not been invested. ⟨fol. 62v⟩ A man invested with the income from mills, coinage, tolls, vineyards, rents, or similar things can have it renewed by a new lord and pass it on, even if the lord controls the place itself and can invest someone with it. Whatever these men lose on their holdings while the lord controls the place in which the fief is situated and bestows it to someone, they shall be compensated by the lord for their loss. However, if the lord bestows more in fief than the property produces, then those who were first to receive enfeoffments shall retain them in the same place, and those who are enfeoffed later and cannot obtain theirs shall claim compensation from the lord.

12 Unless a man has a half hide from his lord or a property that is worth five shillings and has been invested in it, he cannot be a witness in feudal court. The testimony of an excommunicate or an outlaw, whether in royal or local outlawry, can be dismissed by the court that outlawed him. He cannot act as spokesman. If he brings a suit against someone, that person need not respond if he can prove the claimant's outlawry or excommunication. In contrast, the outlaw must answer to all who bring a suit against him.

13 If a lord expels his man from a fief that the man has held in his possession for six weeks and ⟨fol. 63r⟩ a year without any rightful opposition from the lord, then even though the man is able to prove his right of possession with seven men, he corroborates his right of possession simply by means of an oath on the relics and keeps the property without witnesses because he cannot be dislodged from his possession without a lawsuit. Whenever someone needs the testimony of seven men, he may ask twenty-one men for their testimony.[23] However, no one may hold a castle fief as a regular fief without proof of witnesses, even if the person is in possession of the property. Should a lord allow a man to remain in possession of his property for a year and a day without contesting it in court as he by rights should, and if the man then exceeds his renewal limitation period during which he must claim his property or clear it,[24] he cannot detach the property from his lord on grounds of possession or by appealing to another lord for it unless the [second] lord acquires it lawfully. Land on which a person pays yearly rents cannot confer feudal rights on him. But if the man claims feudal rights, and the lord offers to confirm the land as his rent property in front of witnesses, possession of the property does not help him unless he can win with witnesses his feudal rights with respect to the lord. The man

has a greater right to do this if he completes the proof than the lord does to maintain the property without feudal rights. ⟨fol. 63v⟩

14 By swearing an oath on the relics, a man may retain a farmstead, a *morgen*,[25] or a man among his other property with respect to his lord if he has this property renewed by another lord as long as he has right of possession. A property can have several users such that one receives it from another. However, one of them must have right of possession. The person who has use of the produce or revenues and collects rents from it, be that person man or woman, has right of possession.[26] One must also answer to this person if someone commits an improper act on the property. However, it is not called rightful possession when someone takes control of a property by force if the injured party brings charges for the violent deed and can prove it with witnesses. If a man claims he holds property from a second lord in the presence of the lord from whom he holds it, and if his lord has the testimony of his men [to prove it], then the man forfeits his right to the property unless the lord from whom he originally claimed to hold it acquires it.[27] No man shall name the warrantor of a fief in front of the overlord as long as he may refuse [to do so] according to feudal law because the man is not duty-bound to answer to the overlord for his own lord's property in his possession as if he were the [overlord's] man. But if the overlord can prove that his man[28] has alienated the property or that a court judgment has revoked it from him, then the person in possession of the property is liable for it and ⟨fol. 64r⟩ must, together with the lord, have the property renewed by the overlord. Should a man deny his lord's property and disclaim before his [lord's] men that he holds it from the lord, then the property reverts to the lord. But if he has bestowed it further, and the overlord obtains control of it, then the man in possession shall admonish his lord with a court ruling that the lord himself is to represent his property in court and settle the overlord's claims according to law. This the lord shall do within six weeks time in fulfillment of the law. But if the lord unlawfully refuses to comply, the man shall have his holding renewed by the overlord himself. In this way he does not lose possession of the property even if his lord acquires it. If a lord denies his man's property to the overlord or does not identify it when he receives it as he must lawfully do, then the man shall request renewal of the fief from the overlord within the lawful limitation period.

15 The lord may misspeak and hinder his own legal position, but he cannot do so with his men as long as they answer for their holdings according to proper procedure. If a man has his property renewed by the overlord

and requests investiture or attornment,[29] he must identify for the overlord the property and the lord from whom he had received it before he can attorn and be invested. ⟨fol. 64v⟩ Also, if the lord wants to transfer him, the man will execute the attornment with respect to the [new] lord using the testimony and oath of the overlord's men [establishing] that he has come to the overlord for the sake of justice and attornment. If the man proves this before the overlord, then he needs no proof for the lord to whom he is transferred.

16 Once a lord has granted a property to someone who then alienated or sold it and then procured it again, that person may not acquire that property a second time unless he remained without possession for a year and six weeks.

17 If the lord takes a man's fief and in his presence grants it to another, and the possessor does not contest it legally, then he no longer has any right to the property afterward.

18 If the lord summons his man to the feudal court, and if during the hearing the man brings a suit against the lord, he is not required to respond to the man while his own suit is pending judgment. But if the lord's feudal court hearing is postponed by a ruling, and meanwhile the man inherits a property, be it a fief or reversion, and wishes to obtain it in fief from the lord or offers to establish it by legal means, the lord must accord him feudal rights by law within the proper time period, even though his own suit remains unresolved. If this were not done, the lord could delay the man with his own suit until the limitation period on his request for investiture had expired.

19 If a litigant rejects his spokesman's statement, and yet the lord holds the spokesman ⟨fol. 65r⟩ liable for it, then he must pay a fine unless he swears that he spoke according to what the man to whom he has been given as advocate had requested. The litigant himself may avoid any culpability with his cleansing oath if no one can prove that he said it in court.

20 When the son survives after his father's death long enough to be heard within the four walls of the house, he inherits the father's fief and cancels thereby the rights of all those who were enfeoffed with the property in reversion. The son who dies before his father is not a successor in fief because he never inherited a fief, and so he never cancels anyone's reversion of his father's fief. If a person's property has been revoked, or if he has alienated it, then he loses whatever claim of reversion he had along with the property. When the son is not of equal birth to the father, and the men refuse to have their fiefs renewed by the son, then even if the son survives

the father, the son cancels no one's right to a reversion of his father's property. If a lord repudiates his man wrongly, and the man does not do likewise, the man loses neither his fief nor his reversion and keeps his property without service during his lifetime but may not have it renewed by another lord.[30] The king must bestow a bishopric and a banner fief in its entirety and undivided. Whoever is invested by the prince of a banner estate ⟨fol. 65v⟩ need not accept a fief from anyone who lacks a banner fief, even if that person is a prince by birth.[31]

21 A son who is of equal birth retains his father's status in the orders of knighthood according to feudal law as long as he does not lower his status with homage.[32] If however, the son does not wish to succeed to his father's place and become a vassal, he does not raise his status in knighthood.

22 Nothing raises one's status in the orders of knighthood except to be invested with a banner estate. No one passes a fief by inheritance except a father to his son. After the father's death, the son shall present himself to the lord within days[33] and offer him homage with folded hands. If the lord is standing, he shall approach him so near that he can touch him. And if the lord is seated, he shall kneel before him. Many people say that he should move [his hands][34] toward the lord, but that is not correct because the man moves his entire body and with it his hands as he walks toward the lord if he is standing, or kneels down if he is sitting. The man speaks thus as he requests his fief with folded hands: "Lord, I desire of you the property that I have lawfully brought before you and offer my homage[35] in return, for the first time, the second time, and the third time, and designate these your men as witnesses." If the lord refuses unlawfully to accept him as his man, the man keeps the property and holds it without feudal service since he had offered his homage for it. ⟨fol. 66r⟩ In addition, he need not seek the investiture again as long as he has living proof;[36] he may pass it on to his children[37] and make grants in fief upon it to his men because he proved his property by lawful means when justice was denied him. The man need not offer his homage a second time unless his witness dies. But when a man's property is taken by force, he shall renew his complaint yearly because he has lost possession. But if the lord offers the property to his man, he must accept it immediately or the limitation period expires, because the lord cancels the term with his offer just as the man extends it with his petition.

23 The lord must not reject homage offered by anyone except a person without knightly status, an imperial outlaw, or someone of the same district placed in limited outlawry. The lord shall refuse homage from someone he himself had brought charges against in territorial law for reason of robbery

or any felony, and who had already been summoned by a court order. While the trial continues, the lord may not accept his homage. Once the lord does accept the man's homage, he may not refuse to bestow on him the property that he has had renewed lawfully and for which he offered his homage. The lord may invest his man with property at any time and in any place when the man seeks it lawfully except in a church or churchyard.

24 When a lord asks his men for a ruling ⟨fol. 66v⟩ whether a person has offered homage in such way that he must accept him as his man, and the men decline to hand down a judgment, then it is not the lord's fault as long as they justify it according to law. Consequently, the lord is guiltless toward the man even though the man receives nothing with his enfeoffment request. If the lord accuses him afterwards of missing his deadline for the request, then the man can clear himself with an oath all the more securely. When the lord invests a man with a fief that the man had lawfully renewed with the lord, the man is duty-bound to identify the property immediately so that the lord may know it. But if he does not know it, he shall identify it for the lord within a fortnight, at which time the lord shall schedule a hearing with his men for the man. If the man cannot name the estate at that time, he no longer has any right to it; and if he identifies it, but the lord does not accept it, then he may retain it if he has proof of witnesses at hand. If he cannot prove it right away, he has a fortnight to do so but must immediately name as his witnesses as many of the lord's men as he wishes. He shall bring seven of those whom the man chooses and not those the lord chooses. If seven of the named men are present at the time, then they need not be summoned to the next hearing because he can ask them to testify right then. Should one of lord's witnesses fail to appear, the man wins his case against the lord. ⟨fol. 67r⟩

25 However, the man cannot bring witnesses to prove a case against his fellow vassals[38] in this way. If legal hindrance prohibits the lord's designated witness from coming, and this is verified with proper procedure, then the lord loses nothing. But if the lord summons his own witness as the law requires, and the witness does not come, the lord shall summon him to court for justice and finally divest the man of the property he had bestowed on him. In this case the lord is without fault and without disadvantage if the man does not appear since in feudal law the lord cannot force him by additional means. The man can still justify his case with another witness. But if the named witness is not the lord's man, or the lord does not admit that the witness has received property from him and affirms it on the relics, the lord need not ask him about any evidence nor bring him to court.

Should the lord swear this in the man's presence, and it is not challenged according to legal procedure, then whatever property the lord had granted the man reverts to the lord. But if the lord wishes to bring evidence against his man, and if the man believes that the lord's witness is not his man in a way that qualifies him to be the lord's witness, then that witness must prove his investiture with an oath on the relics and identify the property if he wishes to testify. ⟨fol. 67v⟩ The man shall choose for the specified court day seven men who will be asked about the evidence from among all those whom he and the lord bring.

26 If the man obtains supporting testimony of two men from among them all, he wins the case, and if he does not, he loses. Should he fail to appear at the feudal court, he also loses. If the lord fails to appear, the man wins the property, even without evidence. However, a legal excuse can release either of them from blame. A legal excuse is captivity, illness, service to the empire, and war if the land is attacked and the man is called with the hue and cry.[39] When a legal hindrance prevents someone from attending the feudal court, he must send his messenger to prove the legal excuse with an oath on the relics. If the lord doubts that the man is in fact that missing person's true messenger and actually sent by him, the messenger can prove it on the relics, be he servile or free. He cannot be dismissed. Nevertheless, the lord has the right to decide whether to accept the messenger's oath immediately or wait for the man to give his oath in court once the legal impediment has passed. If he is prevented from attending the feudal court by incarceration and sends no messenger, then by court ruling a date shall be set for him for a time after he is freed. He shall then appear before this court as he was obliged to attend the earlier one. As stated earlier, the man must have his property renewed by the overlord ⟨fol. 68r⟩ and offer him homage when his lord dies, or when he sells his property, or if it has been withdrawn from him. He shall ask the lord to invest him with the property or transfer him [to a lord] where he will receive the fief with the same high honor he held it in from his first lord because it is not right that one lower another's status by means of his property.[40]

27 If within a year and a day after the request for attornment the lord does not transfer the person to another lord by spoken word, he may no longer shift him to another but must invest that person with the fief himself. Should a lord die who has a son, the fiefholder may not request his invested property from the overlord while the son is within his limitation period to renew his inheritance, but if the child misses his own limitation period, the man's time limit to renew his holding begins from that time on.[41] In order

to renew a holding, a person is allowed as many periods of a year and six weeks as he is removed from the king in the levels of military shields.

28 Each man's limitation period [for renewal] begins with the investiture of his lord in the property that the man holds from him because no lord may enfeoff anyone with any property without having first been invested with it himself unless the [over]lord refused the investment contrary to law. Also, if the lord is outside the country or in captivity so that the man cannot petition[42] for his property, then he fulfills his rights under feudal law by taking control of the property and using it for his own benefit as if he had actually been granted it, as long as he is of age. ⟨fol. 68v⟩ If he then lends it further before he has been invested, he must fulfill his obligations consistently.[43] When a lord receives a property, and the overlord dies or transfers the property afterward, each man who then holds property from the lower lord may exceed his limitation period for renewal of his own grant while the lower lord has not confirmed his fief, as long as he has not missed his own deadline for renewal. The reason is that during this period the lord may not remove any property from his own lord by an act of enfeoffment unless he is forced to do so by law. The limitation period for children to renew a fief is thirteen years and six weeks after their birth.[44] However, that age is inadequate if someone should sue them for their fief in court while they have not yet reached their majority, which is twenty-one years. In this case, they can have one of their lord's men as guardian who represents them in feudal law. They shall promise him with finger and tongue[45] to abide by the decision regardless whether the court finds for or against them. The child's age is not to be calculated according to conception, but according to the time the mother gave birth and brought the living child into the world. Should anyone claim the child's fief during his minority, and that claim is contested, then in place of the child the child's lord must make the determination with the child's men or guardian whether right of use has been transferred to the child or his lord.[46]

29 The lord is always the child's guardian for property the child holds ⟨fol. 69r⟩ from him as long as he has not transferred right of use to the child.[47] He shall collect the revenues from the land until the child comes of age. During his minority, the child forfeits nothing in feudal law if he misses a deadline. Should the lord not believe that the child has attained his majority, it can be proven on the relics by the child, his guardian, or one of the lord's men. This proven, the lord may no longer take income from the property. No one may be a witness for another in a feudal court if he himself is under age. Regardless of a child's age at the father's death, when the

guardian presents him to the lord and requests the lawful transfer of the fief to the heir, the lord shall grant it to him. In addition, guarantors shall be assigned for him in case there are several children, so that the lord will not be sued for the fief. The limitation period in which the men are to renew their fiefs from the child begins at the time the underage child is enfeoffed. They shall, however, serve the overlord if the child or his guardian calls upon them by law, as long as the lord has granted him right of use.

30 Right of use includes no feudal or renewal rights. Nevertheless, right of use can be granted in court, but it cannot be renewed; it cannot devolve upon a son and ends when the child granted right of use dies or enters his majority. As long as the child does not have ⟨fol. 69v⟩ right of use by agreement or by law, he is not obligated to identify the property received from the lord. No one can acquire right to a child's property by investiture, pledge, or conveyance of property inherited during minority—be it according to feudal law or territorial law—for the purpose of invalidating the child's earlier and lawful possession that had devolved upon him. Nor can anyone who inherited the property unlawfully cancel the child's right to it while he is under age. If one transfers an invested property to the child with the stipulation that he bestow it on another, and if the child does so and upholds it[48] when he reaches majority, then the enfeoffment is legal. However, if he cancels the contract legally when he comes of age, then the property reverts to the one who had transferred it because he had stipulated at the time of the transfer that it is to be bestowed upon another person and disposed of in no other way. For this reason, when the investiture is nullified by the court,[49] then the transfer also becomes invalid because it was made upon the condition that the fief be granted to another. Should the child refuse his men their feudal rights once he reaches majority, then they should request reconfirmation of their fief a second time; otherwise they exceed their limitation period with respect to the child.

31 If a man who has a son dies during the renewal period for his property, the son does not lose the property, even if the father had not had it renewed, as long as he had not missed the renewal deadline. ⟨fol. 70r⟩ If a lord's son dies during the reconfirmation period in which the men are to receive their fiefs from him, they have their property renewed by his successor and do not lose it.

32 The [lord's] son may not divide a man's feudal property by transferring [part] unless he himself holds it from more than one lord.[50] But if he transfers a holding from one overlord only in contradiction to the law, then the smaller portion follows the larger one.

33 If the lord transfers the man's property, then the man himself need not accept the smaller segment that the lord holds from his lord from anyone but that overlord.[51] Also, the man may receive his property from only one of the lord's sons if all have been enfeoffed. If the sons cannot agree among themselves, then it is the [over]lord's prerogative to choose the son to whom the man must go. After a man dies, the lord is not required to grant the man's fief to more than one of his children.[52] Before the children are of eligible age for full enfeoffment, they may select the feoffee, but after they reach the eligible age,[53] the lord has the right to choose the one he wishes to enfeoff of those who have rightfully applied to him. If the lord grants a property to a child according to his own desire and not according to law, that does not hinder others from accepting their own property [in subfief]. If one of the children misses the deadline to renew his own fief, the lord no longer has an obligation to him unless he clears himself with an oath on the relics. If a man's son comes of age, requests a property from his lord, and ⟨fol. 70v⟩ has brothers still in their minority, then before he is invested, he shall vow to the lord that his brothers renounce their claim and will not sue the lord for it when they come of age. Later, if the brothers break the pledge anyway and claim the property in feudal court, the lord shall sue them along with the oldest, who made the pledge relinquishing his brothers' right to sue, and divest him of the property if they do not give up their claim.

34 If anyone tries to void his lord's or his child's claim, or a man's contract of expectancy for his fief[54] by granting it anew or transferring it, he does not damage the person who receives and retains it in his possession until he dies.

35 When a man makes property over to his wife with the oath of the sons who are all of age, no one, not the lord nor the children, can nullify it if she has witnesses. However, if the children pledge this before their majority, then they may indeed cancel it although the lord may not.

36 A lord may enfeoff several brothers with a property jointly if they accept it and wish to have possession in common. Should they separate within the property, they may divide it as they wish without permission from the lord. Once the division is made, no brother has any right to another's portion when that brother dies unless he had been granted the reversion while they still had possession jointly. If one of them dies, the child inherits his father's position and holds the property with his uncles[55] just as his father had done. ⟨fol. 71r⟩ As long as those invested with a single property hold it in common, no individual of the party may invest or trans-

fer a portion without the consent of the others because he deprives them of it. A man granted undivided property jointly with others may not invest or transfer sections. However, if he has invested or transferred it, he cannot revoke it. Only one of the others with whom he holds the property in common can revoke it. When more than one person is invested with a single property, and they hold it undivided, then if their lord dies before one of them does, no individual can have the property renewed by another lord.

37 Should a lord by his own choice enfeoff his man when he cannot act as guarantor for the grant, he must make restitution so that the man does not exceed his renewal limitation period. But if he takes possession of the property granted to him, and then someone takes it from him, he must present his lawful suit within the legal limitation period. If he fails to do this, the lord does not compensate him for his property. But whenever a lord is ordered by the feudal court to grant a fief, and then the court rightfully denies his capacity as warrantor for his man's property, then he need not make restitution to the man. However, if the lord states that he will be warrantor for the man and tells him to take possession of the property and then is not able to provide warranty for the grant, he must make restitution unless the man himself missed the deadline and lost possession by not bringing his claim to court within the allotted renewal period. ⟨fol. 71v⟩

38 Married or unmarried women fiefholders are not obligated to perform military service. Instead, they must pay military dues according to enacted law[56] and are freed from the military campaign according to feudal law. If the lord invests children with their father's property during his life, and it remains in the father's sole possession until his death, then after the father's death the children shall come and ask the lord to confirm his granting of the property to them. This they must do within their limitation period. Should the lord not acknowledge his grant of the property to them in fief, they shall request permission to claim the property with proof of witnesses. Now the lord may deny this proof since the children lack possession. They may, however, prove the investiture according to the rules of reversion.[57] In that case, they must request renewal of their father's property by offering homage to the lord because they cannot obtain the property any other way unless the lord were to acknowledge his grant to them. When, however, the father and children have joint and equal share in the property, the children retain the property after the father's death if they prove the investiture before the lord within the renewal period.

39 If a man transfers property to his lord with the condition that he

grant it to another, then if the lord wants possession himself and does not enfeoff that other person, he has no right to do so because the property was transferred to him only in order to invest the other person. ⟨fol. 72r⟩

40 If the father transfers to his son property he holds from his lord, the son does not receive it as a heritable fief, even if it was his father's, because he has not inherited it. Whoever transfers his heritable fief and receives it from another loses the right to pass it on to heirs.[58]

41[59] A man who claims to have a type of right concerning a property that he does not indeed have, and then is not able to prove it, loses all right to the property. The person who has rightful possession of a property has more right to it than someone who lacks rightful possession.

42 If a person transfers to the overlord a property he holds from the lower lord, and he receives it back in fief, or another receives it, and the recipient occupies it for a year and a day without lawful challenge, but the lower lord who has right to the property knows nothing about this, then the lower lord does not lose his property if he brings his complaint within the renewal period explaining that he was uninformed about the man's transfer of the property. If the lord presents his suit when he first hears of it, then whoever of the two parties can prove to the overlord the earlier investiture of the fief with six witnesses from among the overlord's men obtains the property. However, if the man can prove that his lord's property has been stripped from him by a feudal court, or that he had transferred it, then the lord's proof is dismissed. Even if the man had had right of use to the property, that right does not set aside the lord's feudal possession. No one can be witness for feudal possession except a person who has been enfeoffed by the same lord. ⟨fol. 72v⟩ Concerning ordinary right of possession, however, any man with full legal capacity can be witness.

43 No one may expel a person from his right of possession unless he lost it by a court decision. If a person's property is revoked in a feudal court, or if he transfers it, he forfeits possession. However, he may deny within a year and a day that he transferred the property if he dares to swear a cleansing oath before his lord. But if the lord grants the property to another in the presence of the man who transferred it, and he does not contest it, then he may not swear a cleansing oath. Should a lord force his man in breach of trust[60] to transfer his property to him, this does not cause that man any loss if he sues the lord within the renewal limitation period for using force and convicts the lord. Intentions and words are not considered force unless an action follows. If a man transfers a property to another before his lord, then

the recipient right away gains possession of the property that had been the transferor's. A man may function as witness for his fellow vassals in many more legal actions than the lord.[61]

44 When two parties make equal claim to a property and offer equal proof to achieve possession, and neither one has received the property from the other, then both shall go to the location of the property to prove right of possession. ⟨fol. 73r⟩ They shall ask the villagers and local people about possession. The party with the majority of witnesses gains right of possession. The lord shall hear the witnesses, or he shall delegate two of his men who by their fealty oath accept responsibility to report who wins. If right of possession cannot be determined because of the local community's lack of unity or knowledge, then the litigants shall be required to swear that they will prove that no one other than they has right to this fief. When both assert their claim and swear equally on the relics, then the property shall be divided between them, or a determination shall be based on a trial by water.[62] A trial by ordeal[63] may not be used except where the truth cannot be ascertained by the fact-finding process.

45 If a lord and his man claim possession of the same property and offer proof of witnesses, the man's witnesses are first because he does not withdraw the property from the lord even when he holds it from him in fief. But should the lord accuse the man of missing his deadline for petitioning renewal of the investiture or for clearing the property from incumbrance,[64] the man can win his claim with a cleansing oath unless the lord can prove in front of his men that the request for renewal had been denied the man after the deadline. This the lord must accomplish with six men. Should the lord state that he denied his man all claim to the property, and the man state that he had indeed requested renewal or that he had cleared it ⟨fol. 73v⟩ within the term limit, then if the man can establish his case, his proof voids the lord's proof.

46 If the lord sequestrates his man's property[65] because of another man's suit, the lord shall award the plaintiff possession of the property that had been occupied by the first man before it was seized. Nevertheless, the first man has his year limitation period to release his property. If he clears it, then the lord must provide a court date with his men for him, and the date shall be made known to the plaintiff a fortnight before. If the man arrives and the plaintiff does not, the man is declared free of the accusations as long as the plaintiff is not prevented by legal hindrance. If the legal excuse is proven, the plaintiff has lost nothing. Should the man attempting to regain his property die within the limitation period, it devolves upon his son, who

has it renewed by another lord when his own lord dies, transfers, or sells it, or repudiates him. The son may not, however, grant in feudal tenure an available property to anyone until he has cleared his property with the lord. But if the property is confirmed by another lord, then the man need not clear it with respect to the new lord. He must nevertheless have it renewed according to feudal law. After the father dies, the son need not clear the property in his father's stead.

47 Each time a man's fief comes to another, the confirmation time period begins anew. A man may grant property and transfer inheritance to his son when the lord calls a court into session. ⟨fol. 74r⟩ The son does not answer to the lord in place of his father unless he holds property where his father is being sued; or if the lord's court has levied a fine on the property, he must pay it or clear it according to proper procedure in his father's stead. If the man claims from the lord a fief to which he does not have right of possession, and the lord sets a court date with his men for that man, then the man may not make a further grant of any property while the court is in session. If a court revokes a person's property in his presence, and he does not challenge it, then he may no longer clear and recover it.

48 A lord can be witness against a man in three instances only. Whatever a man claims, vows, or does in feudal court, the lord can prove against him if he denies it. If the man has been commanded to imperial service by decree,[66] and the lord has proof of this from his men who heard it, he can easily convict the man with his testimony.[67] Likewise, when the lord summons his man to the feudal court individually and has it announced from person to person by means of proclamation, [he can prove it].[68] It is easier for the lord to prove these three conditions with two of his men who saw and heard than it is for the man to exonerate himself. If a man has two lords or more who command him by decree to join in the imperial campaign, he shall go with the one who called him first, and to the others he shall pay military dues that amount to the tenth shilling or the tenth pound that he receives annually from his lords.[69] ⟨fol. 74v⟩ A lord may not call his man to imperial military duty until he receives the decree himself.

49 If a man has his property renewed by another lord and not by his [first] lord's son, and if that lord refuses to recognize his fief, then the man must win his case with the first lord's men. They shall be required to answer upon their fealty to the first lord and shall not be forced to swear more. But if the fiefholder does not believe that they have indeed sworn homage to their lord, they shall swear to that before they give testimony, or they shall confirm their testimony with an oath on the relics. The lord shall summon

these witnesses to a hearing only if they are also his men as well. Anyone who lacks men himself but is born high enough in the knightly orders to convey feudal rights and is himself the lord's retainer,[70] may avail himself of the lord's men instead. He employs the local men where he has need of them wherever his property is located.[71]

50 If a lord transfers a man's property to his own lord but without the holder's knowledge, then the holder shall have his property renewed within the term limit even if it has been granted in fief to another. A man's term limit begins when the lord declares before his men that he has transferred the property, or when the person to whom it has been granted notifies the holder or takes possession himself, and this is proven to him by the lord's envoy. ⟨D fol. 73r⟩[72] *No one may request enfeoffment of his lord's property from the overlord until he hears his lord's answer whether he has transferred it or missed his renewal date. If the lord does not confirm anything, the man shall caution him in front of his men with a court order that the lord must answer for his property before the regular court hearing—that is, within six weeks—and thus be the man's warrantor for the fief. Should the lord wrongfully refuse, and the man has proof, his property is renewed, and he keeps it without damage even if the lord regains it afterward.*[73]

50b[74] *If a lord confiscates property from his man, or refuses him feudal rights, or fails to be his warrantor as is required, the man shall bring the complaint to the overlord in the presence of his men. The overlord shall by court order command the lord to fulfill the law and be warrantor for the property. This shall be done by the overlord either in person or via an envoy so that two men hear it. If the lord does not comply, then the overlord shall enfeoff the man and be his guarantor when the man proves his claim according to feudal law.*

51 *If the lord leaves the country during the man's renewal limitation period during which he must confirm his property, it does not damage the man's rights. However, when the lord returns, the limitation period is reactivated. If the man sees his lord at his house, or at court, and in feudal court within the renewal period after the lord's return and does not renew his property from him, he loses his claim to it.* ⟨D fol. 73v⟩ *Should the man himself also leave the territory during his renewal period, this does not extend his time limit. The time period is extended when the man requests investiture, and the lord refuses unlawfully; in the same way, the lord shortens the time period when he offers it. If the lord withdraws or sequesters himself in a castle so that the man cannot reach him, that does not damage the man's rights as long as he has proof that he has sought his lord in court and at home, at both entrance and exit, and offered him homage for his property or rightfully cleared it. If a man dies in the Holy Land*[75] *or elsewhere, then for his*

children, the confirmation limitation period for their fief begins when they receive word of their father's death. If a man's lord dies without the knowledge of his men, then their renewal period is calculated from time they first learn of his death.

52 *One may, within the legal limitation period, clear himself of all fines to his lord that were levied in his absence by swearing on the relics, unless the lord proves his case with witnesses as was said earlier.*

53 *If a man claims a property but does not have right of possession and holds no other property from the lord, then if the lord refuses to grant him the property, he must first set guarantors for his fine and compensation payment to the men if there is cause before the lord will set a court date for him to pursue* ⟨D fol. 74r⟩ *his claim. However, if he does have right of possession to the property, it shall be his surety if he wins it with witnesses in court.*

54 *If a lord grants his man's property to another, and even though he is that man's warrantor and swears with finger and tongue,*[76] *the first holder of the fief shall not lose his right of possession because of this unless the lord can prove that he had been denied and stripped of the property by a feudal court. The lord may not invest anyone with property nor give anyone right of possession unless he himself has that right already.*

55 *Should a lord diminish his status by pledging homage* [to an equal], *he loses all his men's fiefs that are not part of his own allodial land. His men shall then receive their fiefs from the overlord, or he shall attorn them to someone who is the equal of their former lord.*[77] *The man must follow the same procedure if his lord lowers the status of his property by accepting it from a different lord than the one he had had earlier.*[78] *However, a man's knightly status is not diminished when he becomes the man of an equal because of homicide and receives his property from him as long as the subordination is not passed on to heirs.*

56 *If a man is granted a property upon his word of honor*[79] *that he will relinquish it if his lord redeems it within a specified time, the lord may redeem the property whenever he wishes or he may leave it* [unredeemed]. *If the man dies without a successor to the fief, the property reverts to the lord, who is then not required to pay the man's heir the redemption money for the property. But if the person to whom the property is granted upon his* ⟨D fol. 74v⟩ *word of honor then breaks his word and denies that he must give up the property, he can swear a cleansing oath unless it can be proven that he made the pledge in feudal court. All suits within a feudal court that can be settled with a fine can be won by the lord if he has proof of two of his men as witnesses against his man. But when the man stands to lose his fief, the lord must prove his case with six other witnesses.*[80] *When a man is granted a holding based on his word of honor, feudal law allows him to enfeoff his men with it and to pass it on to his sons. The sons need not return it to the*

lord upon the lord's redemption payment unless they themselves have pledged to do so. The man is not duty-bound to fulfill his lord's pledge that the man relinquish a property, nor is a child required to fulfill his father's pledge that the child do so.

A lord may place a property in security without feudal service.[81] *The lord's goodwill*[82] *then determines whether he lets the person have the property permanently. If the lord wishes to regain it with a cleansing oath, he can do that, unless the man can prove that the lord had given it as security in court. But if the lord grants something with feudal service, it depends on the man's goodwill whether he stands by his oath or not, unless the lord can prove that the man had sworn it in feudal court. Whoever receives a property in this manner is not required, after the lord redeems it, to relinquish it to a son or a man to whom it reverts after the lord's death* ⟨D fol. 75r⟩ *unless he had sworn beforehand to do so. Whoever asserts that he has been enfeoffed with property as security speaks incorrectly because no property can be granted in feudal tenure as security. For a proper outcome, a property must be placed in pledge before the judge of territorial law so that the members of the judiciary can witness it. In contrast, when an investiture is to be made, it must be performed before the lord's men, who are then witnesses for the man. An enfeoffment in security* [is neither].[83] *What the lord bestows with the condition of feudal service is a proper fief, heritable fief, castle fief, or a fief in reversion of specified property that will revert to the lord.*[84]

57 *In addition, a man may receive property together with a woman such that he represents her regarding it. He has the property renewed by another lord if their lord dies, because a woman's fief cannot be renewed since she lacks the military shield.*[85] *The man possesses the military shield and holds the property on behalf of the woman, and for that reason has the right to have it renewed by another lord. But if the woman for whom he holds the property dies, his own enfeoffment also ends because he had acquired it in the function of guardian, unless he received it as a proper fief or a reversion. Anyone who asserts that there are more types of fiefs with feudal service than outlined earlier is wrong, be he man or lord.*[86] *Similarly, if the woman transfers her property, or if it is seized by feudal court, the man who received it with her no longer has any* [claim] *to it.* ⟨D fol. 75v⟩ *But if he transfers it, or it is seized by feudal court, then she loses nothing because she has right of possession. He is also prohibited from subinfeudating to anyone without the consent of the woman unless a fief reverts to them, or if he is ordered to do so by a feudal court.* [What reverts] *is hers and not the lord's or the man's who was granted the fief with her.*

58 *With the woman's consent, the man may certainly bestow a reversion on a property already granted as well as what becomes free because they both have full feudal rights based on the joint investiture of the property.*[87] *He has the enfeoff-*

ment and the military shield; she has the same enfeoffment and right of possession. If a lord enfeoffs a woman or man with a reversion in a person's property, and the fiefholder with right of possession dies thereafter, then possession passes to the person enfeoffed with the reversion because it was already his fief, granted under the condition that the holder dies without a successor to the fief. The fiefholder who died had held the property unconditionally. Should the lord not recognize the grant, the feoffee of the fief in reversion should caution the lord within the renewal limitation period, using the testimony of two who saw and heard the enfeoffment, that he was enfeoffed without right of possession.

When the fiefholder dies without heirs, the lord can positively take control himself if he forgets that he has enfeoffed someone with the reversion. ⟨D fol. 76r⟩ *If the person enfeoffed with the reversion or in expectancy also takes control of the property, but before the lord, he does no wrong as long as he immediately answers for it and assumes his duty with respect to his lord if the lord accuses him or calls him to court for it. He must not wait for the limitation period to begin, for as much as he extends his time limit with his request for confirmation, the lord reduces the time period by as much if he offers the man confirmation. If a lord dies, or if he transfers his man's property within the renewal period just when the property devolves upon the man, and he must remind his lord of the investiture, the fiefholder shall have his property renewed, not as a reversion, but rather as a proper fief when he is directed to the lord for justice. He must offer the first lord proof of his right to the property by means of witnesses. If the lord opposes the man unlawfully, he nevertheless retains his rightful property and the right to renew it because justice was refused him. However, if the property was transferred during the holder's lifetime, and if it was properly and rightfully conferred on the recipient, or if the recipient had been invested by the holder, these events invalidate the reversion of the property the first lord had granted.*

59 *A child may invest another child with property and also with feudal succession in fief or inheritance while both are minors as long as he has first been invested with it. The succession in fief or inheritance disallows renewal if the lord who made the bestowal dies. The lord takes from his men right of use of property that is in feudal succession or inheritance for use just as his own property* ⟨D fol. 76v⟩ *while the children are under age. Whoever grants property fraudulently must pay a fine to his lord unless he clears himself according to proper procedure. He must then cancel the investiture legally within six weeks or be divested of his property.*

60 *It is a fraudulent grant whenever a man grants something because he expects to die, suffers from illness, or wishes to quit his lands while intending, after he recovers or returns, to resume possession of his property.*[88] *Whoever grants prop-*

erty in this way acts against God, the law, and his own word because he owes his lord constant fealty and support. He grants not what is his, but what is his lord's or another's after he dies simply because he does not want to lose it during his lifetime. However, if a fiefholder promises to transfer a property to another who refuses to accept it in fief, but the fiefholder gives him right of possession anyway, and then if the recipient follows the holder's request and grants the property in fief to his man in order to strengthen the recipient's illegitimate possession, then the lord may bring the fiefholder to court for it. The lord may accuse him before his own men for having granted property in that way. If the man admits it, he loses the property because he had given away his right of possession to a person without enfeoffment. This is the same as if a man were to claim to hold property of another lord in the presence of his own lord and his men. And if the fiefholder is accused of this three times in feudal court, his property is seized by court order. Unless he ⟨D fol. 77r⟩ *clears it within six weeks and fulfills his legal duty for it, he is denied all claim to the property because he lacks right of possession, and no one holds it in fief from him. Persons who have been enfeoffed with property in this way have no right to renew it because they lack right of possession, and no one holds it in feudal tenure from them.*

61 *Any enfeoffment without investiture lacks right of renewal, and any right of possession granted without enfeoffment is unlawful. Neither* [condition] *is lawful without the other; a man must have both.*[89]

62 *But if the man to whom property has been granted in feudal tenancy claims right of possession, he must prove it before the overlord with the majority of the neighbors. This is done after the accusation* [has been made] *and once the lord's rights have been suspended.*[90] *If the lord who granted the property in this manner denies it, he shall clear himself on the relics and command his men upon a court order to take control of the property within six weeks and withdraw right of possession from the feoffee either by amicable or lawful means. If the lord does not accomplish this within the legal time limit,*[91] *his cleansing oath becomes invalid, and he is stripped of the property unless unlawful force had prevented him, and he brings charges before the court.*

63 *If a person in possession of a property lacks right of possession and enfeoffment and attempts to acquire the property as if it were his leasehold, and if the person he appeals to confirms it, then let it be known that no one may lease out a castle, town, judgeship, or the service of a man bound to feudal service, but not* ⟨D fol. 77v⟩ *one's equals or a man with higher status. This cannot be done in such a way that the lord, or the people, or the men subject to the court or to feudal service cannot reverse it. Mills and mints, however, and all types of tolls, hides, and property let out for lease or for service cannot be let out a second time for rent* [i.e., sublet] *in a way that leaves people without a remedy.*[92]

64 *Anyone who wants a leasehold legally must work it himself or have his servant do so for food and a wage. If he lets it additionally for rent or service, then he himself becomes an illegal renter on the property.*

65 *No priest, woman, or man with diminished legal capacity*[93] *may be invested with a judgeship.*[94] *No one may preside as judge until he has been invested with the powers of the office. Once he has been invested, then even if his lord dies or transfers it, he can still preside within his renewal limitation period until he is granted the jurisdiction anew.*

66 *No one who is steward*[95] *of his lord's estate can usurp that estate from him with right of possession, even if he claims it in fief because the lord had entrusted control of his entire property to him.*[96] *However, if the lord grants the steward a property in fief that he later does not acknowledge, the steward must prove it with those who saw and heard it, just as a person must do who lacks right of possession, although he cannot have the property renewed by another lord and cannot pass it on to his son during his stewardship.*

67 *Whenever a property is granted to someone without feudal service,*[97] *it is not considered* ⟨D fol. 78r⟩ *a proper fief. The same holds for property that the lord bestows on his ministerial,*[98] *not with feudal service, but with service according to household law.*[99] *He must serve for the property according to household law and not according to feudal law. According to household law, each ministerial must be a seneschal, butler, marshal, or chamberlain by birth.*[100] *Given the multiple permutations of the law, one does not speak of the law of ministerials separately because they claim different rights from each bishop, abbot, or abbess they serve.*

68 *A man must request each property with an offer of homage even though he is* [already] *the lord's man. A man can establish his fealty with an oath on the relics if the lord questions it. He must, however, obtain the relics himself.*

69 *The lord shall summon his man to feudal court for any wrong if the deed carries a fine. The lord can definitely hold a court session before noon, excluding peace days, and in all places except in churches and churchyards. When the lord wishes to begin the hearing, he shall ask his man in such a way that two or more of his men hear whether he can call one of his men to answer for a complaint. Once that determination*[101] *is affirmed and agreed to,*[102] *then, based on the ruling, the lord shall set him a court date in a fortnight; the time is to be calculated from the day of the ruling or six days later. The hearing shall be held in a specified village and farmstead that is free or enfeoffed to the lord.* ⟨D fol. 78v⟩ *Should the man ask where the village chosen for the hearing is located, the lord shall inform him, because many villages located far apart have the same name. If the man holds imperial property* [the hearing is set there].[103] *And if he holds his own property in fief, then the lord shall set the hearing on the owned property. But if the man holds a*

property from a lord who also holds it in fief, then even if it is owned, the lord may locate the hearing on any proper fief the man holds. When the lord summons his man to court in this way, he can then command the men present to attend the feudal hearing. If someone fails to attend, he is judged liable to pay a fine to the lord unless a legal excuse prevents him from coming. The man is not fined if he arrives in court before noon, even if the hearing has already begun. The defendant must pay a fine to the lord if the summons was made in his presence on the basis of the court ruling and he does not appear in court, unless lawful hindrance prevents him. The lord shall demand his fine from the property he has granted the man in fief. A leaseholder shall not suffer any attachment by his lord beyond the amount he pays annually, and then only if he has not yet paid for the current year.[104] ⟨D fol. 79r⟩

In a case where the lord cannot attach property for his fine from the fief he had granted to the man, he may seize the entire fief. The property is then revoked by the court if the man does not challenge the fine within a year and a day. If the man is present when his lord calls him before the court, or close enough to hear his summons, then even if he holds his ears so that he does not hear it, he is nevertheless obligated to appear in court. But if the man is not present, the lord or his envoy shall inform him of the court date so that two of his men hear it, either in his presence or in his yard where he enters and leaves. If he is not found, or he lacks that type of yard, then the notice is to be given at the fief he holds from the lord a fortnight before the scheduled date. The lord must bring six of his men there and one messenger who is to summon the man to the court hearing. When the lord opens the session, he must first ask if it is time for the hearing. Once that is affirmed, then he asks whether he may have one of his men be spokesman for him in feudal court. After the judgment is given, then he must ask each of his men if he agrees. If the men cannot determine a judgment right away, they are given a fortnight time ⟨D fol. 79v⟩ *if each, when asked, swears an oath on it.*[105] *Once this is done, the court is adjourned for a fortnight. During this time, a judgment must be determined. The lord may not adjourn a hearing according to his own discretion without the consent of the defendant and plaintiff.*

If the lord wishes to bring a complaint against the man for another matter while the first case is postponed by court ruling, then according to law, the man should not make a plea as long as his first case has not yet been decided. As the day ends and the sun sets, it is no longer necessary for the defendant to answer in court, or for the men to determine a judgment. But if the case is not resolved, then, upon a court ruling, the lord must adjourn and recall the defendant to resume the hearing in a fortnight. The lord must begin the session before noon. After the opening of the session is agreed to and the lord has appointed a spokesman, he must ask if he may have his man, the one he has brought a complaint against, summoned before the court. Once that is decided, he must ask who is to bring him forward. Next a messenger is designated so that two men at opposite ends of the yard can hear him say the following: "On behalf of my lord, I order N once, twice and three ⟨D fol. 80r⟩ *times to answer to those complaints for which he has been summoned here." If the man is not present, then the envoy shall return to the lord and say, "He was not there, nor anyone else who could prove his legal excuse." When the messenger states this, the lord shall ask what is lawful and proper. The lawful ruling is that the defendant shall be ordered* [to respond] *a second and a third time. This must be done with a messenger, whoever it may be. However, it is necessary to have a different man each time the defendant is ordered to appear. Once the defendant has been called three times and still does not come, the lord asks what is lawful and proper. The lawful ruling is that he must wait for the defendant until the sun begins its descent, and that occurs at noon. After that the lord asks whether he has waited according to feudal law. If the court upholds this, then the lord summons the man to a second court date and waits for him as he did the first time. This must be done a third time.*

Should the lord miss any of these court days himself and fail to pursue his legal action according to feudal law, he loses the entire case. The man has to be informed of the first court date but not of any subsequent ones. The lord may not convene a feudal court in a locked yard, under a roof, or in a castle.[106] *After the lord has waited for his man three days until the sun begins to descend, he shall ask what is lawful and proper. The court shall find that he must prove that he summoned the man before the law the first, the second, and the third time.* ⟨D fol. 80v⟩ *He must prove this with different witnesses for each summons from among his own men. The witnesses say, "Lord, I testify upon my duty to you that you have served N a summons at this place and have waited for him as feudal law requires. I saw and heard it and am your witness." The lord then asks after each testimony whether his proof is complete and can bring him justice. If the witness says upon his fealty to the lord what he knows concerning the suit he is asked about, or claims upon his fealty to the lord that he knows nothing about it, then one should not continue questioning him. The lord may ask as many of his men as he wishes until he completes his proof. Once the lord proves the three summonses to the scheduled hearings, he must ask what is lawful and proper since the defendant did not appear. The court shall decide to divest him of the property received from the lord. Next, the lord asks whether he or one of his men must do it. After that the court rules that one of his men will do it. He says, "As the court has found for my lord, I dispossess the man of the particular property he holds from my lord." Then the lord asks what he is to do with the property revoked from his man. The court finds that he should take control himself or send an envoy to do it accompanied by two of his men. He must retain it without cultivation or rents for a year and*[107] ⟨fol. 75r⟩ a day.

If the man does not clear the property by the end of that time period, all rights to the property shall be revoked. The lord will take control of the property the man thus forfeited. But if a village or hides of land belong to a castle fortification, or a manor, then if the lord takes control of the manor, he also has control of all the land and all the castle fortifications that belong to it.[108]

70 If the man comes to the lord within the limitation period wishing to clear his property, and the lord hides or locks him out of the castle he currently occupies, and if the man has fellow vassals to witness that he would come before his lord willingly if the lord would permit him, then he recovers his land in the presence of his peers in the way he should have done with his lord. But when the man does appear before his lord, he must first of all request a spokesman, then the relics, and the official to administer the oath in order to clear his property.[109] If the lord refuses, then he must provide the relics himself and swear without the court official that his right to the property was not rescinded for so grave a matter that he should permanently forfeit his property for it, so help him God and the saints. This must not be done unless the lord refuses him justice. Whether the man clears his property without a judgment or with a judgment, the lord must serve him a summons, and if the man does not appear at the hearing, he forfeits all rights to the property. ⟨fol. 75v⟩

71 When the lord makes his response to the man, or the man to the lord, in feudal court on the first, the second, or the third day, and the ruling is made to adjourn, then the litigant who fails to appear loses the case or forfeits the property, and the person who appears and pleads obtains it.

72 On days when the man holds the stirrup for his lord,[110] determines judgments, or serves him with a gift or other things, he is not required to answer for anything in court. Nevertheless, the lord may make a determination when two of his men lay claim to the same property, regardless whether only one of them or both are in his service. If the person to whom the property is thus denied clears it and appears at the set court date, he may not bring anyone into the yard except the lord's men. Should he bring any men who are not the lord's men, he must pay a court fine for each one separately.

72a[111] Before the man comes before his lord, he must divest himself of his sword, dagger, spurs, hat, hood, cap, and all weapons. If he fails to do this, he pays a fine. According to the opinion of stupid people, he shall also remove his ring, breastplate, all iron rings, belts, and buckles. No one shall be placed in this compromised position except the person the lord has called to defend himself in court based on the accusations the lord made against him. In contrast, when the man brings a claim against the lord and receives a court date, he, like all the lord's other men, is not to be ⟨fol. 76r⟩ compromised in this way. The man is not required to answer to the lord, or the lord to the man, in feudal court for any damages one may have caused the other before the man became the lord's vassal.

Once the lord has opened the session and enlisted a spokesman, he must ask the man for whom the hearing was set whether he has come to defend himself against his lord in feudal court. He may consult [with others] regarding this or refuse to defend according to law, if possible. If refusal is not lawfully possible, then he must come again and say, "Lord, I have come to fulfill the law and attain justice to the extent the law permits." Next, the lord may bring accusations against him one by one and ask him to reply. The man then requests a spokesman and [time for] deliberation.[112] The person who makes his plea immediately after the lord's accusations and before he has taken a spokesman shall [later] be denied one. But if the man speaks without a spokesman while he is refusing to defend, claiming he need not do so, he has not yet pled.[113] After each response the litigant must be asked whether he is in agreement with his spokesman's words. If the spokesman has not spoken correctly, then as long as the litigant does not accept it, it does no harm. After the plaintiff and defendant have each had a turn, the lord must ask for a ruling on the law. Should he ask according to his own opinion and not according to procedure, that causes the man no harm. However, if someone asks for one judgment ⟨fol. 76v⟩ before another, then that judgment must be determined first. In feudal court, the man need not speak out loud but may instead whisper quietly to his spokesman. But when his lord asks if he agrees to his spokesman's statement, he must speak aloud to declare a "yes" or a "no," request a consultation, or challenge a ruling. Once the litigant requesting the consultation has withdrawn for deliberations and returned, he must bring a response to the question for which he had requested consultation: he shall accept or deny.

If the man invites his fellow vassals to the deliberations, the lord shall allow all [to do so] except three, so that if they deliberate too long, the lord can recall them. One of the three acts as a judgment finder and the other two support or oppose him. It is not the lord [but the man] who determines which three men remain with the lord. The man may freely choose his spokesman and other participants for the consultations as long as he leaves his lord three men and a spokesman. The man must pay a fine for each mistake that calls for a fine unless he clears himself on the relics. However, the lord can call his man to task for anything for which he cannot take an oath or that does not require a fine. If, on the other hand, the lord accuses him of speaking or acting to the lord's humiliation or detriment, he shall clear himself with an oath or pay a fine. ⟨fol. 77r⟩

74 If a man takes property from another, and the first holder who had received it from his lord does not inform his lord and does not pursue the loss with lawful complaint, then he is fined by the lord. If a man gives his fief as security without permission of the lord who granted it to him, the lord can command by order of the court that the man redeem it within six weeks. If he does not comply, he is fined. If a man takes unlawful control of his fellow vassal's fief, or if he abuses him with word or deed, all the while knowing that the man is in his own lord's service, or if he commits a felony against one who is born to that property or against one who holds it in fief from him, then the malefactor must pay a fine based on the property he himself has been granted by the lord unless he can clear himself on the relics. However, the lord is not required to answer to his man before the overlord unless he had earlier refused the man justice in the presence of his own men. Nor does the lord have to answer to his leaseholder before the overlord unless he had refused him justice in the presence of his fellow tenants.[114] The man pays no fine if he has the property renewed [by another lord] and if the renewal itself is rejected, unless his proof for the property fails.

If during the court hearing the man wipes [his face], blows his nose, spits, yawns, coughs, sneezes, stands on the side of his spokesman opposite to the side he stood on first, looks around with propriety, brushes away flies, ⟨fol. 77v⟩ mosquitos, or horseflies, he shall not be fined. Only stupid people think these acts are fined. The fine paid by a man to his lord is ten pounds. A prince with a banner estate pays the king a hundred pounds in pennies of common currency in the mint where the fine is levied, a pound being twenty shillings. Every lord's man is entitled to compensation payment at the level of his birth. The table for each man's payment can be found in the book that discusses the territorial law.[115] But if a man has forfeited his rights, he loses the compensation amount he was born with. Both indemnity payments and fines are to be paid within a fortnight at the lord's dwelling closest to the place where the court made the ruling. The man may not sit down when a feudal court is in session without the lord's permission, but if he cannot stand any longer, he may lie down. If the lord takes issue with this, he shall claim that he can no longer stand and swear it on the relics. A man cannot incur a fine from his lord more than three times in one day. After each argument, the man may have three consultations and may remain in consultation until he is recalled three times by the lord's ruling.[116] He must be able to hear the recall, and he must remain in the yard in which the court is being held. ⟨fol. 78r⟩

75 Those who lack knightly status may not challenge the judgment of someone who has knightly status. A person with a half hide of land or five shillings yearly from his lord may challenge a judgment and be a witness for someone who lacks these things. If he challenges the entire judgment or only a part, he must offer a guarantor that he shall win his argument or accept the final judgment with a fine to the judge and a compensation payment. His guarantor must be someone invested by the lord. However, if the person reaches a judgment on behalf of his lord, and then someone objects, that person must propose an alternative judgment when the lord commands him. The judgment that has the support of the majority succeeds, but the person whose judgment is discarded pays neither fine nor compensatory payment as long as he did not appeal the [previous] judgment. If a person appeals a judgment and is accused of doing this, not for reason of justice but in order to delay the trial, he must clear himself on the relics or pay the court fine.

When a man appeals a judgment, he names the person and says the following: "If your name is X and you are X then you have given my and your lord, and me and yourself a false judgment in feudal law, and I shall appeal it where I lawfully must and request a judgment there where I make the lawful appeal." After that a lawful judgment shall be made in the court of the overlord of the property. Both parties request messengers and the lord shall choose two of his men to go with them to witness whose judgment is accepted and whose is not. ⟨fol. 78v⟩ The lord shall provide these envoys with plenty of beer and bread, and three courses at each meal, and a cup of wine. The servants receive two courses.[117] The horses shall be shod in front and not in back; they are to be fed five sheaves each day and night or as much threshed fodder as appropriate. There shall be eight horses, six servants, four riding and two on foot. Their number may be fewer but certainly not greater. The judgment finder, the appellant, and the envoys will set out in three days and must return with the judgment within six weeks.[118]

However, if the lord to whom the appeal is brought is out of the country, then once returns to German territory within the Holy Roman Empire, the envoys have six weeks from the time they learn of his arrival to return with a decision. The accused shall then come forth to plead as he did the first time when notice of a new court date is given him personally at his dwelling or at a property he possesses from the lord, as was discussed earlier.[119]

If a judgment is appealed because of a fief that is also the lord's allod, then one may ultimately take it to the royal court because the king has rightful jurisdiction over each man's life and property held in ownership and in fief; the reason for this is that territorial law and ⟨fol. 79r⟩ feudal law begin with the king because the orders of knightly status begin with him, too. A man is required to perform the same service for his lord when he holds the lord's allod in fief.[120] Now if one were not allowed to make a ruling concerning a grant in fief of allodial land before the king, then the fiefholder thus invested could not determine a judgment on someone who is invested with an imperial estate, nor another fiefholder on the previous one. If a decision is appealed in a person's suit for which he has been summoned to feudal court, and if he has two or three types of property, then the appeal is taken to his highest overlord to whom the greater part of the property is traceable. That lord shall preside over the final appeal.

If peace days hinder the required service for his imperial holdings so that the judgment cannot be determined within the legal time limit, then the judgment shall be handed down in six weeks time once the peace days end.[121] If a man appeals a judgment after the consensus is reached and fails,[122] he must pay a compensatory fine to the person who had determined the judgment and to all those who had supported it, unless he had requested a consultation before the consensus was established. The lord may only levy one court fine for the case because it is unlawful to fine a man two or three times for the same legal action. A person who breaks the peace and the holy days against a man must pay two court fees for the same act: one to the secular and the other to the ecclesiastical court. The injured party ⟨fol. 79v⟩ receives only one compensatory fine because he must pledge a guaranty that he will not pursue the case further before he can be awarded compensation.

76 When two villages dispute a boundary, the neighboring villages shall make a determination based on testimony of witnesses. The side with the greater number of witnesses wins the case. But if the witnesses are equally divided so that a decision cannot be reached, then the final judgment shall be made according to the territorial law explained previously.[123]

Everything discussed up to this point concerns general feudal law. I shall now delineate to you three types of fiefs and describe how they differ from the general feudal law.

77 Judicial power held in fief from the king cannot be further invested beyond the third level down with the single exception of the *Schultheiss* office because no count's court is legal without an invested *Schultheiss*. No person may grant further (in subfief) a judicial fief granted him unless it is a separate court that exists within his own jurisdiction as, for example, a county within a mark or in another banner territory.[124] He may bestow it and may not leave it ungranted for more than a year according to law. Two men may not hold a judicial fief jointly. However, a person may be enfeoffed with the reversion as with any other fief. If the king places someone in royal outlawry, that person may no longer preside over a court of law, nor may a person preside who has lost his fief by court ruling until he is able to recover it. A person who succeeds to the fief upon the fiefholder's death may not preside ⟨fol. 80r⟩ until he has been invested with [judicial authority] unless a legal hindrance prevented him from receiving the grant when he reached his majority.

78 When someone holds allodial property in fief in this way, he may not have it renewed [by another lord]. The investiture, however, can be granted further down to the seventh level, just as any fief that is part of imperial property. No one may deny the right to renew these nor deny anyone feudal rights to the property except the highest lord who owns the property. The lord who grants the property may also reclaim it if he needs it as long as he replaces it with an equivalent property on imperial land. If an allod reverts to the empire or is given to an ecclesiastical house, the person who holds it in fief cannot be prevented from renewing it.

A reversion and fine apply to a castle fief just as to any other fief. The castleholder[125] may not grant the castle in subfief. But if the holder does grant it to another, then when the lord discovers this, he can rule that the castleholder answer for and regain control of the fief within six weeks. If he fails to do this, the lord can revoke the castle. If the fiefholder of the castle dies before this is done, and the invested man has had right of possession of the fief without any legal opposition, he may have it renewed within the year by the overlord as long as he can prove it in feudal court with witnesses. He must swear that he did not know about the relation of the property to the overlord when he accepted the fief. Likewise, the lord may not transfer his man's fief and receive it back as a castle fief. ⟨fol. 80v⟩ But if the lord does so against the law, then the men can request investiture from the overlord or attornment to the person who can accord them proper feudal rights to the property. Should a man die while his wife is pregnant and another have right of reversion to the property, that person with the reversion shall assume control of the property until the mother gives birth to a son. The son cancels a man's reversion only if he is born alive and lives after the father's death.

If a lord grants a castle in toto, or if he conveys it to someone of lower rank, the men of the castle need not have him renew their own castle fiefs. They retain their holdings from the lord who granted them as their rightful fief, or they renew them with the man to whom their lord granted the castle as a legal fief. Should the castle men not wish to remain, they shall be reimbursed for their buildings. A castle fief includes right of use,[126] the lord's fines, and reversion, just like any other fief. If a fiefholder lends his castle fief to another in subfief, he may not cancel it in feudal court, but the holder of the subfief has no right to have it renewed unless it is done as described earlier.[127] The man has a castle fief renewed and bestows it on his sons even when the castle, or the castle fief, or both are owned by the lord who had invested him with it. Should a man having men and castle die, the castle men are required, like every vassal, man or woman, to swear fealty and homage to the heirs while the children or other heirs have not yet divided up the castle according to land or feudal law. ⟨fol. 81r⟩ The castle men also swear to protect the castle against others according to law. Each person must do this if he wishes to keep his fief. He may, however, accept his fief from no more than one of the heirs. It is quite possible to grant a castle fief on imperial property even if the castle itself is held in free ownership. A man with a castle fief is not required to perform military or court service for his lord. Instead he shall live in the castle and defend it when necessary. He shall also act as judgment finder for his lord in a castle court. The lord of the castle can hold a castle court nowhere but in his castle. No one can be a witness, or determine a judgment unless he holds a castle fief from the lord. And no holder of a castle fief may testify as witness or render a judgment concerning someone who holds a proper fief; nor may that person render a judgment concerning one with a castle fief. But for every other kind of fief excluding a castle, a man with uncompromised military shield can indeed make a judgment about another and be a witness except in the case of a prince with a banner fief. In the last case, the prince may determine a judgment and testify regarding any man in the realm.

A prince is a prince of the realm because he receives his banner fief directly from the empire alone, and no one holds it above him. When someone who is granted a banner fief bestows it on a second person, then that person is not the first in the subinfeudation process and cannot be an imperial prince.[128] Whoever holds a banner estate and is a prince shall have no ⟨fol. 81v⟩ layperson as lord except the king. Any man with uncompromised knightly status who has been enfeoffed by his lord shall be a judgment finder and witness on any prince's fief except for a banner fief. No one may refuse to determine a judgment or to be a witness or spokesman; the lord may not refuse to do so concerning his man, the man concerning the lord, or the kinsman concerning his kinsman. The king shall summon a prince to his feudal court held in a specified place in six weeks' time by means of his letter and seal. He may not name any court in his summons because the court is located wherever the king himself presides in public. The king may even hold feudal court on peace days and in all towns, but not in churches.

When the lord of the castle holds a court hearing, the gates to the castle must be open. No one may render a judgment under a roof or within a walled enclosure. The lord may bring his man with a castle fief to court on three grounds only: if he is disloyal to the lord, or if he fails in his duty to the castle, or if one of the men brings a suit against another for a castle fief. When the lord calls his castleholder to answer before the castle court for one of these reasons, he himself or his messenger shall inform the man in person or in his yard where two other men hear it. He shall then prosecute him in castle court in the stipulated location as the feudal law outlined earlier. ⟨fol. 82r⟩ But if the lord revokes the man's castle fief, he must clear it [of incumbrance] within six weeks, or his claim to the fief is also rescinded. If a fiefholder of the castle leaves with his household, and the lord orders him to come back, and he is informed personally or it is proclaimed in his yard so that two of the lord's fiefholders of the castle hear it, then if he does not return within six weeks, he forfeits his castle fief unless legal hindrance prevents him. However, if the fiefholder does return within six weeks and spends at least one night there, his castle fief cannot be revoked. But if the lord brings him there by court order, he may not depart with his household until the lord gives him leave.

A man may be invested with a proper fief and a castle fief at the same time, but with separate witnesses for each fief. If a castle is demolished by force when the holder of the castle is innocent of the felony, he shall not do without his fief because of it. His castle fief is a proper fief while the castle is being rebuilt with walls or palisades until it can be secured with a gate. However, a castle razed by court order may not be rebuilt. When a castle and a castle fief are not part of the same jurisdiction, so that after the lord's death they revert to different lords, and the castle fief is separated from its castle, the castle men renew their fief where it belongs because it becomes their proper fief since they have been freed of their duty to live in the castle. ⟨fol. 82v⟩ If the lord rescinds his fiefholder's castle fief, it then becomes his proper fief without the castle court, and it is renewed by the overlord as previously described. The fiefholder will be compensated for his buildings. No one may claim a castle as a proper fief where the lord pays the gatekeepers and sentries. If the lord grants a property that contains tenants born to the soil or those who have bought [rights to] the rent property, and these people owe service for these rights, then the lord may retain their service for himself as long as he stipulates this when he grants the property.

79 But if it is a freehold, and no one has right to the rents, and no one was born to it, and if the lord leases it to an outsider, it is unlawful for anyone to demand service, payments, or shelter from the leaseholder. He shall not perform any service except what he had agreed to do for the lord. He must, however, attend the secular and the ecclesiastical law courts.

80 Should a man possess property in guardianship for a woman or child but without enfeoffment, or should a man place a property in his brother's possession without the knowledge and approval of his lord, and should the fiefholder die while the other person has right of possession, then that person may claim the property. If he does so, he cannot establish his claim by swearing on the relics by himself, but instead he must prove it with witnesses when someone has a claim in reversion for it, or the lord to whom it reverts offers to prove with witnesses that the man had held the property in fief until his death. The right of possession to enfeoffed property must be proven with the testimony of six of the lord's men. Simple possession is proven by ⟨fol. 83r⟩ [the oath] of the claimant with six others who are uncurtailed in their rights, whoever they may be.

81 It is desirable for a lady to have a relative be granted her property with her so that if the lord dies, and she may not have the property renewed if she lacks the military shield, then the man has the right to renew his property as long as he enjoys knightly status. Whoever outlives the other retains feudal rights to the property with respect to the lord who bestowed it. But if the man receives the property from the lady's hand only, then when she dies, he has no claim to the fief once the property transfers to another

lord. But if the (new) lord enfeoffs them both with it, as is proper because they both have feudal right to it, then they hold it from him the same as they did from the first lord. But if the lord denies the lady's right of renewal and invests only the man, he has full feudal rights over it and may grant and transfer it with the lady's consent because she has possession, although he may pass it on to his children. If a lord lays claim to a lady's property when she has right of possession or when a man who lacks knightly status has right of possession, the lord can declare it free after the man's death. But if the lady claims the property from another who is still alive, and the lord accepts it in accordance with feudal law, then she retains it.[129]

82 The man may demand security from his lord for a debt or sue him in court when the lord denies him justice before his men, ⟨fol. 83v⟩ and he has witnesses. But if the lord robs the man, he may bring charges against him for all felonies to the judge in territorial law. The man may most assuredly protect himself from the lord and does not have to relinquish the property because of [the case] if he has accused the lord of denying him justice in front of his men. If the man repudiates the lord, the property he holds from him reverts, and if the lord repudiates him, the lord also loses the property that the man held from him unless it is the lord's allod, and the man renews it with the overlord.[130] If the property is owned by the lord or by an ecclesiastical institution from whence it cannot be removed, and the man may not renew it, he still retains the property for life, but without service, and passes it on to his children. He fulfills feudal law even if the lord repudiates him while he does not repudiate his lord. When a person transfers property to his lord, or repudiates him, or when his property is revoked, the man forfeits usage rights as well as all the property that he holds from the lord. By law, the man may not repudiate the lord, nor the lord the man, except in person. After that, neither may cause harm to the other for a day and a night. However, the action is traitorous if the lord collects his forces against the man, or the man against the lord, before the one has repudiated the other, and repudiates him only after he has armed himself ⟨fol. 84r⟩ in order to injure the other, and sets out against him with his forces. This act is traitorous because the lord may not injure the man, nor the man the lord, with advice and deed[131] before one repudiates the other. The advice of man and lord is equal to a traitorous act.[132] If the man requests an escort to go to and from the lord when he wishes to repudiate him, it shall be granted him. If the lord refuses unlawfully to grant it, then the man shall repudiate him in his nearest house or court so that those

present hear him. Or he may repudiate him where the judge and the lord hold their next court hearing and transfer the lord's property in the same place. The man should have two witnesses of the repudiation from among the lord's men in case he needs them. The lord may not injure the man for six weeks thereafter. The lord shall do the same when he repudiates his man. Should the man deny that he had repudiated his lord in this way, it is easier for him to cleanse himself with an oath than it is for the lord to prove it against him, unless he had repudiated the lord face to face, and the lord had invested someone else with that property in his presence. If a man clears his revoked property with respect to his lord, he also recovers all his enfeoffed usage rights. If the lord grants him the justly revoked property a second time, he does not receive it with usage rights unless they, too, are lent a second time. ⟨fol. 84v⟩

83 A fief granted to the office of village headman is inherited by the son even though he lacks knightly status and renews it with a succeeding lord. However, he may not lend it further in fief. With this fief, he may attorn to another lord, but he cannot refuse any lord when the fief is renewed, be that person woman or man. He may not act as witness or judgment finder based on the fief regarding any man of full knightly status.

84 I have come to the end of the entire feudal law. However, many people say there are additional investitures that terminate at a specified time, such as a military fief that expires with the shield,[133] and a dwelling fief that expires when the person no longer lives in it.[134] But all this is incorrect because any fief a lord grants to a man is valid for life if the man does not transfer it or lose it in a feudal court decision. It would be easy to explain the law if there were not so many who desire lawlessness, commit unlawful acts for their own gain, and even call it right and proper. If one were to do the same to them, they would consider it wrong because no one is so unjust that he would not think it wrong if someone did him an injustice. This is why a lengthy explanation is necessary for people to understand what is lawful conduct and to learn how to replace wrong with right and establish justice. A person who speaks justly in all things wins the anger of many. May the righteous man console himself with this thought for the sake of God and his own honor. ⟨fol. 85r⟩ This book shall make many an enemy, for all those who strive against God and Law will be enraged because it pains them to see that the law is always revealed.

85 Whenever a lord calls his man before the feudal court and commands his men to attend, then during this hearing he may not assign an-

other hearing that they must attend. Nor may any of their other lords set a court hearing during the same period because they are in imperial service for their property while they assist in the lord's feudal court. They must prove this with their oath sworn in person or by messenger. But if the command for military campaign or court duty is made by decree, and if the man who was called to answer before the court is given proper notice, he is excused from appearing at the hearing because the need of the empire excuses him by law as long as the legal hinderance is proven according to proper procedure before the feudal court. Under territorial law, a man is not released from a court summons for imperial service because he is subject to territorial law during his entire service to the realm.[135]

86 If a person who requests an investiture or attornment of his property is transferred by the overlord to someone who is not the equal of his lord, and discovers this before the renewal limitation period has passed, he may contest the attornment before the overlord. If the lord asks,[136] he must tell him immediately why he ⟨fol. 85v⟩ may not renew the fief. If the lord wishes, he can give him a single court date before his men and not more unless a judgment is challenged or a continuance is needed for rendering judgment. The plaintiff must then state whether he refuses the attornment because of the person's lower birth status[137] or because of the men who lowered the person's status. The man must then either renew with that lord or appeal the judgment.[138] But if the court finds for him that he has a lawful argument, he shall prove the case with witnesses. If he refuses the attornment because the lord is of lower birth, he must prove this with six others who have full legal capacity, whoever they may be. But if he refuses the attornment because of the men who lowered the lord's status to whom he is attorned, or his father's or his grandfather's status, he must prove this with two others who were born into knightly status, be they the lord's men or not. If they are the lord's men, the lord dictates that they bear witness in fealty. If they are not his men, they must prove with their oath as witnesses that the lord to whom the man is attorned is not equal in military shield status to the man's previous lord. If that person comes forth against whom the testimony is given and offers to clear himself, he cannot negate the man's proof with his cleansing oath. If he then offers proof that he is indeed the equal of the man's previous lord both in birth and knightly status, he cannot with his proof of witnesses invalidate the man's proof ⟨fol. 86r⟩ because the man can more easily withdraw himself and his property from a lord using proof of witnesses than the lord can gain such property with his

proof. If by means of a court ruling someone without proof of witnesses cancels his lord's proof with witnesses, the lord may attorn him a second time. But if someone voids the attornment with testimony of witnesses, the lord cannot transfer that person anywhere. Instead, he must grant the fief himself because the man is not required to give proof with witnesses more than once for a property held from the lord.

Glossary

Each entry contains a term used in the translation along with its Middle High German equivalent(s) and an explanation. When the MHG term has been retained for use in the translation, it is listed along with a rather lengthy description. In cases where the original term is ambiguous or encompasses several meanings, several possible translations are provided. The book and chapter numbers show where a term is used in a definition or in a significant or typical context. Not all occurrences for each term are listed, and no references are given for extremely frequent terms.

Advocate. *Vogt* n.m. A secular judge and magistrate for an ecclesiastical foundation, a monastery, or a bishopric. He presides over a superior court. I 2; III 64.

Alienate. *Geben* v. To transfer or convey real property held in complete or limited ownership; to transfer right of possession. I 9, 21, 34. See "freehold," "possession," "sell," "transfer."

Allod. *Eigen* n.n./m. Inheritable real estate held fully in one's own right, not subject to feudal duties or burdens. I 2, 9, 29, 34; II 5, 43; III 56. See "freehold."

Appeal. *Schelten* v. To appeal a verdict and take the case to the higher court; to challenge a claim by producing contradictory evidence in the form of witnesses or charters; or to attempt to reverse a court ruling. II 12; III 70; IV 75.

Arrest. *Vrone gewalt* n.f. Seizure and detention of a person by the judge's authority. I 61.

Attach. *Phenden* v. To take property as security for a debt, a fine, or a pledge until the person performs his obligation, when authorized by a magistrate. I 53; II 27; III 20; IV 82. See "seize."

Attainder. *Ubiracht* n.f. All rights and capacities are withdrawn whenever a person who has been tried and judged guilty of treason or a felony receives a sentence for his crime. Within the scope of the *Sachsenspiegel* the concept of attainder comes under the rubric of outlawry. *Ubiracht* presumes guilt and can therefore be called "irrevocable attainder." Unlike attainder, however, it can be imposed in place of a sentence against a convicted felon, or imposed on a person who has evaded judgment for more than a year. Outlawry is normally imposed before conviction, and attainder after judgement. The result is loss of all rights, including loss of property and loss of legal protection since a person imposed with attainder may be killed on sight without penalty. III 34. See "legal incapacity," "outlawry."

Attornment. *Wisunge* n.f. Attornment or transfer is the process by which an overlord transfers a vassal's enfeoffment to another liege lord, who then invests him in the fief. IV 15, 27, 86.

Bailiff. *Fronbote* n.m. An officer of the court who served as a herald, warrant officer, convener of a law court, and executor of court decisions and enforcement orders. I 8, 28, 53, 61, 63, 68, 70; II 22, 41; III 46, 61.

Ban. *Ban* n.m For the Roman Catholic Church ban means imposition of anathema or major excommunication (III 57) (*HRG*, 1, c. 306–7). See "royal jurisdiction," "royal judicial authority."

Banner estate. *Vanen len* n.n. The king's investiture of the large imperial principalities on the crown vassals of the empire, who then owed fealty to the emperor only. These territories were called banner estates because the formal ceremony of enfeoffment was accomplished with the banner of the territory for lay princes, and with a scepter for ecclesiastical princes. III 53, 53a, 58, 60; IV 20, 78.

Bench. *Bank* n.f./m. The bench or seat on which the *Schöffen* and judge sit during a court session (II 13).

Bondage. *Eigenschaft* n.f. Servitude, serfdom. III 43.

Bondman. *Eigenmann* n.m. *Eigene lute* pl. Any servile person, a half-free person, or most often a serf. The "Imperial Landpeace of Mainz" distinguishes this term from *dinstlute* (fol. 1r). There were two groups of bondmen and women. The *dagewerchten* ("day laborers") served their master constantly and had no land of their own to work but paid no tithe. The remainder were all peasants who also had at least one hide of their own to cultivate for which they paid a duty (*HRG*, 1, c. 877–78). I 16; II 20; III 43; IV 26. See "ministerial," "hide."

Breaking on the wheel. *Radebrechen* v. This was a uniquely German form of execution. First the person's limbs (and sometimes the back) were broken, then woven through the spokes of a cart wheel which was then placed horizontally on top of a pole. The procedure caused a slow, excruciating death. II 14 (*HRG*, 4, c. 135–38).

Burgrave. *Burgreve* n.m. A magistrate and judge ruling a castle and its adjacent lands by hereditary right. III 53; IV 78.

Castle fief. *Burglen* n.n. A castle and surrounding lands were bestowed as a whole or in parts to men who were required to perform constant military service protecting the castle and aiding the lord in battle when needed. Since these fiefholders were castle guards, they were required to live in the castle and their fief typically consisted of an income with housing in or near the castle. Castle fiefs were held more frequently by ministerials than free vassals (*HRG*, 1, c. 562–64). IV 2, 13, 52, 57, 64, 70, 78. See "fief."

Champion. *Kemphe* n.m. A fighter hired by a court or individual litigant to fight in a trial by combat. Because it was a despised occupation as was minstrelsy, these fighters suffered from curtailed legal capacity. I 38, 48, 49; III 46. See "legal incapacity."

Charge. *Rügen* v. To make an accusation or bring charges against someone. This is the responsibility of the local judge and village headman in the case of misdemeanors. I 2; III 86.

City code. *Weichbild* n.n. An urban, municipal law code. The early codes drew heavily on the *Sachsenspiegel*.

Claim. *Beredin* v. To make a claim or demand one's rights in court; to pursue a remedy. IV 17 (*DWB* 1, c. 1492–94).

Cleansing oath. *Unschult* n.f. The act of proving one's innocence by means of an oath sworn on a reliquary; an oath of innocence. I 14; III 23; IV 24.

Clear. *Entreden* v., *Entsagen sich* v. refl. To clear or exonerate oneself of a charge with proof. III 23.

Clear. *Uszcien* v. To release a property, usually a fief, from encumberment in a court of law, or to reinstate full rights to it. III 1; IV 13, 45, 46, 47, 52, 70, 78, 82.

Commons. *Marke* n.f. A common meadow and woods to which families in the village had pasturage rights. II 48.

Compensation. *Buse* n.f. (OE bote) An indemnity or compensation payment; may also be levied as a fine. It was paid as compensation or restitution made to an injured party. Often listed as a money payment, it can also mean restoration of property to its original condition. Initially, it was an act or payment to reinstate property in its previous condition, but then a split developed between the idea of restitution and a public penalty or fine paid in a money amount. This double meaning led to the distinction between *buse* and a court fine (I 53).

Buse retained the meaning of compensation. It was also used in cases where the initiator of a law suit paid a fine to the winning party. In these situations I translate *buse* as a fine (I 8, 42). The amount paid was established according to a fixed scale; see the entire scale of wergeld and compensation payments due to people (III 46, 47) and animals (III 52), and fines (IV 74). The word is related to *bessern* (v.)–to make good, improve, or compensate–which provides the moral component of improving oneself. See "court fine."

Concubinage. *Kebis* n.f. A marriage-like relationship between a freeman and a bondwoman in common law because it was public (*HRG*, 2, c. 695). *Kebiskint* is the illegitimate offspring of this relationship. I 51 (*HRG*, 2, c. 817–18).

Consensus. *Volburt* n.f., *Folge* n.f. After each ruling or judgment in land or feudal court, the entire body of judgment finders was asked if it agreed to its lawfulness. The *Schöffen* performed this function in the superior court under territorial law. If the members agreed, the judgment was confirmed. II 13; IV 70, 75. See "judiciary," "judgment finders," "*Schöffe*."

Consultation. *Gesprech* n.n. At every stage in a trial, each litigant could ask for a consultation with his spokesman, his family, and, in the case of feudal law, his fellow vassals. They removed themselves from the court to deliberate and returned when they were ready. If the deliberations took too long, the judge could recall the group. I 62; IV 72a, 74, 75.

Convict. *Beredin* v. To convict someone of a felony. I 40, 48, 49, 50; II 14, 16, 72.

Count. *Graf* n.m. The judge of the superior court invested with the king's jurisdiction. This means that a count tried all cases regarding allodial land (I 2), and all crimes including capital offenses (I 59). The judges of the high court also included the *pfalzgraf, landgraf*, and certain advocates (III 52). At this level the judge dealt with all disputes regarding allodial property including the tenants and sharecroppers (I 59; III 80). The only limiting stipulation was that people of *Schöffen* class had to be tried under the king's authority at the legal court venue. I 67; III 61. See "burgrave," "margrave," "advocate."

Country people. *Lantlute* pl. The free residents in a rural community and judicial district. All were members of the judiciary at the local level. They were required to attend the count's court and to respond to the hue and cry in the event of a crime. II 4, 71; III 56, 64, 68 (Planck, 9). See "villager."

Court assembly. *Ding* n.n. The assembly of the court in the place set aside for that purpose; *echtes ding* was the regular court that was assembled at fixed intervals; the *gebotenes ding* was a court called for special purposes; *dingen* means to call a court into session. I 19, 41, 52; II 13, 42; III 44, 61.

Court fine. *Gewette* n.f A fee or fine levied by the court and paid to the judge. I 53; II 14, 40; III 9, 46, 53a.

Court of law. *Gericht* n.n. The judiciary power and jurisdiction of a law court; the hearing itself; the judgment determined by a court; or its jurisdiction. I 57, 62; III 53. See "court assembly," "district," "sentence."

Defend. *Entworten, Entwerten* v., *Beredin* v. To defend oneself against an accusation in court; to answer for failure to do something; to make a plea (II 15; III 16, 25) (Schmidt-Wiegand, "Rechtswortschatz," *Facsimile W*, 3, 225). In this meaning *bereden* is found in the "Landpeace of Mainz" (fol. 1, 2r,r). See "clear," "cleansing oath."

Disreputable occupation. (*unechtes*) *Ammechte* n.n. The occupations of champion or fighter (*kemphe*), prostitute (*fahrend wip*), and minstrel (*spilman, spillute*) were considered disreputable (*unecht*), primarily by the Church, but the practitioners also suffered legally because their rights were curtailed to the extent that they had no right to a spokesman (III 16) and had no means for seeking legal remedy if any action was taken against them, but they were not totally without legal capacity. III 28, 46, 47. See "legal capacity," "legal incapacity," "champion."

District. *Gericht* n.n. The territorial jurisdiction of a judge. I 13; II 71; III 53, 63.

Enfeoff, Grant. *Lien* v. To enfeoff or grant possession in fief, where tenure is dependent on service or dues. Fiefs in reversion, expectancies, and castle fiefs were types of investiture that carried restrictions on renewal or inheritance. I 52; IV 5. See "expectancy," "fief," "fief in Reversion," "investiture," "renew."

Enfeoffment. *Lenunge* n.f. A grant or transfer of property held in feudal tenancy; the contract of enfeoffing someone with a landholding, usually a fief. It did not automatically include but was normally accompanied by investiture and, consequently, control or possession of the property. III 59; IV 7, 8, 77, 78. See "fief," "fief in reversion," "investiture."

Exonerate. *Entschuldigen* v. To clear, exculpate, or exonerate oneself with an oath. II 34, IV 73.

Expectancy. *Wartunge* n.f. A promise to invest a man with the first available property. III 84; IV 34, 59.

Family estate. *Hantgemal* n.n. The hereditary estate of a clan from which a family took its name. Naming the estate served as proof of identity for nobility (*HRG*, 1, c. 1960). I 51; III 29.

Felon. *Vridebrecher* n.m. A criminal; someone who commits a grave crime or a breach of the peace. I 69, 72; III 1.

Felony. *Ungerichte* n.n. A grave criminal act; a crime. II 12, 13, 64, 72.

Feudal law. *Lenrecht* n.n. Law and judiciary process pertaining to the properties, privileges, and duties of the nobility. It covered only relations between a lord and his vassals and subvassals and not issues between two vassals of different lords. I 3, 4; IV 1, 2 (primarily book IV of this translation).

Fief. *Len* n.n. Any grant or transfer of property rights that produces continuous income; e.g., real property or rents. In book IV the term refers primarily to a contract of mutual obligations that included the terms of the responsibilities of lord and feoffee to each other and to the property rights granted. The term *gut* ("property") designated the actual property, and *len* ("fief") the contract. Hence, feudal property held from an overlord came with the responsibilities of military and advisory service. In fact, it was this service that made a man legally eligible to hold a fief in the first place and defined the personal relationship of fealty and reciprocal duties involved (*HRG*, 2, c. 1711, 1722–25). According to the feudal law in Germany, any object could be given as a fief, and it was the relationship of the two parties that determined the type of grant involved and not the status of the fiefholder. It follows then that peasants, too, could be fiefholders and, consequently, subject to the feudal laws (I 14; IV 2) (*HRG*, 1, c. 321–22). W uses the term freely in all four books, apparently for almost any tenancy seen as a lending or leasing but not for the sale of property. In the feudal law of book IV, several types of fief are mentioned: proper fief (*recht len*), heritable fief (*erblen*), fief in reversion (*gedinge*), and castle fief (*burglen*) (IV 57). The proper and heritable fiefs were normally not distinguished since they carried full rights. The castle fief is discussed in IV 2, 13, 52, 57, 64, 70, 78. Reversion is enfeoffment with delayed possession. See "castle fief," "fief in reversion," "expectancy," "leasehold," "freehold," "lend," "renew," "revoke," "repudiate."

Fief in Reversion. *Gedinge* n.f. An actual enfeoffment having three predetermined conditions: the person would receive possession of the specified property upon the death of the current possessor as long as the property had no other legal successor; the property could not be passed on by inheritance; and the investiture itself ended with the death of the investing lord or fiefholder (Janz, 144; *HRG*, 2, c. 1696–98). This last stipulation meant also that the fief could not be renewed or confirmed by a new lord. III 75; IV 5, 7, 20, 38, 59, 82. See "castle fief," "fief," "expectancy."

Flogging. *Hut und har* n.f./n. Minor corporal punishment consisted of caning or flogging in addition to cutting the convicted person's hair. This penalty, although it applied to all ranks of people, could be ransomed with a money payment, which means that a distinction was growing between wealthy and poor–those who could pay and those who could not. II 14, 28 (*HRG*, 2, c. 1777–90).

Flogging. *Kuniges malder* n.m. A specific form of corporal punishment reserved for the bailiff consisting normally of thirty blows with a green oak rod of a given length although actual dimensions varied. II 17.

Food supplies. *Musteil* n.n. The stored foodstuffs on hand after the burial of the deceased. These supplies, along with the rest of the estate, were divided among the heirs after the thirtieth. Fifty percent of the foodstuffs belonged to the widow. I 24; III 74. See "thirtieth."

Free. *Vri* adj. Means both immunity or exemption from, and privilege or eligibility to; thus it refers to someone who was free or eligible to do something. Members of the *Schöffenbarfrei* class were eligible to become *Schöffen*; certain groups were exempt from tolls, etc. (II 27). Alternatively, *vri* could be negative and express that someone was free from, or outside of, legal protection, such as an outlaw. It also means free, the opposite of servile. I 16; III 54. See "bondman."

Freehold. *Len* n.n. Real, heritable property held in qualified ownership (for life or for an uncertain duration). II 43; III 75, 76. See "allod," "fief," "ownership."

Free lord. *Vrier herr* n.m. The old class of free knights of the fourth level of the *herschilt,* who took the title of count as the ministerials climbed into their ranks. I 3; III 46.

Guarantor. *Bürge* n.m. A bondsman; a person who guarantees that someone will do something such as appear in court or pay some amount. A bondsman can also guarantee the truth of a person's claim in court. I 6, 61; II 37; III 9.

Guarantor. *Gewer* n.m. A person who testifies or has proof of a person's claim or statement in court. I 15; II 42; III 7; IV 14.

Guaranty. *Gewer* n.f. Evidence or proof for a claim; security offered until legally pledged or required actions are fulfilled. I 63; II 17; III 14; IV 28.

Guardian. *Vormunde* n.m. Tutor; protector; one who has legal responsibility for a minor, a woman, or anyone who lacks legal capacity in a court of law. The guardian managed that person's property and was his or her legal spokesman. I 41; II 65; III 46; IV 29.

Hide. *Huve* n.f. Originally a peasant holding; gradually became a unit of land measure. It was a parcel of (normally arable) land held in ownership or in tenancy that included usage rights to the common grazing areas. In Saxony, one hide contained twenty to thirty *morgen*, or about twelve to twenty acres (Kuchenbuch, 155). Some of the hides (*mansus regalis*) given out in eastern clearance areas (including eastern parts of Saxony) may have been twice the size of the older hide (*HRG*, 2, c. 248–50). The peasant tenants on the land were required to pay rents. I 29; II 48, 54; III 46, 61.

Homage. *Hulde* n.f., *Manschaft* n.f. Formal acknowledgment of feudal tenure and its accompanying duties; feudal service; the ritual of humbling and subordinating oneself to a lord (described in IV 22). It includes acceptance of the reciprocal duties: the lord is to protect and support his man, and the vassal is to provide court and military duty when called upon. III 19, 56; IV 3, 21, 24, 26, 56, 67, 68, 86. See "fief."

Household law. *Hoverecht* n.n. This law circumscribes the duties and rights of those persons and groups within and subordinate to a manor or court. These people were usually referred to as *familia*, hence the terms *lex familie* ("law of the household"). Household law was most prevalent in ecclesiastical foundations (*LexMA*, 5, c. 77–78). Discussed only in book IV, it is distinct from feudal and general territorial law. IV 69 (*DWB*, 4, 2, c. 1696; *BMZ*, 2, 1, 624). See "feudal law."

Hue and cry. *Geruft* n.n. A distress call; an alarm to gather the members of the community when danger arose and when someone was caught either in flagrante or red-handed so that they could make an arrest. The hue and cry, since it required the inhabitants to rush to the scene, accomplished two things; it provided witnesses and initiated the legal proceedings. I 2, 53, 62; III 1. See "red-handed."

Imperial judge. *Hoferichter* n.m. The judge who presided over the royal or imperial court, called *Hofgericht*, in place of the king or emperor himself. This judgeship was instituted by Frederick II in the "Imperial Landpeace of Mainz" in 1235 (fol. 3r,l). W mentions only the royal court. I 34; II 13, 25 (See "Hofgericht," *HRG*, 2, c. 206–9; and "Reichshofgericht," *HRG*, 4, c. 615–26).

Indict. *Vorzugen* v. To bring someone to trial with the testimony of witnesses; to prove something about someone with witnesses. III 71.

Inheritance. *Erbe* n.n. The property that devolves upon the heirs. The concept of the heritable estate is composed of several subgroups, each with its own rules of inheritance. *Erbe* refers to undifferentiated heritable property. In a more limited sense, it refers to the real property owned and passed on in the family as well as property held in tenure where the right to possession can be inherited. Other subdivisions of estate passed on individually are the *gerade*, which consisted of the mother's personal possessions and dowry; *hergewete*, the father's personal military equipment; and *musteil*, the food stores divided among family members. II 56; III 16. See "food supplies," "military equipment," "woman's personal belongings."

Investiture. *Bewisunge, Wisunge* n.f. The process of placing a feoffee in legal possession of a feudal property. IV 6, 10, 15, 78. See "attornment," "enfeoffment," "possession."

Judge. *Richter* n.m. Supervises the proceedings in a court of law and requests a judgment from the judgment finders. He did not make a determination himself (III 78), but he did proclaim the final judgment. At the end of the legal procedure the judgment was not what bound the parties; instead it was the order of the judge based on that judgment, because he had the authority to carry out the judgment to resolve the dispute or injustice done. In the person of the judge, the knowledge of the law and the power to carry it out were united. To be effective, he needed the help of the members of the judiciary to track and seize transgressors and to control any unlawful opposition (II 24, 25, 54) (Planck, 90). In feudal law, the judge was the liegelord who regulated only the property relations and feudal obligations of his vassals. See "judgment finder," "judiciary."

Judge. *Richten* v. To sit in judgment; to preside over a hearing; to pronounce and execute a sentence; to bring about a judgment. I 57, 59, 69; III 1, 55.

Judgment. *Urteil* n.n/f. Judgment; decision; ruling; determination; verdict. The system recognized that one decision laid the foundation for the next in building a case until a final judgment was reached. I 14, 53; III 54, 69, 70. See "consensus."

Judgment finder. *Dingphlichte* n.m. In the lower court of territorial law, the full members of the judiciary were responsible for determining a judgment. In the lower courts and in the marches, any free landed man of full legal status was obligated to attend the law court and help the judge by determining judgments by majority agreement. In general then, for each court hearing at each level of jurisdiction, judgment finders were responsible for attending the court and helping the judge by producing a judgment. The *Schöffe* determined a judgment in the high court, and the other *Schöffen* had to concur (Planck, 263–66). There are special cases, however. First, members of the clergy could not fulfill these functions in a secular court. Second, a Wend could not hand down a verdict on a Saxon, and vice versa (III 70; Willoweit, 88). The primary purpose in all cases was to ensure that people knowledgeable in the law reached judgments. The law stipulates that appeals to the king's court had to be heard within Saxon territory so that members of the judiciary familiar with local custom could attend (Planck, 101–2). Also, judgment finders had the right to withdraw in certain circumstances; for example, a *Schöffe* could refuse to give a decision in cases where breach of loyalty to kin or lord would occur (II 13; III 19). However, he was not required to do so (i.e., he could not be excluded from the judgment by the opposing party). See "*Schöffe*," "consensus."

Judiciary. *Dingpflichtig* adj. Describes membership in the judiciary. In territorial law this included all free landed men in their own judicial district who were required to attend the regular court sessions based on their status as having property in freehold or leasehold. In feudal law the judiciary consisted of the lord's vassals. In both territorial law courts and feudal courts, the members of the judiciary were the ones who needed to reach agreement for a verdict or ruling to be valid. Among the judiciary, the most important people aside from the judge were the *Schultheiss*, bailiff, and the judgment finders (Planck, 98–99). I 69; II 22; III 61, 88, 89. See "country people," "judge," "judgment finder," "consensus."

Jurisdiction. *Gericht* n.n. Designates the superior court that tried capital offenses, or the lower court that tried only petty crimes and the civil cases of peasants. I 57.

Land. *Lant* n.n. Territory (e.g., Saxony); or a rural region or community; also, arable land, a field.

Landpeace. *Vrides recht* n.n. A peace ordinance or landpeace was a compact enacted at the royal, and often at the territorial, level (see "Imperial Landpeace of Mainz" in this volume). Its purpose was to end private feuds and delineate crimes. It also provided immunity from assault and violent breaches of the peace to certain people (including clergy, Jews, women, and peasants) and to certain places for fixed periods of time. I 69; II 66, 71; III 8. See "peace days," "sworn peace," "truce."

Law. *Recht* n.n. Law; the norms of conduct established by custom or a code;

also, the justice achieved by means of a legal judgment. The phrase, *noch gesazteme rechte*, refers specifically to enacted laws (IV 38). I 1, 3, 6, 17, 18, 19; III 19, 30.

Leasehold. *Zinsgut* n.n. A property leased for a fixed or unlimited period of time. In Saxony, a heritable landholding on which the tenant paid ground rent. II 21; III 76; IV 13, 64, 65.

Legal capacity. *Recht* n.n. Having full rights and privileges before the law; *Vollenkumen in sime rechte*: having full legal capacity; undiminished rights (I 5, 14; II 12, 34). *Unbescholten* adj. Never having been in conflict with the law; a person unblemished in his legal and social status. I 49, 51. See "law," "legal incapacity."

Legal hindrance. *Echte not* n.f. Legally acceptable grounds for failing to appear in court; permissible exigencies are given in I 38, 70; II 7, 42; IV 26.

Legal incapacity. *Echtelos* adj. Complete loss of legal rights and protection under the law; the condition of attainder; having no safety of person. This was much more serious than *rechtelos* because it encompassed additional limitations. The consequences were inability to enter into legal marriage, have legitimate children, and own or inherit property. Often the terms *elos* and *erlos* are used in place of *echtelos* indicating that the terms were not yet stabilized, or that the concept was still in flux. I 38, 39, 48, 50, 51, 64, 69; II 14, 26 (Janz 263–64). See "legal incapacity," "attainder."

Legal incapacity. *Rechtelos* adj. Diminished legal capacity before the law due to birth, a dishonorable occupation, criminal conviction, or failure to stand trial. The result was that the person lost the right to indemnity and wergeld and was excluded from the judiciary. However, the major consequence of limited legal capacity was that the person lacked the right to use normal channels for a defence if criminal charges were brought against him or her (I 50, 51). However, if anyone injured or killed one of these people, the perpetrator was held liable for a criminal offense. W sometimes interchanges this term with *echtelos*. I 38, 39, 48, 50, 51, 64, 69; II 14, 26; III 28; IV 80. See "legal capacity," "legal incapacity."

Life estate. *Libgeding* n.n. Guaranteed legal lifelong use of a property. I 21, 32; III 74. See "right of use."

Limitation period. *Jarzcale* n.f. Refers to the period of time allotted to initiate a legal action. Most often, however, it refers in book IV to the fixed duration of one year, six weeks and one day in which the vassal had to reinstate himself or renew his fief. I 38, 70; IV 29, 30, 37, 38, 43, 46, 47, 52, 59, 66, 70, 86.

Local judge. *Gougreve* n.m. The local elected judge. Three villages together could elect him temporarily as need arose, or for shorter or longer tenures. It is unclear whether he was invested with the king's jurisdiction. I 55, 56, 57; III 64 (see introduction). See "judge."

Lord. *Herr* n.m. A person of status or nobility (III 55); the lord or landlord of a fief or territory with legal jurisdiction over free tenants and serfs on his holdings (III 33); a feudal or liege lord. II 21; III 52, 58, 84; IV 22, 26, 28, 42, 45, 67, 72a, 82. See "master."

Man. *Man* n.m. The several meanings found in this text are adult male, full member of a community, husband, vassal, or some type of subordinate.

March. *Mark* n.f. A German border province, ruled by a count called a margrave. II 13; III 62.

Margrave. *Margreve* n.m. The count and judge of a march. III 53.

Marriage. *Ewe* n.f. *elich* adj. A marriage that resulted from a contract between the families (or guardians of the betrothed). The consent of the bridal couple and their union completed the contract, and at that point the husband assumed guardianship of his wife. W does not use the noun for marriage but instead contains circumlocutions for taking a wife or a husband. I 3, 45 (*HRG*, 2, c. 810–15).

Master. *Herr* n.m. The owner or master who had tutelage and other control over his serfs and day laborers. I 9, 22; II 32, 38; III 6. See "lord."

Military equipment. *Hergewete* n.n. A man's military equipment, including weapons, charger, and field equipment. It could only devolve on the man's closest male relative. I 22, 27, 28; III 16.

Military shield. *Herschilt* n.m. Originally the order of military shields, or escutcheons, consisted of those men who were eligible to bear such arms and provide military service. Gradually the shields came to designate the feudal ranks distinguished by their arms. These arms symbolized the right to feudal enfeoffment. From an originally three-tiered system of king, crown vassals, and their men, the levels expanded. Eike lists the seven levels of noble status that became the model for most of the German territories. We know this because his hierarchy was retained in the other lawbooks. *Herschilt* as a legal designation brings with it the privilege or legal ability of holding feudal tenure because it fulfills the requirement of military service. A distinction is made between legal rights and one's place in the order of military shields because one may lower himself in the ranks by becoming a vassal of his peer (III 65) (*HRG*, 2, c. 1732–34). I 3, 25, 27; II 22; III 59, 71; IV 1, 2, 21, 22, 83.

Ministerial. *Dinstman* n. *Dinstlute* pl. A person in someone's service, mostly of servile status. Frequently, the term refers to the unfree knights in the service of a lord, but where the context does not provide additional information, it is difficult to determine if W uses the term consistently for ministerials. For the plural form see I 52; III 43, 72; in the singular I have translated it as "ministerial" (I 38; II 42; III 19) or "an unfree person" (III 42); some occurrences are ambiguous (III 41, 72); a clear distinction between serviles and ministerials is in III 81. See "*Schöffe*."

Morning gift. *Morgengabe* n.f. A gift given by a knight to his new wife the morning after the marriage was consummated. This gift was given to her in sole ownership, or it may also have included whatever was bestowed on the bride as part of the marriage agreement. She does not, however, gain control of her morning gift until her husband dies (III 38) (Rummel, 148) or upon divorce (III 74). The widow's right to her morning gift was not questioned, so we may conclude that the gift provided her with critical economic support. I 20, 21, 24; II 21 (*HRG*, 3, c. 678).

Oath. *Eit* n.m. A binding statement or promise sworn with one hand on a reliquary as part of a legal procedure. II 48; III 11, 54.

Oathhelper. *Gezugen selb sibende*. To prove with seven others. An oathhelper was a compurgator, one who strengthened a person's oath by swearing to his upright standing but not to the content of his oath. The text has no precise term for the concept; it is normally rendered by the phrase *selb* plus the number of oathhelpers required in the given case. I 8; II 34; III 5, 39.

Outlawry, *Achte* n.f. Pertains to a fugitive from the law. In general, it was like attainder to the extent that it meant the withdrawal of rights so that anyone could openly pursue and capture the person outlawed. Rights were usually withdrawn before judgment but were also withdrawn at the time of, and as a result of, sentencing because the rights of a person had to be withdrawn before the sentence could be executed. However, outlawry was more significant than the modern concept of attainder because the malefactors often escaped before a trial could be held, or a verdict reached, or a sentence executed. In these situations, the court revoked or limited a person's legal capacity. The accused could be seized and brought to trial on sight. He was, however, still able to appear and testify on his behalf to release himself from outlawry and stand trial. Outlawry was necessary in times when court hearings and sentences were not always enforceable. There were three types of outlawry. *Vorvestung* was local outlawry, limited to the judge's judicial district. *Acht* was royal or imperial outlawry and extended to the entire empire. The outlawed person had a year and a day to release himself by appearing in court. If he failed to do so, his outlawry became permanent, called *obiracht*, with the result that the person had no legal protection whatsoever, and all his property was confiscated. I 38; III 16, 17, 18, 23, 24, 34 (Janz, 264–67). See "outlawry," "attainder."

Outlawry. *Vorvestung* n.f. Limited, or regional, outlawry because it was limited to the jurisdiction of the specific court that outlawed a person. The outlawed person maintained some legal capacity (i.e., the right to appear and testify before a court on his own behalf), but he could be captured and brought forcibly to court, where he could neither ransom nor appeal the verdict (especially in the case of capital crime). I 64; II 4; III 16, 17, 18, 23, 24, 34.

Pardon. *Losunge* n.f. A release from prison or a sentence bestowed by the king. III 43. See "ransom."

Peace days. *Gebundene tage* pl. Binding or peace days. Specified days and periods of time were set aside as peaceful or nonviolent days. They included the major feast days (Easter, Pentecost, Assumption, All Saints, Christmas), Sundays, Wednesdays, often the entire period from Thursday or Friday to Sunday, and certain longer periods (Advent, Lent, Holy Week). Market days were also peace days. Exactly which days were fixed varied regionally. If a crime was committed on a peace day, then, in addition to the type of crime itself, the deed also counted as a breach of peace, making the fine or penalty that much greater. All legal actions except summary trials and oaths of truce were prohibited on peace days (II 10, 11, 66) (*HRG*, 1, c. 1424–26). Heinrich IV produced the earliest imperial decree concerning the so-called "truce of God" (1085), upon which the definition found in *Sachsenspiegel* versions builds. (A translation of Heinrich's text is found in Henderson, 208–11.)

Plaintiff. *Cleger* n.m. The person who brings a suit or charges against someone and prosecutes the case. II 25, 42, 72; III 18.

Possession. *Ledicliche gewer* n.f. Primary, unmediated right of possession to a property. II 57.

Possession. *Gewer* n.f. The right of possession to a property; legally established rightful investiture and, consequently, possession or occupancy.

It also means "in someone's control or care" (III 91; IV 66) (Ishikawa 81–82). I 15, 20, 32; IV 36.

Possession. *Rechte gewer* n.f. Right of possession. II 44; IV 6.

Proof. *Gezug* n.m./n. Testimony or evidence of a witness validated by an oath in court. II 33; III 4, 24, 64.

Proof. *Urkunde* n.f. Information confirmed by a spoken or written notification; knowledge based on written or oral evidence. II 54, 61; III 5, 42; IV 22.

Prosecute. *Beklagen* v. To bring suit; to bring to trial and to an ultimate conclusion. II 17, 19; III 9, 86.

Prove. *Behelden, Behalden* v. To prove a case in court, to win a suit (I 4; II 42; III 83); to establish the validity of a claim or charges made; to establish legal grounds for a suit. I 15, 22, 34; III 21, 54; IV 14, 15, 22, 44, 69, 74, 80.

Prove. *Beredin* v. To substantiate with an oath. I 34; III 84; IV 38.

Prove. *Gezugen* v. To prove a case with witnesses or other evidence substantiated by an oath; to convict. I 8; II 41, IV 13.

Ransom. *Losen* v. To redeem or free oneself from a sentence of corporal punishment, even a death sentence, by a payment of money. I 64; II 14; III 56.

Realm. *Riche* n.n. Empire, realm. As a collective noun, it refers to the empire in the jurisdictional meaning of dominion. It is ambiguous because it frequently refers to the emperor himself as the corporate body, and thus the terms for emperor (*keiser*), empire, and realm are interchangeable. Just as often, however, a passage shows the "realm" actually performing an act that only an individual person can perform on behalf of the whole. I 29, 38, 40; III, 53, 54, 64.

Recover property. *Anevangen* v. The legal meaning builds on the literal, "to seize or grasp." By grasping a piece of property, one initiates a legal claim to ownership of that property. This was the remedy if someone found his own goods in the possession of another. It also means simply to initiate a suit (II, 33). In its strict sense, it indicates the initiation of legal action for claim of property in place of a summons. This procedure did not bring charges against the person in possession of the goods because the possessor could prove that he acquired them legally or even prove original ownership. II 34; III 4 (*HRG*, 1, 159–63).

Red-handed deed. *Hanthafte tat* n.f. A criminal act in which the marks of the crime identified the perpetrator and made a conviction possible. II 9, 33; III 9, 78.

Redeem. *Losen* v. To redeem a rent due in kind (especially dues on animals) by making a money payment (II 48); to redeem a pawn or pledge by making the appropriate money payment. I 24; IV 74. See "ransom."

Release. *Erlassen, Irlasen* v. To release someone from court duty or other responsibility. III 56.

Renew. *Volge* n.f, *volgen* v. In feudal law, it primarily refers to the renewal or confirmation of a feudal contract with a succeeding lord, particularly when one's own lord died or failed in his duty. It also entails the right to pass the fief on to one's heir (III 14). This privilege applies to the standard feudal contract (*HRG*, 2, c. 1696–98). III 63; IV 1, 4, 5, 10, 26, 30, 59, 81. See "fief," "fief in reversion," "seize a fief."

Repudiate. *Enzcagen* v. To reject or renounce the feudal relationship of fealty and homage between lord and vassal. Either party could repudiate the other, but possession of the fief was not relinquished unless both parties renounced it. IV 20, 46, 82.

Right of use. *Anegevelle* n.n. The process by which a property or right of use was transferred to someone either as inheritance or according to feudal law, which limited it to right of use. It is different from a woman's life estate because right of use is of limited, fixed duration. II 58; IV 28, 29, 30, 78. See "life estate."

Royal judicial authority. *Ban* n.m. The ruler could delegate his authority, such as his judicial jurisdiction of the superior court to the nobles. It was invested like any fief but could be extended only to the third level below the king. I 57, 71; II 13; III 52, 53, 64; IV 77 (*HRG,* 1, c. 308–10). See "judge."

Royal jurisdiction. *Ban* n.m. The king's territorial jurisdiction. He dispensed over specified areas or territories in several ways. He could either ban certain people from an area (e.g., hunting preserves) or give designated people certain privileges within an area (e.g., monopoly on a mill). II 61.

Schöffe n.m. *Schöffen* pl. Normally referred to as lay judges, jurors, or judgment finders, these people were roughly equivalent to the doomsman in old English law. *Schöffen* functioned primarily but not solely as jurors in a court of law. They rendered judgments while a case is being pled and were also responsible for the final decision in a case. Hence their work required extensive knowledge of the law of the territory. In Saxony, the task of the *Schöffe* eventually became a hereditary office in the count's court, which normally met under the king's jurisdiction. The *Schöffen* came from land-owning families that were long-time residents of the county and, according to W, belonged to the ranks of the fifth level of knighthood (I 3) (Planck, 99). The symbol of the office was a chair (*Schöffenstuhl*) because judgments were reached while seated (II, 12; III, 69). The *Schöffe* passed his privilege on to his first son or, lacking a son, to his closest and oldest agnate male relation (III 26). The actual status of *Schöffen* has been determined. Kroeschell and others have claimed they were previously freemen owning hereditary lands who became ministerials, thus losing their free status. However, they did retain their freemen privileges, one of which was the right to be a judgment finder (Kroeschell, "Rechtsaufzeichnung," 359–61). *Schöffen* were necessary in the higher courts, beginning with the count's court held under the king's judicial authority. The qualifications for the *Schöffen* were essentially the same as for the other judgment finders, but they also had to be full landowners, which means they owned nontaxable, inherited land of at least three hides (III, 65). Their class was called *schöffenbarfrei*, precisely because they had duty-free land at their disposal (Planck, 99) and the freedom or privilege to become *Schöffen*. Within the rural districts, the *Schöffen* class became the measure for full and complete legal capacity in territorial law because this class had so many legal privileges and duties, whereas other groups had fewer. Consequently, in a court of law, the *Schöffe*'s words (i.e., his application of the law and his spoken judgment) were worth more than any person's who was not his equal because the individuals in this office had the right to determine a judgment concerning any man (II 13). On the other hand, no one could reach a judgment concerning a *Schöffe* who was not his equal (III 19), and only a person of equal status could challenge his judgment. In the judicial process, only a single *Schöffe* was called upon at any one time to make a ruling, but no mention is made of a requisite number of *Schöffen* in a hearing. Thus they did not function like a jury in any modern sense. I 3, 51; II 13, 41; III 18, 45, 64. See "judgment finder," "ministerial."

Schultheiss n.m. The count's appointed court officer and judge (III 61). His presence and rulings were necessary for holding a regular court session. The judge specifically required the *Schultheiss*'s ruling to convene the session before the proceedings could begin (I 59). Witnesses swore before the *Schultheiss* instead of the judge if the monetary value of the decision was high (II 22) (Planck, 7). In Saxony, however, the singular and primary function of the *Schultheiss* was to be a check on the system. He was judge over the count when a complaint was made against the judge claiming that he refused to carry out the law. Only in this special case did the *Schultheiss* have power over life and limb because he was otherwise not invested with the king's juridical authority (III 52).

The *Schultheiss* was also judge at the level of the second class of freemen, which included the tenants and sharecroppers. He judged in small cases concerning family land, but no criminal deeds, and only when the case was carried over from the regular court. Whatever was not settled at the count's court was adjudicated by the *Schultheiss* at a session six weeks later (I 2; III 45, 64) (Planck, 8–9). In addition, he initiated legal proceedings and prosecuted every breach of peace, damage to property, and other transgressions of the law. Only one *Schultheiss* was allowed in the count's jurisdiction (I 2). He was selected from the free landholders born in the area who were totally unblemished in their legal capacity, and he received certain rents for his services (II 12). In addition, any plot of land less than three hides in size possessed by sharecroppers without issue devolved on him (*HRG*, 4, c. 1519–21, 1702–3).

Seize. *Bevronen* v. It was the bailiff's duty upon the judgment of the court to detain a person lacking property or seize a person's real property with the purpose of bringing it within the custody of the court to ensure satisfaction of judgment. This meant that the property could be sold by the court in due course of law to pay the judge's fine. The person whose property was marked with the sign of seizure (a cross) had a year and a day to make restitution. If this was not done, then what was seized was immediately sold. II 41; III 56. See "attach."

Seize a fief. *Vorteilen* v. When property held in fief was sequestrated or seized by a court decision in feudal law, one did not lose the right to a fief; one lost possession and right of use (IV 43). The lord then retained the property uncultivated for a year and a day to allow the fiefholder to rectify the problem and regain possession. IV 8, 14, 20, 43, 70, 78, 82. See "clear," "fief."

Sell. *Verussern* v. Alienate; dispose of property. II 62. See "alienate," "possession," "transfer."

Sentence. *Gericht* n.n. The final outcome of a criminal hearing; the penalty handed down or required for a specific crime. II 14.

Servant. *Knecht* n.m. A boy or man in general; a free or unfree servant; apprentice; soldier; but certainly someone in a subordinate service relationship since the terms *herr* and *knecht* form an opposition. In clearly specified instances it may also refer to a page in service of a knight. I 20; II 13; III 6 (*HRG*, 2, c. 895–96; *DWB*, 5).

Sharecroppers. *Birgelden* n.pl. Free tenants who paid rents in kind and attended the same court as the *lantsesen*. III 45. See "tenant."

Spokesman. *Vorspreche* n.m. Spokesman; speaker; a person who acts as pleader for another in court. Each litigant needed someone to speak on his behalf in both territorial and feudal court. I 59, 60, 61; II 63; IV 9.

Successor. *Erbe* n.m. The person or persons who inherited the estate of the deceased. I 6, 15, 28; II 21; III 78.

Successor. *Lenerbe* n.m. The successor to a fief in feudal law. I 9; II 21, 58; IV 5.

Summons. *Vorladung* n.m. A call or summons to a court session designating the time and, when necessary, the place of the next court session to be held. The summons was given by the bailiff to all members of the judiciary and gave the litigants time to prepare their case. I 41, 62; III 5.

Sworn peace. *Geswormer vride* or *Gelobter vride* n.m. A peace agreed upon and supported by an oath. The feuding parties could do this voluntarily, or the court could also force a peace agreement on parties, who then had to swear peace or incur a penalty. II 71; III 8, 64 (*HRG*, 1, c. 1288).

Tenant. *Lantsese* n.m. A free tenant leaseholder; a free peasant in the fourteenth century who owned no land but could lease it from a landowner for three-year periods. Multiples of three were used for the lease because of the three-field agriculture (Rösener, 166–67). The tenant was free to move and settle anywhere, so the community tended to consider him an outsider. II 16; III 45, 72.

Tenant. *Phlechafte* n.m. A free tenant on the king's land who paid ground rent to the count but was under the king's wardship. This group of peasants developed during the colonization of Saxony. They passed on their land to their heirs but could not transfer the land in any way. The bailiff was selected from among their number. I 2; III 46.

Territorial law. *Lantrecht* n.n. The land or territorial law pertaining specifically to rural regions. Books I-III of this translation. I 3, 4.

Thirtieth. *Drisigister* n.m. Celebrated on the thirtieth day after the funeral, this mass signified the end of the mourning period, and the time when the heir or heirs were allowed to take possession of the inheritance. I 22; III 15 (*HRG*, 1 c. 785–87). See "inheritance," "food supplies."

Transfer. *Uflasen* v. To convey, cede or transfer property. I 9, 45, II 24; IV 8, 49, 78. See "alienate," "possession," "sell."

Truce. *Orvede*, *Urvede* n.f. An oath of truce; abjurance of all vengeance. It was a promise of truce by the injured party who abjured revenge.

Usually both parties swore, and the oath was valid even when sworn under duress. I 8; III 42.

Village headman. *Burmester, Burmeister* n.m. The primary administrative official of the village. He directed the village commune, an entity that combined the functions of both a jurisdictional community and a neighborhood association. Its authority extended to the fields as well (Rösener, 164–65). The village headman made decisions in accordance with the majority of the local peasants in a village council (II 55). He also represented the village in important legal and administrative affairs, and in its relations with the outside world. I 2, 55, 68; III 56.

Villager. *Gebur* n.m. Normally translated as "peasant," it really means "community member," "neighbor." These people were the residents of a village and worked the fields. The term may have included both free and servile men and women. I 13, 20, 68; III 44, 65, 80, 86; IV 44. See "country people."

Weistümer. n.pl. A collection of dooms or judgments based on local practice and intended for local use. Based on oral practice, they contain strictly oral formulations in unsystematic arrangement, referring to specific legal cases in the form of question and answer. The written collection began in the eleventh century. They are important because they provide information about actual legal practice.

Wergeld. *Wergelt* n.n. The value of a man in terms of a criminal tariff. In W (and other *Sachsenspiegel* manuscripts) it specifically means a compensation for homicide or damages and can therefore be applied to animals and levied according to wergeld tables. III 46, 47, 48, 49, 52.

Witness. *Gezug* n.m. A person who gives testimony under oath. I 9; II 22; III 54; IV 22.

Woman. *Wip* n.n. A married female adult; wife; used in contrast to *maget*, meaning "an unmarried female." In comparison to *vrouwe*, *wip* and *maget* are used throughout the text. See "woman."

Woman. *Vrouwe*, *Frouwe* n.f. A female adult; a married woman. In contrast to *wip, vrouwe* implies noble status, especially in a courtly context (IV 81), but it is not at all certain that the distinction between the two terms was consistently made. The plural form always means "women" in general. I 20, 21, 24, 46; II 16, 21; III 75, 76.

Woman's personal belongings. *Gerade* n.f. A woman's dowry and personal belongings; her personal household items and clothing, which devolved on her closest female relation on the cognate side (I 24, 27; III 74). After 1400, city laws contained catalogs of *gerade* (*HRG*, 1, c. 1527–30).

Notes

Introduction

1. When I refer to the Wolfenbüttel manuscript and this translation, the Roman numerals indicate books I-IV, and the Arabic numbers, the chapters.

2. The slightly earlier *Mühlhäuser Reichsrechtsbuch* (1223–1231) containing the code of that imperial city is much more limited in scope.

3. The *Sachsenspiegel* manuscripts describe a somewhat timeless Saxony that is not historically exact. For example, they are written as if Westphalia were part of Saxon territory and as if the Duchy of Saxony were still intact. The fourteenth-century manuscripts do not clarify or correct this image, nor do they mention the Duchy of Braunschweig-Lüneburg (Lieberwirth, *Entstehung*, 9, Theuerkauf, 415–16).

4. On the importance of Magdeburg as legal center, see the section "Context and Reception" below; see also Johanek 409–11.

5. According to Karl Kroeschell, it is now accepted that those designated as *Schöffenbarfreie* were originally free nobles who retained the right to their allodial land, and their function as *Schöffen* when they became ministerials. Their status in the *Sachsenspiegel* manuscripts appears to be elevated above those who are ministerials only; "Rechtsaufzeichnung," 360–61.

6. Lines 274–75. According to Ruth Schmidt-Wiegand, we have no reason to doubt the statement in the text that the lawbook was initially written in Latin even though none of the general law survives (*Cimelien*, 197). Eike's Latin version of the feudal law is thought to survive in the *Auctor vetus de beneficiis*. See Kroeschell, *Deutsche* vol. 2, 424, and his longer discussion in "Rechtsaufzeichnung," 352. Others are less inclined to attribute the *Auctor* to Eike because no positive proof exists (Johanek 405; Schmidt-Wiegand, "Sprache und Stil," 203).

7. Lines 97–280 of the rhymed preface are found in the earliest manuscripts and are therefore considered to have been written by Eike. The rhymed preface is not in the Wolfenbüttel manuscript on which the present translation is based. See "Choice of Text" in the introduction.

8. Most scholarly discussions about Eike's reason for writing the lawbook cite the rapid change in customary law and view Eike's work as an effort to preserve tradition (Kroeschell, *Rechtsgeschichte,* 267). Rolf Lieberwirth, for example, points out that many kinds of specialized courts with overlapping jurisdiction were proliferating; he concludes that customary laws had become so complicated that it became necessary to fix them in a written version (*Entstehung,* 34).

9. For a complete summary of the manuscript transmission, see Schmidt-Wiegand, "Überlieferungs- und Editionsprobleme," 66–69.

10. Some novellas were already added by Eike in his second German version, and they continued to accrue until the fourth German version (Homeyer, *Rechtsbücher*, 6). The apparent loose organization of the chapters may be a result of added novellas; see, for example, IV 76.

11. For evidence of citations from Wernher von Elmendorf and Freidank's *Bescheidenheit* in the rhymed preface, see Eckhardt, *Lndr*, 44–46.

12. Herbert Kolb has shown that Eike's discussion of bondage is formulated as a theological *quaestio* employed to work out contradictions within the faith by rational means (300–303).

13. Criticism of bondage was not new: similar ideas can be found in the writings of the church fathers, for example, and are also consistent with Gratian. According to Lieberwirth, the argument put forth by Eike in the *Sachsenspiegel* is particularly memorable in its clarity and its unique placement within a custumal (*Entstehung* 29; see also Kroeschell, "Rechtswirklichkeit," 6). It certainly dares to point out falsity in contemporary legal practice and also questions the value of accepting custom without rational questioning. Herbert Kolb's genetic and structural study demonstrates that Eike's theological argument on law fits the genre of mirror literature, the intention of which is not merely to present customs in practice but rather to present the ideal that fulfills God's purpose (309–10). See also Kisch, *Bible*, 133–46.

14. The genitive in the original formulation denotes possession but also defines the group: they are Saxons because they live according to Saxon laws.

15. References to *Saxon Mirror* indicate the present translation.

16. Additional information on the influence of Honorius can be found in Ignor, 197, Köbler, "Vorstufen," 101; and Drescher, 385–91.

17. W lacks the rhymed preface.

18. Given that the text grounds Law first in the Old Covenant and then in the New, I interpret this statement to mean that Law comes from God first, and that justice is achieved once the law, in this case God's law, is in place. Gerhard Dilcher agrees saying of Eike's statement, *Dahinter aber steht Gott als Ursprung aller Schöpfung und damit auch des Rechtes* [Behind all of this is God as the source of all creation and therefore of Law] ("Ursprung," 151). Furthermore, when the second prologue states that God is the beginning and end of all things, he is clearly the ultimate lawgiver who will judge mankind at the Last Judgment. In contrast, Ulrich Drescher sees the phrase as referring to God as judge and therefore representing justice, but he bases his interpretation more on the image in the Wolfenbüttel manuscript than on the text, which is ambiguous (98).

19. Ulrich Drescher even attributes an eschatological dimension to the mirror metaphor as a reminder that man must account for his sins at the Last Judgment (20–21).

20. All citations of the *Sachsenspiegel* text are taken from the Wolfenbüttel manuscript unless otherwise noted.

21. Alexander Ignor has carefully studied Eike's concept of *recht* and all the meanings and connotations of the word family; for prepositional phrases see 136–49.

22. For a discussion of typical marks of orality in the *Sachsenspiegel* texts, see Dobozy.

23. Of course, not all courts were alike. The courts of the territorial princes and the royal court made use of their chanceries and tended to commit all types of information to parchment; this practice was not so in the count's court or the local judge's court. The clerk of the royal court was explicitly directed to keep written records (see the "Imperial Landpeace of Mainz," fol. 3r, in this volume).

24. Once the claim is made that the lawbook is not exhaustive, it follows that each subsequent copy and redaction of the *Sachsenspiegel* does not necessarily present reliably the judicial system's legal practices of its period. Nevertheless, one may dismiss neither the adaptive potential nor the normative effect of the several hundred manuscripts copied and amended with novellas over a three-hundred-year period. Although many texts were reworked because legal rules changed, nevertheless, the various versions were read as an authoritative guide.

25. Recent scholarship questions Kern's thesis that long-standing tradition legitimizes and fixes customary law (Schulze, 9).

26. This designation was first suggested by Kroeschel *Rechtsgeschichte*, vol. 2:84).

27. See Dilcher, 27. According to Gerhard Theuerkauf, the *Saxon Mirror* as we know it developed after Saxony had been converted to Christianity. Consequently, the Saxon lawbook incorporated both canon and Germanic law (417). The *Sachsenspiegel* manuscripts describe a system of ecclesiastical courts already in place (I 2, 5; II 14) and a reliance on Christian relics in the practice of oath taking.

28. For information on the special privileges created in clearance lands, see "Scope and Content" in the introduction.

29. According to Hans Hirsch, the local judge may well have been acquiring greater jurisdiction in the fourteenth century (Hirsch, *Gerichtsbarkeit*, 217). If his jurisdiction was changing, it would explain the discrepancies in the *Sachsenspiegel* texts (I 57, 71; III 52).

30. The text explicitly states that since a homicide can also occur without the shedding of blood, trials regarding such killings are also assigned to the superior court (I 68).

31. To what extent the *Mirror*'s description corresponds to actual practice has not yet been determined because, according to Reiner Schulze, scholars are still unsure what the exact procedures were for determining a judgment (16). In contrast, Kroeschell is more confident and points to a number of proven correspondences between practice and the paragraphs in the *Mirror* ("Rechtswirklichkeit," 4–5). The obvious conclusion is that each chapter must be considered and corroborated with external evidence separately to determine the exact congruence of lawbook and practice.

32. The princes of the realm who were directly responsible to the king certainly had their own jurisdiction. Nevertheless, the territorial law appears to speak only of appeals from the count's superior court going directly to the king (II 13) even though the text rarely specifies the higher court to which the appeal had to go.

33. For a discussion of the relationship of the Latin and German versions of the imperial landpeaces, see Schmidt-Wiegand, "Recht und Gesetz," 157–66, and Ursula Schulze, 35–42, 195.

34. Heinrich IV produced the earliest imperial decree concerning the so-called

"truce of God" (1085) designating fixed peace days. The *Sachsenspiegel* versions build on this and subsequent peace ordinances. See "peace days" in glossary.

35. On the different types of outlawry, see "outlawry, attainder" in glossary.

36. The *Sachsenspiegel* texts and other medieval lawbooks consider the work of a hired champion who fights for payment in a trial by combat a despised occupation, but an occupation nonetheless (I 38). See Danckert, 9–15.

37. Scholars like Hirsch and Bar who used these modern concepts to discuss the medieval lawbooks because they sought the roots and origins of modern German law forgot that these concepts do not explain how and why this transition took place. Current scholarship is now reevaluating the terms and has not yet turned to an analysis of the transition itself (Hirsch, *Gerichtsbarkeit*, 212–20; Bar, 99–101; Dilcher, "Ursprung," 153–55).

38. The concept of *Rodungsfreiheit* has been used to refer to these colonists, who supposedly received manumission for their labor. However, it is now understood that "freedom" in the context of colonization in clearance lands can only be used to refer to a gradation of privileges and rights won by peasants in some areas but not in others (Rösener, 228). See H. K. Schulze, 549, and *HRG* 4, c. 1098–1100.

39. See Schmidt-Wiegand, "Mitteldeutsche Bilderhandschriften" 95–98.

40. For additional information on women, see Altenkirch and Kuntschke; and Rummel.

41. For an exhaustive explanation of the uniquely German method of calculating degrees of kinship, see Hüpper, "Ehe, Familie, Verwandtschaft."

42. For information on the reception of the *Sachsenspiegel* in the east, see Friedrich Ebel on Silesia; and Piirainen and Waßer on Poland.

43. See Gönczi on the application of *Sachsenspiegel* texts in Hungary.

44. Eckhardt's precise dating of 1225–35 is now considered by Kroeschell to be based on inadequate information since we do not have Eike's text. For all we know, Eike's text may have contained sections written at different times. Since the extant manuscripts list the electoral princes in terms first used in documents at the election of Heinrich VII (1220), Kroeschell suggests that Eike may have already begun his text at that time ("Rechtswirklichkeit," 3).

45. See Rummel, 40; see also *Weistümer* in glossary.

46. For more information on changes in terminology during the first hundred years after Eike, see Schmidt-Wiegand, "Verhältnis," 7–12.

47. For an example, see the terms in glossary.

48. According to Rösener the significant parallels between privileges of free peasants and city dwellers (230) could well have induced cities to copy a *Sachsenspiegel* text.

49. Johann von Buch (1300-after 1356) was court judge (*judex generalis curie*) for Margrave Ludwig of Brandenburg. For a short summary of his work on *Sachsenspiegel* glosses, see *VL* 4, c. 551–59; and *HRG* 1, c. 526–27; for a longer discussion see Lieberwirth, *Glosse*.

50. Bertelsmeier-Kierst suggests that the very first illustrated manuscript in this hypothetical genealogy should probably be dated much earlier than 1300 because the ruler pictures in H reflect the earlier method of depicting the jurisdiction of the

ruler by using his image. This changes and by the early fourteenth century the image of the ruler authenticates the text, pp. 387–9.

51. This current interpretation stems from Ruth Schmidt-Wiegand and her collaborators, who have studied the images of the illuminated manuscripts in great detail. See especially Schmidt-Wiegand, "Text und Bild" and "Zeugen"; Hüpper, "Bildersprache"; Kroeschell, "Licht," 243.

52. See Schmidt-Wiegand, "Überlieferungs- und Editionsprobleme," 63–81.

53. Schmidt-Wiegand ("mitteldeutsche Bilderhandsschriften") outlines the terminological complexity and variation in the legal language of the illuminated manuscripts that are leveled in Eckhardt's edition.

54. Schmidt-Wiegand, supported by other philologists, expresses strong criticism but also some praise of Eckhardt's text "Von der autornahen zur überlieferungskritischen Ausgabe," 14–15. However, she also has pointed out that the only reason his text is cited so frequently is because it appeared in the Monumenta Germaniae Historica series, whereas far better editions of important, single manuscripts (by Borchling, Holmberg, Homeyer) have gone unnoticed ("Überlieferungs- und Editionsprobleme," 70–71). In contrast, legal historians tend to accept Eckhardt's reconstruction (Kroeschell, "Licht," 237).

55. "The Lineage of the Lords" was not originally part of Eike's text and was added later. It appears in a variety of places in the manuscripts, sometimes in the beginning and occasionally at the end. The names listed have been verified with place names and family names of the late thirteenth and early fourteenth century (Lieberwirth, "Vorrede," 17).

Imperial Landpeace of Mainz

1. A product of the imperial chancery, this landpeace is thought to have been originally formulated in Latin, as were all its predecessors, but this has not yet been proven satisfactorily. See Janz for the debate concerning the priority of the German version ("Reichslandfriede," 246–48) and U. Schulze (35–42). In any case, the German translation was the better-known version in the thirteenth and fourteenth centuries, partly because it is included in several *Sachsenspiegel* manuscripts. Since it differs from the Latin in terminology, and the content varies in sequence, it can be read independently from the original. The Latin text with German translation is available in *Quellenverzeichnis*, translated by Weinrich. See Janz also on the function of the Imperial Landpeace of Mainz in the illuminated manuscripts ("Reichslandfriede"). My paragraph divisions follow the formal divisions indicated in W by rubrication.

2. I render the phrase *wir sezcin unde gebiten* as "we establish and hdecree." Such doublets, typical of German oral style, and not a direct translation from the Latin, are a sign of the stylistic and lexicographic differences between the Latin and German versions of this text (Schmidt-Wiegand, "Recht und Gesetz," 158–59). In her comparative study of Latin and German imperial documents, Schulze maintains that the syntax and wording of each of the two languages demonstrate relative independence and therefore appear to have had limited influence on each other

(69). None of the German syntax is copied from or adapted from Latin syntax, but this conclusion does not exclude more subtle influences such as preference for certain existing German syntactic structures over others (194–95). Janz discusses this as well ("Reichslandfriede," 247).

3. These "loyal men" are the princes; that is, the immediate vassals of the king. I translate *man* as "man" in order to indicate the ambiguity of the original term that can refer to a "male person" or a "vassal."

4. See "oathhelpers" in glossary.

5. *seintbaren mannen*: literally, "men who have full legal capacity in an ecclesiastical court." In context, however, the phrase simply indicates legal capacity in any court. See "legal capacity" in glossary.

6. The father-son conflict described in great detail at the beginning of the German text occurs in the middle of the Latin version. The German sequence is not surprising if we consider that in the year this landpeace was promulgated Emperor Friedrich II had had to return to Germany to arrest his son, Heinrich VII, and have him imprisoned for life for anti-imperial activities (Janz, "Reichslandfriede," 253).

7. *alse hivor gescribin ist*: "as was written earlier." This phrase reflects written legal style. Not surprisingly, the formula is typical for a chancery where written records were the norm. However, this German text contains both literate and oral characteristics throughout, in contrast to the highly oral nature of the *Saxon Mirror* (e.g., I 20, 33) (Schmidt-Wiegand, "Recht und Gesetz," 162).

8. *der selbe ist erlos unde rechtelos ewiclichen*: "he is forever without any legal rights and protection" (I 50, 51). See "legal incapacity" in the glossary.

9. *dinstman*: can be a "servant" or "ministerial" but refers to ministerials consistently in the landpeace; see "ministerial" in glossary.

10. *selbe dritte*: "self three" refers to the litigant and his two oathhelpers who swear an oath with him (see I 8).

11. *achte*: "imperial outlawry," but here "attainder" is meant because it is a total revocation of all legal rights after conviction (I 38); see "outlawry" and "attainder" in glossary.

12. The first folio of the manuscript is written across the entire page but the remainder of the landpeace is written in double columns. I refer to the manuscript text by folio number, recto or verso side, and left or right column.

13. *dem richter sin recht*: literally "to the judge his right." It refers to all the rights and privileges enjoyed by the judge. In this context, it specifically indicates the judge's right to collect the court fine, normally called *gewette*. See "court fine" in glossary.

14. *gebur*: "peasant" or "villager;" see "villager" in glossary.

15. *undirgenos*: "a person of subordinate rank."

16. *widersagin*: "to declare a feud against someone."

17. *scintbaren luten*: "people with full legal capacity in an ecclesiastical court."

18. *zcolle*: "toll," the amount paid for use of a road, etc. Here it specifically refers to the right and responsibility of maintaining a structure and collecting a toll.

19. *richten*: here "to sentence;" it can also mean "to try a case;" see "judge" (v.) in glossary.

20. *sine lute*: "his men, vassals;" that is, those under his control.

21. *lantlute*: "residents of the rural areas;" see "country people" in glossary.

22. *hantvride*: "a sworn peace" designates a cessation of armed conflict agreed to by two feuding parties and secured legally by a handshake. This term is not used in W. See "sworn peace" in glossary.

23. *das her im sins rechtis gehelfe*: literally "that he help him to [achieve] justice."

24. The penalty for this refusal to cooperate is loss of a hand; *so si he dem keiser der hant schuldig*: "then he owes the emperor his hand." "To owe someone something" is a typical way of expressing a punishment in the *Saxon Mirror*.

25. The term used here is *gericht*, "a court of law," but it also means the judicial authority to preside over a court of law, a "judgeship;" see "court of law," "judge," and "jurisdiction" in glossary.

26. The term is *buse*: "compensation payment" or "punitive fine"; see "compensation" in Glossary.

27. The term for these people, *phalburgere*, refers to those citizens of the castle or town who lived just outside the gates. Because they saw themselves as citizens of the town, they claimed the same privileges. The nobility disliked the practice because it siphoned people away from their influence and away from the rural communities (*HRG*, 3, c. 652–57).

28. *lant* in the singular refers to a territorial principality or duchy and not the entire breadth of the German kingdom.

29. *hoferichter*: the "imperial" or "royal" judge. The judgeship was instituted by Frederick II, and his Imperial Landpeace is our first record of the position. The emperor appointed the judge, who traveled with the emperor throughout the German lands of the empire and represented him in the imperial court first called *Hofgericht* and later *Reichshofgericht* (*HRG*, 4, c. 615–26; 2, c. 206–9).

30. *gericht*: here, "judgment."

31. *us den schulden kumen*: "to be cleared of an accusation."

32. The shift to the first-person plural pronoun is significant because it further distinguishes the jurisdictions of the king's judge and the king's own court. The passage also reveals that the royal court systematically recorded the hearings and decisions in writing and to what purpose it maintained those records. In contrast, the *Saxon Mirror* mentions almost no recourse to written records at the village or even count's courts (Schmidt-Wiegand, "Recht und Gesetz," 162–63).

33. *unde nemelichen allen boten, di wir selbe nicht gehes vorriten mugen*: in *Facsimile W* Schmidt-Wiegand corrects *boten* ("messengers") to *luten* ("people") which makes better sense. Nevertheless, W contains a more complete text of the Mainz landpeace than the other illuminated manuscripts, and I have used it for this translation (Schmidt-Wiegand, "Recht und Gesetz," 159).

34. See I 2, n. 8.

35. The term is *vogt*; see "advocate" in glossary.

36. *ubir zcuget*: "to convict with the testimony of witnesses."

37. *ubir redit*: "to convict."

38. This section is not part of the Mainz landpeace nor is it part of the earliest versions of the *Sachsenspiegel*, but it was added later to several manuscripts, often somewhere in the front but sometimes in the back. See Lieberwirth's discussion of this genealogy ("Vorrede," particularly p. 17).

39. The manuscript reads "*heinrich iudas der voyt. albrecht von spandouwe*" with a dot between *voyt* and *albrecht* usually separating the elements in the list and here, separating Albrecht from the designation *vogt* ("advocate"). Attributing advocacy to Heinrich is consistent with standard syntax. In contrast, Schmidt-Wiegand based her edition on Homeyer's text and amended it to: "*Heinrich Judas [von Snetlinge], der voit Albrecht von Spandouwe*" thereby designating not Heinrich but Albrecht as the advocate.

40. *kint*: "squire" (Lexer I, c. 1575–76).

41. *vanlen*: a "fief which makes the holder directly subordinate to the king"; see "banner estate" in glossary.

42. *herschilt*: "the feudal ranks and hierarchy of the nobility" (I 3; IV 1); see "military shield" in glossary.

43. *unde mag wol orteil vinden unde urteiles volgen*: this means that he may hand down a judgment like a *Schöffe* and also contribute to a majority decision to accept or reject a judgment.

44. In the text I use the standard modern spelling of the proper names. Since the spelling in the manuscript is not always easily recognizable, the manuscript spelling for each name in the original sequence follows: Anehalt, Brandinburg, Orlamunde, Missene, Bren, Hakenburne, Gnercz, Mochele, Tubule, Edeleresdorf, Heinrich Judas der voit, Albrecht von Spandouwe, Alverig unde Cunrat von Snetlinge, Strapen von Jersleve, Anne von Irkesdorf, Herman von Meringe, Heidolv von Winninge, Sedorf, Doringen, Regenstein, Blankenburg, Vinni, Clodene, Druzke, Kotebus, Brunswig, Luneburg, Poppenburg, Ostirburg, Aldenhusen, Werningenrode, Arnstein, Besenrode, Emersleve, Gevekenstein, Halbirstat, Suselicz, Lichtenberg, Obin, Limborch.

Book I

1. This paragraph, or prologue, is known in the literature as the *Prologus*.

2. Alexander Ignor interprets this passage, and especially the key word *sin*, as relating to the gifts of the Holy Spirit. Four of these gifts—*sapientia, consilium, intellectus, scientia*—apply to *sin*, which translates as "understanding, comprehension, mind" (175).

3. *alle gute lute di rechtis gern*: "all good people who desire justice," but I translated it as "law-abiding." Ulrich Drescher explains that "good people" implies that they are good because they obey God's laws, see also II 29.

4. *das si das noch rechte bescheiden noch irme sinne, so sis rechste wissen*: I have translated *recht* as "justice," indicating the desired outcome, although "law" would be the more literal translation. Given Planck's assessment that as far as the German judiciary were concerned the "established set of laws had already organized and accounted for all events of life" (87), "following the law" (*noch rechte bescheiden*) is to be understood as the proper application of law to a particular situation in order to achieve justice.

5. *Got is selber recht, dar umme is im recht lip*: I translate this as "God is Law" because Eike's text specifically derives all law from God in the two prologues. A

literal translation with *selber* would read "God himself is Law" but I feared that Law would appear to some readers as an attribute instead of equating Law and God as the text does. *Recht* includes what in English are distinct concepts of law and justice. The connotation "justice" as found in the text derives from proper functioning of the law court (see third sentence of the first prologue). Furthermore, *recht* also implies the moral component of righteousness, which is no longer part of our modern concept of law. Hence a person is just and law-abiding because he or she is morally good. With this statement, Eike grounds German legal custom in Judaeo-Christian theology and morality. Kisch (*Bible*, 67) has shown that this phrase does not have a parallel in Deut. 32:4 as Eckhardt states (*Lndr,* 13), but rather in Psalm 11:7: "For the Lord is righteous, he loves righteous deeds" (*New Oxford Annotated Bible*). See Kisch, *Bible,* chap. 3, "The Problem 'Bible and Secular Law'" 21–26; Drescher, 83–84; the short discussion of *recht* in the introduction to this volume; and II 66.

6. This paragraph, or introduction, is known as the *Textus Prologi*.

7. This public act of homage (subordination), supposedly first fulfilled by Charlemagne, was the basis for strife between the papacy and empire, but Eike downplays the implied superiority of the papacy over the emperor's temporal power.

8. The idea of cooperation between secular and spiritual is also mentioned in III 63.

9. *vriheit is abir drierhande*: "freedom is of three kinds"; *vriheit* here means "obligations" as well as "privileges." No one enjoys a freedom or privilege to do something without having a concomitant obligation; thus I translate "freedom" as "obligation" for the most part because this is what the context normally requires; here the text speaks of "three kinds," but the next passage makes clear that it refers to three legal ranks of people who are obligated to attend different types of courts according to their legal status.

10. *Schöffen* are judgment finders in a court of law (see "*Schöffen*" in glossary). They belong to the lowest class permitted to bear arms (cf. I 3, 51). The German term is often translated as "lay judge" or "juror," but because these terms do not adequately describe their function and even mislead, I use the original German throughout.

11. The *phlegehaftin* were the king's tenants, and *lantsezin* were tenants and sharecroppers on local land; for their status, see III 46, and "leasehold," "tenant" in glossary. The dean of the cathedral was the bishop's magistrate and judge in ecclesiastical court. The archpriest was normally the priest of a major or central parish church who served as ecclesiastical judge at the local level.

12. *di schepfin des greven ding ober achzcen wochin undir kuniges banne*: *ban* (E "ban") means that the king invests his delegated judicial authority to the count, who then has the right to preside over a superior court in the king's stead and judge capital offenses (see II 13; III 52; and glossary). I normally translate *under kuniges banne* "under the king's jurisdiction" or simply "high court." See "royal judicial authority" in glossary.

13. *hi mite habin si vorvangin ir eigen kein den richtere das is allis dingis von im ledic is*: This statement indicates that the inherited land of the *Schöffen* makes them eligible to give verdicts in a law court but also requires them to contribute actively to the

judicial process and implies that their land may be encumbered if they fail to fulfill their legal obligations.

14. The *Schultheiss* is the count's appointed magistrate and court officer; see I 59; III 52; and "*Schultheiss*" in glossary.

15. A *fronbote* is an officer of the court. The older term is "beadle," now obsolete so I translate it as "bailiff"; see I 8, 28, 53, 61, 68, 70; II 17, 22, 41; III 46, 61; and "bailiff" in glossary.

16. The *gougreve* is the "local village or district judge" who serves a group of three villages that elected him; see I 55, 56, 57, 58, 71.

17. As members of the judiciary, the free landholders in each of these groups were required to attend and participate at the specified court determined by their status. This judicial duty is a requirement of the land itself and applies no matter whether the land is an allod, a freehold, or leasehold and no matter whether the tenancy is inheritable, life-long, or fixed-term.

18. The "advocate" (*vogt*) was a secular judge and magistrate for an ecclesiastical foundation, a monastery, or a bishopric.

19. The "headman" (*burmeister*) is one of the villagers chosen to serve as leader of the village; see "village headman" in glossary.

20. The source for this discussion of the seven ages is not Origen, but Isidor of Seville's *Origines*. It could have been picked up by Eike directly or indirectly from any number of sources, quite likely from Honorius Augustodunensis (*PL* 172, c. 855–56) or possibly from a twelfth-century vernacular sermon. See Eckhardt, *Lndr* I 3, p. 72.

21. *herschilde*: "military shields," also translated as "orders of knighthood"; see I 25, 27; IV 1, 2; and "military shield" in glossary.

22. *di leienvursten den dritten, sint si der bischove man worden sin*: the *man* (pl. "men") here are clearly subordinates in the sense of vassals in this section.

23. The term again is *herschilt*, "knighthood." This passage stresses the right to participate in the orders of knighthood by bearing arms; thus I have rendered the term as "the right to bear arms."

24. The text here is drawn not from Origen, but from Isidor of Seville's *Origines*, which contains the pattern of representing kinship relations used in canon law. The schema that follows here represents the unique German procedure and metaphor of the human body for calculating consanguinity. See my article "From Oral Custom to Written Law: The Sachsenspiegel," and for a detailed analysis of the method for calculating kinship, see Dagmar Hüpper, "Ehe," 140.

25. *nemen zcwene brudere zwu swestirn und der dritte bruder ein vremde wip*: "if two brothers marry two sisters and the third brother marries a foreign woman." In this case *ein vremde wip* contrasts with the two sisters to indicate someone unrelated to anyone in the clan.

26. *ebinburtig* means "of equal birth" in the sense of having the same level of rights and obligations before the law.

27. *Erbe* refers to the estate or inheritance although certain types of property are considered separately; see "inheritance" in glossary.

28. *Uf altvilen unde uf getwerge irstirbit noch len noch erbe*: A distinction is made between *len* (G *Lehen*) and *erbe*. The *len* can refer to any kind of land tenancy, to a

hereditary leasehold for which the tenant pays ground rents, or a feudal tenancy. This passage does not specify which is meant. The word *altvil*, which I translate as "feebleminded" (following Lübben), has not yet been adequately defined, see Janz, *Rechtssprichwörter*, 69–70.

29. Here *len* translates as "fief" because the context is specifically feudal law.

30. *veter* specifically meant "father's brother."

31. *gerade* refers to heritable, personal miscellaneous belongings of a woman including her dowry. It is not considered part of the estate; see I 24 and "inheritance" in glossary.

32. *mit welchem gute der man stirbit, das heist alles erbe*: "the property with which a man dies is called his estate;" see Inheritance in glossary.

33. See Oathhelper in glossary.

34. *uf den heiligen*: "on the relics." Oaths were sworn on the relics of saints.

35. *eime manne gezugen wil an sin recht oder an sinen lip oder an sinen gesunt*: this passage refers to bringing a complaint against someone (e.g. theft or robbery) for which he loses his legal capacity, life, or health if a judgment is found against him.

36. The amount awarded as compensation payment or punitive fine is called *buse*; see "compensation" in glossary.

37. Wergeld is a criminal tariff, see table of values for humans, III 46, 47 and animals, III 48, 49 and glossary.

38. *sune aber unde orvede di der man vor gerichte tut di gezugit man mit dem richtere und mit zwen mannen*: *sune* is "reconciliation," and *orvede* is "abjurance of all vengeance." Both were accomplished by a solemn oath that was often required by the court either while a case was in process or after a settlement had been reached in order to prevent a feud.

39. *selb sibinde*: translates as "oathhelpers;" this is a frequent construction throughout, containing *selb*, meaning "self," plus a number that already includes the person himself. Thus *selb* and *sibinde* (seven) equals the person himself and six others; *selb dritte* is literally "self three;" i.e. the person himself plus two others. See I 15; IV 57.

40. *lehnserbe* is an "heir" or "beneficiary" who receives property according to feudal law but not land law.

41. *herr* in the original has multiple meanings. I translate it as "lord" unless a more specific term such as "landlord" or "master" is meaningful in a specific context. See "lord," "master" in glossary.

42. I translate *liunge* as "enfeoffment"; it literally means "a lending."

43. *Gelobet aber der man der das gut lasin sal das he ieme di liunge irwerbe unde [tut] he das und kundigt hes ieme mit gezuge das he da zu kume und he das enpha, und weigirt des iener ane rechte not stirbit der herre oder weigirt he des sider zu liene unde mag hes nicht irwerbin als er he is von im ledig des inritens unde nicht des uflasens ab is iener da noch irwerbin mag*: Since the pronouns do not clearly distinguish the three parties involved, I have replaced them with agentive nouns. The term *inriten* means he is thus released from "riding in to transfer possession."

44. *Sundert der vater oder di muter einen iren sun oder eine ire tochter von in mit irme gute, si zweien sich mit der kost oder nicht*: "If father or mother separates a son or daughter from him or herself by a transfer property regardless of whether they carry

separate [household] expenses or not." *Sundern* (v.) refers to the official separation of offspring from the parent by transferring to them their portion of the inheritance.

45. *umme bescheit oder ane bescheit*: "with or without stipulation" of a fixed duration for the loan.

46. *Wer deme andern sine varnde gut liet oder seczt odir zu haldene tut umme bescheit oder ane bescheit wil is im iener da nach besachen oder sin erbe noch sime tode dirre istis nehir zu behaldene selb dritte denne ienir der is in gewern hat sine gezug dar an gezugin oder sin erbe gut oder hat he des geweren*: As I understand the passage, *dirre* refers to the lender of the property; hence it was easier for him to prove his ownership than *iener*, who held the property in his possession. The lender needed only to swear with two oathhelpers whereas the other will have difficulty winning even if he brings proof of witness, or bases his case on his own landholdings, or if he has a guarantor. *Gewer* (n.m.) may indicate a "guarantor"; or *gewer* (n.f.) may mean "surety" or "possession" (Lexer, 1, c. 983–85). See "guarantor," "guaranty" in glossary.

47. *des enket he mit siner unschult*: *unschult* is "innocence," but the term refers to the process of proving one's innocence by means of a cleansing oath.

48. *recht* means "rights" here; See I 50; the discussion on *recht* in the introduction; and "law" in glossary.

49. Here *dinstwip*, "woman servant," is the only noun and stands for both the father and mother. I translate it as "servant" because the term does not necessarily mean "serf" even though this sentence, as it contrasts to the previous one, implies a permanent status lacking freedom.

50. This passage refers to the situation when no heir exists in the direct line of descent.

51. *ganerbin* are "common heirs"; that is, the collective members who inherit equally. This is an old concept deriving from OHG *ge-anervun* (a dative plural form), with its prefix meaning "the collection or sum of heirs," and dates from the ninth century (*DWB* 4, pt. 1, c. 1215–16).

52. The term *buseme* used in its specific, legal meaning indicates the heirs in direct line of descent or ascent from the deceased.

53. Swabian here refers to people living in Saxony who are descended from Swabians.

54. I translate *geschlecht* as "tribe" here.

55. *Der Swabe enmag ouch von wiphalbin kein erbe genemen wenne di wip in irme geslechte alle erbelos sint gemacht durch irre vordirn missetat*: "Swabians may only inherit through the agnatic side of the family because women who have been disinherited and thus have nothing to pass on except a dowry and the woman's personal miscellaneous belongings."

56. This reference to Charlemagne's law probably derives from Otto IV's Landpeace of 11 November 1208, now lost. It presented itself as a renewal of a law originally promulgated by Charlemagne. See Eckhardt, *Lndr*, 53.

57. *das swebissche recht durch der wibe has*: "the Swabian law resulting from their anger with women." This passage refers to custom continued by the Swabians living in Saxon territory and concerns specifically the rule restricting women's ability to inherit mentioned in I 17.

58. *wil is ein Sachse scheldin unde zut he des an sine vordirn hant unde an di meiste*

menie: "a Saxon challenges a decision calling upon his right hand [*vordir hant*]." A person fulfills his legal rights and obligations (including oath-taking) with the right hand, which indicates full legal capacity. Thus the person appeals to his right hand to challenge a judgment and requests a ruling of the court by consensus. See II 13; IV 70 and "consensus" in glossary.

59. *widervichtit he das urteil selb sibinde wider andere sibene*: in general, *widerfechten* (v.) means "to fight against or contest," but here it specifically refers to the legal process of contesting a judgment by means of legal physical combat when the majority in court also agree to contest the judgment.

60. *hergewete* was the man's personal military equipment, passed on separately from other items in the estate. It could only be inherited by a male relative on the father's side of the family. For a full list of items, see I 22, 23; see also "inheritance" in glossary.

61. The agnatic side is literally called the "sword half," *swerthalbin*. The relative himself, called *swertmage*, has several obligations to the family; see I 23.

62. *binnen schwäbische art* includes the meaning "territory" as well as "lineage" in this context. This usage underscores the belief that the territorial boundary (of Swabia in this case) is congruent with the space inhabited by their ancestors. The same thinking is inherent in the phrase *binnen sechsiche art*; see I 34.

63. Swabia was located in what is now the southwestern part of Germany, mostly the northern and eastern part of Baden-Würtemberg, but not limited to that state.

64. *dingstat*, legal venue. A law court may be convened anywhere for certain crimes, but for each level of jurisdiction there exists a specified venue; see I 59.

65. On personal or tribal law, see I 30 and III 73.

66. *nu vornemet* means "now hear this" and is reminiscent of the oral proclamations, the primary means of making ordinances and edicts public. The author and subsequent scribes may well have imagined a speaking voice.

67. *was ein iclich man von ritters art muge gegebin sime wibe zu morgengabe*: *von ritters art* indicates a man who is a knight by birth; *morgengabe* is the gift made by a husband to his new wife on the morning after their union.

68. *einen knecht odir eine mait*: *knecht* has multiple meanings: "(free or unfree) servant, apprentice, soldier." It can also mean an "upright" or "dependable" man, and simply "boy" or "man" in general. In most cases in W, a *knecht* is in a subordinate service relationship since the terms *herr* and *knecht* form an opposition in MHG. In clearly specified instances it also refers to a page in service of a knight, and in one case it refers to the princes of the realm; see I 20; II 13, 66; *DWB* 5, c. 1380–96; *HRG* 2, c. 895–96).

69. *zune unde zimmer*: This is somewhat difficult to render precisely. Basically, it refers to the house and the enclosed yard containing an area for the chickens, geese, etc. and the vegetable garden.

70. *vrouwe*, meaning "lady," is seldom used. Here it indicates a lady of noble status and wife of a knight rather than simply a married woman, or *wip*, which is the customary term used in this text. See "woman" in glossary for a complete list of occurrences.

71. Originally a Germanic custom to celebrate the deceased ten, twenty, or

thirty days after the burial, the "thirtieth" (*drisigister*) was christianized early on and became a mass for the soul of the deceased. The inheritance was divided among the heirs after the mass.

72. The knight's widow must literally vacate the land by taking the building with her. Buildings are owned independently of the land they are built on since tenants may build or make improvements on the land at their discretion. See II 53.

73. *musteil* refers to the stored foods to be divided among family members after the death of the father; see I 24 and "inheritance" in glossary.

74. *unbeschuldene gewer*: "uncontested right of possession." The phrase strongly implies ownership; initially, little distinction between permanent possession and ownership is to be found in the term *gewer* as used in the text. However, Ishikawa has done a thorough word study and defines the term as "possession that requires legal verification" (81–82); see "possession" in glossary.

75. *niftel* is the sister's daughter. Just as the military outfit devolves upon the male side of the family, so the woman's dowry and personal miscellanea devolve upon the female side.

76. A *lipgedinge* is a "usufruct" or "life estate." It designates the right to use a specified piece of land and its fruits. Such land given by a man to his wife is hers to use for life; she cannot be evicted.

77. *Wer uf gnade gedient hat der mus den erbn gnadin manen*: "If anyone had been serving the deceased for mercy or favor must inform the heir to demand the favor." *Gnade* can be rendered as "mercy," "goodwill," "favor," "kindness," or "boon." Schmidt-Wiegand translates the phrase into modern German: *Wer auf Gnadenlohn gedient hat, der soll den Erben an diese Gnade erinnern* (facsimile W, 119). Her rendering is as unclear as the original. The term surely does not designate alms. According to Janz, the phrase refers to service rendered for which no specified amount of compensation had been fixed (*Rechtssprichwörter*, 64–68). It is then up to the lord to pay what he deems appropriate (64–65). She cites the proverb *Wer auff Gnade dient/ soll mit Barmherzigkeit belohnt werden* to support her case (Janz, *Rechtssprichwörter* 65). This proverb does not seem to have existed in the *Sachsenspiegel* tradition in its entirety, and one may question whether it appears later or is even intended in this passage.

It is possible that service without pay may perhaps mean that someone from the neighborhood (a tenant's or even a vassal's child) was taken in for training or even in fosterage. The relationship is not equal because the service is performed for goodwill, thus leaving the extent or form of reciprocation open. (I owe this idea to a discussion with my colleague Peter von Sivers.) Nevertheless, it implies that an alliance of some sort is created. What sort of alliance was established would depend on the rank of the servant's family, but when this relationship is severed by a death, the heir must choose whether to continue the relationship. If he discontinues it, the servant has the right to demand compensation which may be either in the form of a boon or money.

78. *das he hatte zu eines mannes libe da he starb*: "that he had during life, until he died." Significantly, the entire sentence indicates that a man normally owned such equipment and therefore, the widow was expected to account for each item.

79. *swertmage*: see I 19.

80. *di wile is sich selbe nicht vermag noch bedenkin enkan von siner kintheit oder vor torheit oder vor krancheit des libes*: *kintheit* cannot be translated as "youth" because the ward is already of age. It may be that mental incompetence or simply lack of experience is implied.

81. The phrase *bis das si man genimt* is noteworthy because the usual expression allows a man to *echt wip nemen*; that is, the man is thought of as the agent who "takes" a (passive) wife, but here it is the woman who actively chooses to marry and "takes" a man. This phrase may indicate that the consent of the woman was recognized as legally necessary for marriage in conformance to canon law.

82. The text has *wip*, (wife) instead of the expected *frouwe*, (lady) even though the morning gift enumerated must belong to the wife of a knight. See I 20–22.

83. *Musteil*, the food supplies, are part of the inheritance (I 20).

84. A garland of flowers worn on the head is called a *schapel*, or "chaplet."

85. *seltere unde alle buchere di zu gotis dinste gehorn di vrouwen phlegen zu lesene*: I have added the description "devotional" to characterize more clearly what is meant by *zu gotis dinste* (service of God). The books are not likely to belong to the mass itself but are most probably books of hours and courtesy books. The use of *vrouwen* in the plural may, in the context of books, refer to ladies of status or simply women in general.

86. *herschilt* is the term used; see I 3, 27.

87. The gray monks are Cistercians.

88. The verb *begeben* means here "to place in a monastery."

89. *Iclich wip erbit zweier wege ir gerade an ir nehiste niftele di ir von wiphalben zugehorte*: Her *gerade* is inherited by the closest "niece" related on the woman's side (*wiphalben*).

90. The thirtieth day after the funeral; see I 20.

91. *jar und tag*: "a year and a day." The text speaks of the Saxon limitation period as being one year and one day. According to Schmidt-Wiegand, the limitation period is actually one year, six weeks, and three days (*Facsimile W*, 127, note 3).

92. *Hufe*: here, "freehold." In ninth-century Germany *hufe* referred to owned farmland, but by the thirteenth century it had become primarily a unit of land measure like E "hide"; see II 48, 54; III 46, 61; and glossary.

93. *riche* translates as "realm," "empire," and the "office of emperor" or "crown." When it refers to the office, it often implies the person of the emperor, as it does here. I translate it consistently as "realm" to maintain any distinctions implied when *riche, kunig*, and *keiser* are used. When the context refers clearly to the emperor himself or the crown, I note it.

94. The *Sachsenspiegel* custumal is based on territorial law (*landes recht*), as this passage indicates, but it also defers to personal law (*mannes recht*) in a few specific instances. Thus territorial law had not yet completely superseded the personal. See I 19 on Swabian custom, and III 73 regarding the Wends. These correspond in content to the Quedlinburg manuscript of the late thirteenth century (Eckhardt, *Lndr*, I 19; III 73), indicating that remnants of personal or tribal law were still important enough to mention in the mid-fourteenth century.

95. *Man unde wip enhaben kein gezweiet gut zu irme libe*: "Man and wife have no divided property during their lifetime." This is the most common translation. How-

ever, Wilhelm Ebel has construed *zu irme libe* to mean "for their subsistence" ("ungezweite Gut," 187). His translation is equally possible, and likely syntactically, but leads to very different legal implications. I follow Ebel.

96. *das hes durch recht liden durfe*: Literally, "that he would have to acquiesce to it by law." This means that she may not enter into an agreement in which the disposition of real property is irrevocable without her husband's permission; see I 45.

97. The term here is *gewere*, "possession."

98. *wurte*: "yard," "the enclosed land around the house."

99. The modern concept of "gift" should not be read into this passage. The action of MHG *geben* and *gabe* indicate a conveyance, a transfer of control over a property, or primary possession but not necessarily ownership; see "alienate" in glossary.

100. *uf sechsiche art*: "Saxon lineage." Here it is used in its spatial sense of "Saxon territory." The king and his court (*Hofgericht*) were peripatetic. As he traveled from place to place, his royal judge traveled with him and presided over hearings as needed (*HRG* 2, c. 206–9; 4, c. 615–26). See also "Imperial Landpeace of Mainz," fol. 3r,l.

101. *gewint si ein kint e irre rechtin zcit das das kint leben muge*: Literally, "if she gives birth before term when the child is not capable of surviving." I have rendered the original redundancy very freely in the translation.

102. A *kemphe* was a dueler or champion by occupation, employed by the law court or by litigants to fight in a verdict by combat in place of the litigant himself. Considered a dishonorable occupation, its practitioners, like minstrels, were curtailed in their legal capacity and socially marginalized as well (see Danckert, 9–15).

103. *rechtlos*: Designates a person with restricted legal capacity because of occupation, illegitimate birth, or as a consequence of a conviction; see I 51 and "legal incapacity" in glossary.

104. *der och jar unde tag indes riches achte is*: *acht* means "royal" or "imperial outlawry." The person outlawed lost all rights, but not permanently; those outlawed had the legal time limit of a year and a day to comply with the law. See "outlawry" in glossary.

105. The point here is that after the term of a year and a day, the revocation of rights entailed in outlawry was made permanent and irrevocable by court decision. See "outlawry," "attainder" in glossary.

106. Conditions for legal excuse are given in II 7.

107. *Dinstman* appears most frequently in the sense of "ministerial," as it does here (II 42; III 19). However, it basically means "a man in someone's service," "an unfree person" (III 42), or "servant," so it is sometimes ambiguous (III 41, 72). The status of ministerials is complex (III 81); see "ministerial" in glossary.

108. *Eliche kindere enmag der uneliche man sider nicht gewinnen*: *Unelich* refers to revocation of full legal capacity. Lexical confusion arises from the fact that the text sometimes interchanges *echt* and *recht*. In the one case, minstrels and paid champions could have legitimate children even though they had only limited rights, but in the other, convicted felons lost all rights (I 50, 51). See "legal capacity" in glossary.

109. *Wer jar unde tag in des riches achte is, unde im noch der jarzcal vorteilt wirt echt unde recht*: With the terms *echt* and *recht*, this section expresses the need, once someone is convicted, to withdraw all rights before a sentence can be carried out. The grave consequences of attainder are discussed in I 39. See "outlawry," "attainder" in glossary.

110. This degree of outlawry means that the convicted person remains permanently outside the law, suffers attainder, and therefore has forfeited all property and can never regain his legal rights and privileges.

111. *he en zcuschtire vor des keisers schar*: "unless he jousts before the emperor's retinue." Not a specifically legal term, *zcuschtiren, tjostieren* (v.) occurs only once in the text and would designate a "formal joust" as in a tournament (Lexer 2, c. 1451). Admittedly, a joust against a foreign king seems quite out of place here even though its purpose must have been a kind of trial by battle. Contemporaries also understood the passage as a joust because W's illustration to this chapter shows two horsemen facing each other in full armor with lances lowered for the attack.

112. Here I translate *recht* as "legal rights and privileges."

113. *Ere*, translated here as "public status," normally means "public honor," "prestige," and also "legal capacity." It includes a moral connotation as well.

114. The term *balmunden* ("delinquent guardian") used here specifically means "the disloyalty, neglect, breach of trust committed by a guardian." The fact that the definition is also stated in the text reveals that the term was quite old and had a specific legal denotation no longer well understood by the time the manuscript was written (and possibly by Eike's time). The passage itself implies that a woman has the right to bring a suit before the court by herself, but only against a guardian who is not her husband; a wife may not do so.

115. *Kampfwart* is a litigant's guardian or relative who is willing to be his or her champion in a trial by combat.

116. *handhafte tat* is a "red-handed deed." It includes all crimes in which the perpetrator still carries clear evidence of the deed; see definition in II 33, 34, and glossary.

117. *ursale*: "legal and permanent conveyance of property."

118. The definition for the legal beginning of a marriage appears to be the act of entering the man's bed; that is, consummation. This also seems to be the point at which the man takes on his wife's tutelage. See also III 46.

119. Here *vrouwen* in plural refers to women in general rather than ladies of status only.

120. A *vridebrecher* is a felon who breaks the law with a violent act such as an assault on someone on a peace day (II 10, 66).

121. This is the passage that distinguishes *rechtelos* ("diminished legal capacity") and *elos, echtelos* ("attainder, the complete loss of legal capacity and protection"). The terms are used inconsistently. Often *rechtlos* occurs in the meaning of *elos*. See "legal incapacity" and "attainder" in glossary.

122. The terms *kebis*, and *kebsehe* refer to a relationship between a free man and an unfree woman, often considered concubinage. See "marriage" in glossary.

123. *hantgemal* is the hereditary estate of the clan.

124. *underwinden*: "to grab and challenge someone to trial by combat."

125. *dumeln*: "ell." In general, the ell was measured from the tip of the thumb to the elbow; on the Freiburg church it measures 54 cm.; see Kunze, 101.

126. *nimant en wettit um eine sache zwir he en breche den vride unde vorschulde den ban an einer tat*: In this statement, *ban* refers to the ecclesiastical ban of anathema; that is, complete exclusion from the Church, which is the body of Christ.

127. *zcins, zins* is "rent" for use of land, and *zcent* is a "tenth" or a "tithe"; for a list of tithes, see II 48.

128. *das mus he volbrengen selb dritte di is sagen unde horten*: *sagen* (n. preterite) is a variant of *sehen*, "to see."

129. *Alle werltlich gerichte hat begin von kore*: "All secular courts are based upon election." *Kore* means "election" or "selection" of a judge following proper procedures. According to this chapter and the next, villagers had the right to elect their local judge either for a summary court or for a longer period of time.

130. *gougreve*: I translate this consistently as "local judge"; see "judge" in glossary.

131. The *Mirror* is not clear, here or elsewhere, as to the source of the local judge's authority. Either election or investiture by the count may have been sufficient, but it is possible that the elected judge was then invested with the judgeship.

132. It was customary to hold court sessions anywhere necessary depending on the group who needed to attend (see I 62). However, a legally correct place did exist where all regularly scheduled hearings were held. The text stipulates the instances for which this specific location must be used.

133. *vogtei* translates as "advocacy" because the text indicates that the office is limited to a geographic jurisdiction.

134. *vor deme he sich zu rechte biten sal*: I have translated this as "the *Schultheiss* is above him by law" (see III 52). The goal here is to ensure that procedure is followed correctly. If the count makes himself culpable or is accused, then the *Schultheiss* presides over his case.

135. *vorsprechin*: "spokesman, speaker, advocate, pleader." Each litigant did well to have someone speak on his behalf.

136. *vorsumit he ouch kein man des vorspreche he is he mus sich wol irholn mit eime andern vorsprechen*: *Vorsumen* means here a "failure to make a procedurally correct plea."

137. *wo der man recht vordert da sal he rechtis phlegen unde helfen*: I understand this statement to mean "The judicial district in which a man brings charges in court is where he has responsibility to answer when charged and to support the law and the judge."

138. The original states only *da*, meaning "there," so I interpolated "in the judicial district."

139. *den sal di vrone gewalt behalden* indicates that the power of the lord (in this case, judge) shall arrest him; see "arrest" in glossary.

140. *uf eins andern mannes schaden:* The phrase indicates that the sword is drawn with intent to harm.

141. *Rede*: "plea." Each party has the right to present its argument in the following way. A property dispute is the simplest example. First it is decided which

side begins, or leads, the argument. The beginner can be either the plaintiff's or the defendant's side. Then, with each plea, the party presents only the information relevant to the particular law it wishes to invoke in order to win the case. The other party then responds by doing the same; that is, presenting an argument or countering the previous one by applying a different law. The *Schöffen* and other judgment finders must determine the applicability of each law suggested. When each party has had its turn, the judge must call for a ruling on the law. As the litigants take turns, and rulings are made and accepted, the court is able to find for the one or the other party based on its greater right to the property. At this point the winner of the argument must prove the facts with witnesses in order to obtain right to the property. If the proof does not succeed, the court awards the property to the other party (Planck, 228–33).

142. I have retained the syntax here because this type of pithy maxim occurs frequently and is a reflex of oral customs, as are many proverbs and sayings in this text. Conceptual patterns and rhetorical formulations in the *Mirror* rely strongly on tradition and attempt to be faithful to it; see, for example, the section on the mill (II 59).

143. Consultation was permitted between the litigant, his advocate and any friends or relations he invited (IV 72b, 74, 75); see "consultation" in glossary.

144. *kemplich grusen* is the technical phrase for challenging someone to a trial by battle.

145. *zu rechte* in this context of requesting a trial by combat carries a much narrower meaning than the usual "for justice" because it refers to a specific procedure where both words and gesture signify the beginning of a suit.

146. *houbetloch*: "neck opening." Most peasant tunics had merely a reinforced neck opening.

147. *Vride sal man dem kreize gebiten bi deme halse*: *Vride* means "order" in this passage.

148. *di sunne sal man en gliche teiln wen si erst zu samne gen*: "one must divide the sun equally between them when they first come together."

149. *Vervestung* is temporary and limited outlawry. It may be lifted as soon as the outlaw satisfies the law, and it applies only to the local district or, if imposed by the count, to the county jurisdiction; see "outlawry" in glossary.

150. *wer da borgt einen man umme ungerichte vor zu brengen ab he en nicht vorbrengen enmag he mus sin wergelt geben*: In this case the guarantor pays the accused man's wergeld and not his own. The implication is that the guarantor is liable to the plaintiff for damages.

151. *phenninge* ("pennies") were silver coins in common circulation.

152. For jurisdictions and degrees of outlawry, see III 24 and "outlawry," "attainder" in glossary.

153. *unde bewiset hes in der vrischen tat*: this phrase indicates a *flagrans crimen* (a "fresh" or "recent deed") as opposed to a red-handed deed.

154. *ane vleischwundin mag man ouch einen man toten oder lemen mit slegen oder mit stosen oder mit wrfen unde anders*: In this description of the possible moves in a brawl, *stozen* can be a shove, punch, or even a kick. The importance of this point is that all cases of homicide, even those without the shedding of blood, belonged in the superior court.

155. "Peace ordinance" (*vrides rechte*) refers to the peace days first set up in the landpeace and imperial peace edicts; see II 10, 66.

156. *unde wil man is nicht man sal is doch halden sechs wochen unvortan*: The second pronoun *man* does not specify who was to keep the property safe. I assume that the attached property was to remain in the court's custody.

157. The following italicized section has been added from D in order to complete the statement.

Book II

1. Two folios are missing from W between folios numbered 27 and 28. The missing portion would have contained chapters 1 through 11 and part of chapter 12 as listed in the table of contents. I fill in the textual gap from D, printed in italics.

2. This statement implies that any such oath of alliance requires a specific clause acknowledging the overriding loyalty and duty of the parties to the monarch.

3. I assume this regards a man who comes to the court hearing as is his duty but has not been informed that a suit is being brought against him.

4. *Verfestung*: "outlawry." See I 64 and glossary.

5. *und das lant mit vingern und mit zungen als man en in die vorvestunge tet*: "fingers" (*vingern*) refers to the gesture of the oath, and "tongue" (*zungen*) to the spoken words, namely the oral formula of the oath (IV 28, 55).

6. *he mus dem richtere wetten und ieme sine buse gebn*: The court fine is the *wette*, and the payment made to the accused is *buse*. *Buse* here refers to the fine for not carrying through with a suit. See "fine" in glossary.

7. Here and elsewhere, *zu rechte* normally translates "for judgment" or "for justice."

8. *Gebundene tage* are "binding" or "peace days." Certain days or periods were set aside as peaceful or nonviolent days; see I 50, 53; II 66; and glossary.

9. W resumes here. As the text picks up again, the chapter numbering fails to correspond with the numbering in W's table of contents. The scribe has inserted a chapter number here; at chapter 20b the numbering resumes its correspondence to the table of contents.

10. *Busen kuniges banne mus iclich man uber den andern urteil vinden unde urteil schelden der da vollenkomen is an sime rechte*: "[In a court] outside of [i.e., lacking] the king's judicial authority, any man may determine a verdict regarding another and appeal a verdict as long as he is perfect or unblemished in his rights." The phrase "outside the king's authority" refers to the lower jurisdiction of a local judge (*gaugraf*) or village headman. *Vollenkomen is an sime rechte* means that he is unblemished in his legal standing and can participate fully in all legal matters and fulfill his legal obligations as a member of the judiciary.

11. The term used is *bann*; see III 52 on investing a judge with the king's judicial authority.

12. *Garben* ("sheaves") is a measure of grain and, in this case, hay.

13. *Knecht* is generic: *Zwei gerichte den knechtin* means "two meals for the servants"; *Sechse suln der knechte sin*, "the servants shall be six in number." I translate

knecht as "servant" in the generic sense, but when the deputies are *Schöffen*, the term probably refers to pages in their service. See also I 20.

14. The royal judge traveled with the king to the various German territories; see I 34; and "Mainz" fol. 3r,l and "imperial judge" in glossary.

15. The point made is that the customary law of the march is different from that of the count's territory, and therefore the margrave may well stand above the count in legal status, but his court lacks the appellate jurisdiction.

16. *Riche* normally translates as "realm," "empire," or "kingdom" but refers to the royal court in this statement.

17. *sin recht dazu tun*: "to wager his rights on it by swearing an oath."

18. *czut hes an sine vordere hant unde an di meiste menie*: *Hant* refers to his "oath-taking hand," the means by which he exercises his legal capacity and *meiste menie* to the "majority" decision.

19. Presumably, the fight consists of a set of duels performed according to the description in I 63.

20. *Riche* ("empire") implies here either the king himself or his court presided over by the imperial judge. See I 34 above, and "imperial judge" in glossary.

21. *under kuniges banne* means, in precise terms, "the invested judicial authority of the king," which then defines the superior court. The phrases "the king's judicial authority," "superior court," and "high court," are used in this translation; see "royal judicial authority" in glossary.

22. *der aber zu den benken nicht geborn is der sal des stules bitten mit urteiln ein ander urteil zu vindene*: The benches (*benke*) refer to the "chairs" or "benches" of the *Schöffen*, not the judge's bench. German has several permutations with bench (*bank*) and chair (*stuhl*) available–*Schöffenstuhl, Schöffenbank*, *Gerichtsbank* ("court bench")—that distinguish the authority involved. In this instance the passage stresses the fact that the office of *Schöffe* is hereditary (see III 26).

23. *welch urteil iener denne vint das bite he zu behaldene mit sime rechte unde czie des da hes durch recht zien sal*: this sentence indicates that whatever ruling this person makes, he shall offer it for acceptance with an oath based on his unblemished legal capacity and bring it to the proper jurisdiction.

24. See procedures for trial by combat in I 63.

25. *Nu vornemt umme ungerichte welch gerichte dar uber get*: *ungericht* is the term for "felony" in the *Sachsenspiegel* texts but is not used in other law texts. In this passage it is clear that *gericht* and *ungerichte* have to do with right and wrong, with lawful and unlawful processes. *Gericht*, then, actually means the lawful process of arriving at a verdict and sentence. Since this passage lists a penal code, "penalty" rather than "judgment" seems the best way to translate *gericht*.

26. The sentence of *hut und har* consisted of flogging and cutting the malefactor's hair.

27. *Gericht* is translated here as "jurisdiction" because the village headman can preside over greater amounts of money stolen, but only over a summary court. Thus he has the lowest jurisdiction in the system.

28. I translate *roub* as "robbery." It occurs with great frequency and means a violent seizure of goods.

29. *Botschaft* here refers to a person who is given a charge or deputation to represent others.

30. *Radebrechen* was a uniquely Germanic form of execution. The person's limbs (and sometimes the back) were first broken, then woven through the spokes of a cart wheel that was then placed horizontally on top of a pole. The procedure caused a slow, excruciating death ("Rädern," *HRG*, vol. 4 c. 135–38).

31. *man sal im sinen hals nicht vorteiln*: "one shall not condemn his neck." The neck is the most frequent metonym for a capital sentence, perhaps because hanging and beheading were the predominant means of execution.

32. *enmag he der di gewer gelobet hat ienen nicht abe gewisen mit rechte he mus sine vorderunge lasen mit einer werbuse*: *Werbuse*, a serious penalty for failure to produce surety, calls for the loss of a hand.

33. Each person's legal status established his wergeld, and it was on this highest amount that all compensation payments for injury to persons or damages were determined. Book III 46 contains the compensation table for people, and III 52 for animals.

34. See I 52.

35. See II 20b on the wergeld of a disabled person.

36. *Wi dicke man aber einen lamen man anderweit belemt in ein ander glit*: *ein lamer man* has the restricted meaning "lame," but in W it indicates permanent injury in any member, and I translate it as "disability" or "handicap" (see I 48).

37. *Ungesundert* can be rendered as "undetached" or "not separated with an inheritance."

38. *man ensal nicht vinden zu rechte wo man uber einen richten sulle he ensi alrest vor wunden alse verre das man uber en richten sulle*: *richten uber* means "to sentence," and *zu rechte finden*, "to determine a final verdict" for or against the defendant. I follow Ignor (149) in stressing the purposive meaning of the *zu* indicating the outcome of the action. This statement in its entirety implies an awareness of building a case: rulings are made and agreed upon at each stage of the trial as facts and evidence are ascertained and the proper application of the law established; no sentence may be handed down by the judge before the final verdict is reached. The same term, *orteil*, is used for all rulings and determinations made in court, not just for the final verdict.

39. *der herre mus ouch wol usnemen eins sinen eigenen man swen he vorteilt is*: *eigen man* refers to a "serf" or "bondman"; *vorteilt* means "a verdict found against the defendant."

40. The label "a" designates this chapter as the second one numbered 20 in book II.

41. *Ungezweite brudir kint sint ouch gliche na deme geczweiten brudere an deme erbe czu nemene*: The text puts children of siblings at the same level as their parents' half-siblings.

42. *Der czinsman wer he si he erbet sin gebu uf sinen erben uf zinsgute is ensi denne ein man von ritters art*: The *zinsman* is a leaseholder paying both rents and tithes. *Zins* means "ground rent" since it contrasts with the tithe, a 10 percent duty paid in kind from the produce of the land (see II 48, 58).

43. *wen ein iclich man mus wol sin gebu bessern unde ergern uf sime lene wider sins herren willen also mus die vrouwe ouch wol uf irme lipgedinge*: *Man* is any "man," but here a *lehen*, or fief, is mentioned along with a morning gift, which indicates that this

"man" is likely a knight. In addition, the female counterpart of a knightly fiefholder is *frouwe*. See "woman" in glossary.

44. *da sal der richter ouch gezuk sin von der warheit irs gezuges di he gehort hat ab hes wol nicht enweis*: This statement probably refers to the fact that the judge can witness the oaths but not affirm the truth of the testimony itself, which had been confirmed by the *Schultheiss* or beadle and the *Schöffen*.

45. *He hab gehorsam getan oder nicht* means "to take the vows of a monastic order." ("Gehorsam," *DWB*, vol. 4, pt. 2, c. 2533).

46. See I 3, 25, and 27.

47. *wo man mit siben mannen gezugen sal da sal man einunczwenzig man umme den gezug vragen*: I interpret this statement to mean that when the oath of seven men is needed to support the plaintiff's case, it is permissible to take testimony from up to twenty-one men until the requisite seven affirmations are reached. If less than seven are found among twenty-one, the plaintiff loses the case; see III 21; IV 13, 40.

48. This passage regarding witnesses is particularly vexing because the pronoun *he* occurs several times without any clear sign of the intended antecedent. The basic context is that the person building the case is using the opponent as witness. I reproduce the section here: *Zuet ein man sins gezuges uf den selben man uf den der gezug get der sal durch recht sagen bi sime eide was im wissenlich si dar umme oder enzage en das he dar umme nicht en wisse volkumt iener sins gezuges mit im den uber en selbe he en bedarf uber en keins gezuges me he mus san dar umme deme richtere wetten unde ieme sine buse geben alse he ieme solde ab he mit gezuge nicht volkumen enwere wen he en zu gezuge brochte wider recht unde wider sine wissenschaft*. *Gezug uf* means "evidence against," as in *ûf Jêsum dô geziuc begunden sî suochen* ("Bruder Philipps Marienleben," 6612, cited according to Lexer, 1, c. 1005).

49. It was necessary to request a renewal of investiture or tenancy (III 14, 63; IV 1, 4, 5, 10, 26, 30, 59, 81). See "renew" in glossary.

50. See I 34; II 13, and "Mainz," fol. 3r,l, on the king's court; see also "imperial judge" in glossary.

51. The term here is *rechtelos*; see "rights" in glossary.

52. *vint man bi im vierdehalben phenning is get im an di hant*: *vierdhalp* means "half heading towards four," hence "three and a half."

53. *phenninge sal der munczer halden phundisch unde ebene swer unde gliche wit*: the adjective *wit* ("white") refers to the silver content that made the coins white.

54. *ein itel wagen gibt halben czol wider eime geladenen der halbe wain das halbe teil*: I take this to mean that the empty cart pays 50 percent, and a half load 75 percent of the toll for a full cartload.

55. *Wilde wage* refers to open water on someone's property, in contrast to an artificial pond.

56. *Den schaden gildet he uf recht* means he compensates for the damage to satisfy justice or legal custom (Ignor, 140).

57. *das sal man richten mit der wit*: "the deed shall be judged with the noose." A *wit* (n.f.) is a cord or rope made of twined green shoots and refers in this case to hanging.

58. See II 14.

59. *wer von gerichtis halben den lip vorlust*: literally, "loses his life by court order."

60. *sin neiste geteling nimt sin erbe*: a person's closest relative equal in legal capacity is called a *geteling*.

61. Here *knecht* means an unfree, dependent servant or serf because it is he who is being beaten or robbed.

62. *Laster* translates here as "insult" or "shame."

63. *zu schaden sprech ich ab he en geslagen hat das he sins herren dinst nicht volbrengen mag das sal he deme herren bessern alse der knecht solde ab he us des herren dinste were kumen unde mit buse im bessern he enneme sich ab des lastirs unde des schaden uf den heiligen kegen des knechtis herren den he gevangen oder geslagen hatte*: The context here requires that the phrase *mit buse im bessern* refer to the servant who receives compensation because the master is already named as receiving a compensation. However, the concern focuses on the repercussions of the beating on the master, and not on the servant.

64. *So uber den andern tag* means "the day after" the loss.

65. *mit des richters urlobe mus he sin gut wol ane vangen mit rechte*: *anevangen*, "to grasp" or "to begin," verbalizes a specific legal act. In an action to recover stolen property, one grasps the articles and takes them into possession; see "recover property" in glossary.

66. *sin gut werin mit rechte*: "to protect his goods rightfully," i.e., to prevent surrender of the article to the claimant.

67. I have added the word "location" because I interpolate from the following section where it states that the buyer must prove the location of the market, and I am assuming that here, too, the location needs to be proven.

68. *und sin recht dar zu tue* indicates that he places his legal capacity as guaranty for it by swearing an oath.

69. Apparently the possessor leads the claimant to the warrantor, but I see no provision for witnesses.

70. *Selp dritte sal he sich dar zu zien der is geanevangit hat ab ieme bruch wirt an deme gewern under deme das gut gewangit wirt der sal das gut halden in sinen gewern bis is im mit rechte angewunnen wirt*: I would place a period to read "... *der is geanevangit hat. Ab ieme*" and translate the pronoun *ieme* as referring to the possessor in the following clause because this pronoun often indicates a shift from one subject to another. The issue seems to be who retains custody of the disputed article until the final verdict is reached. In my reading, the person in possession remains in possession. In contrast, Schmidt-Wiegand's edition implies that *ieme* in the subordinate clause refers back to the subject (*he*) of the independent clause (*Facsimile W*, 193), suggesting that the claimant has custody.

71. *was der man vint oder dibin oder roubern abejait*: the concept here is the seizure and rescue of stolen goods. It is also found in the Anglo-Saxon laws, where it is called *forfang*.

72. *ab he schuset oder wirfet einen man oder ein vie alse he remet eins vogels*: The activity mentioned is done with a bow and arrow and with something thrown, as indicated by the verbs *schiezzen* and *werfen*. The two verbs are often used together; *schiessen* shoots any sort of projectile, such as an arrow or javelin, whereas *werfen* sets something in motion with the hand and arm, such as a falcon or a stick. David Dalby (93) suggests a throwing stick and cites a passage from the *Prose Lancelot*: *Er* [Lan-

celot] *furt alleweg ein holcz in syner hant, da mit er zu vogeln warff und zu tiern; darzu werff er als gerecht als keyn man geschieszen mocht* (cited according to Dalby, 93, from *Lancelot nach der Heidelberger Pergamenthandschrift Pal. Germ. 147*, Ed. R. Kluge, Berlin: Akademie Verlag, 1948–63, vol. 1, l. 21). This would suggest a simple stick like a boomerang and not one that can be used to throw a projectile. According to Dalby, this usage is unique in medieval descriptions of the hunt. We must qualify this because the sources are not concerned with hunting by ordinary people. Thus when Dalby suggests that this practice could be a childish form of hunting simply because the passage describes Lancelot's childhood, he tells us little about actual hunting by lower classes. A stick of some type should be considered a weapon used by peasants and makes sense in the context of territorial law. But however reasonable this conjecture, other evidence indicates that stick and ball together form a concept. They may even have been used together: *auch sol er haben werfstock und dar zuo werfkugeln* (cited according to Lexer, 3, c. 779, from *Anzeiger für die Kunde der deutschen Vorzeit: Organ des germanischen Museums Nürnberg* (1853), 17, 79 ff.)

73. *wer des nachtis korn stilt der vorschult den galgen stilt hes des tagis is get im an den hals*: the very structure "anyone who . . . " with parallel clauses identifies this statement as a proverb. In addition, the contrasting imagery makes the simple statement that both actions carry a death penalty effectively mnemonic. The two-part distinction is that the daytime thief is beheaded, which is a less degrading form of execution (Janz, *Rechtssprichwörter*, 386). The verb *verschulden* ("to owe, to become encumbered") is the basic concept behind all the penalties. A person commits an act that encumbers him to make amends or pay in some way. Here the thief literally owes his life to the gallows.

74. *werdin des mannes phert oder ochsen unde wagen bestetigit in der hanthaften tat*: the concept of red-handedness (*handhafte tat*), in which evidence of the deed marks the perpetrator or cause, is strictly a legal concept; it is not intended literally and is therefore even applied to animals and objects.

75. *enzut hes nicht us iener des is da is binnen jare unde tage man vor im sin recht dar an*: " . . . if the person to whom it belongs does not release it [from seizure] and one rules to withdraw his right to it." The *vor* makes sense if read as *vorteilt*, meaning "denied by means of a judgment."

76. *gut das ir iclicher im zu lene gijt*: " . . . property that each of the two claims for himself in fief or tenancy." The pronoun *im* is reflexive.

77. *Ir iclicher sal sinen geweren zu dinge brengen wer da geweret wirt der behelt des gewere nicht enkumt der vorluset di gewere des gutis*: *Gewer* may refer to the warrantor himself, or the warranty of enfeoffment, or transfer of property, or actual investiture. In this case, real property is the issue. See "guarantor," "guaranty," "ownership," "possession" in glossary.

78. Normally, *fürsten*, translated as "princes," designates magnates higher than a count, but in this instance it refers to any member of the landed nobility.

79. *senden irn ingebornen dinstman der das vorste an ire stat*: most likely "ministerial" is the intended meaning here, but I chose "subordinate" in order to render the word *dinstman* as nonspecific as it is in German.

80. *Wer ein gut im zu sait* is a typical formula describing a claim to property.

81. The term *eigen* is an "allod" or land held in free ownership.

82. *eigenliche gewer*: actual possession and free ownership of real property. This normally refers to allodial land (Ishikawa, 68); see "ownership" in glossary.

83. *Wer da besaeten acker eins andern mannes anderweide ernt*: "Whoever plows another man's sown field a second time." The phrase is redundant because the field had to be plowed once in order to be sown. It does not mean that a person plowed twice after the field was sown.

84. Usage rights within the common grazing land were carefully regulated, and no one was permitted to graze animals outside the designated sections.

85. *zende*, meaning "tenth," is the 10 percent duty or tithe paid on animals and crops; the *zenender* or "collector," personally collects the tithes paid in kind. The "stand in the fields" refers to the fact that once grain is harvested and tied in sheaves, these bundles are set standing upright.

86. A "shock" (*schog*) is a unit of measure equalling sixty units or six sheaves (see II 13).

87. The passage implies that if the collector wants to take the animal tenth in kind, then he must wait until the animal itself is available. The law clearly stipulates when he is entitled to an animal instead of a money payment (see II 58).

88. *Anderthalb*, "one and a half," literally means half way to two.

89. A *helling* is a coin with half the value of a penny, hence, "a halfpenny."

90. *der sal den da bi haben der ander sit lant da bi hat*: "he shall have that person present who holds the property on the other side [of the border]."

91. *czunet* (v.), *tun, zun* (n.): "to fence or enclose." Fences were normally the woven, wattle variety although *zun* could also mean "hedge" as it does here.

92. The cesspit needed a surround. Many consisted of a wattlework hurdle enclosing the pit, which may even have had a toilet seat.

93. *das sal der herre losen noch der gebure kore entut hes nicht he vuret das eine mit deme andern weg*: "These the lord shall redeem according to the peasants' valuation, and if he does not purchase them, the tenant or his heirs may remove them, too."

94. The *wer* in wergeld means "man," but this literal meaning was no longer part of the concept since wergeld is used in versions of the *Sachsenspiegel* to indicate the tariff set for the value of animals when compensation is paid (see III 48, 49, 52).

95. Here *urkunde* means "proof of witnesses" because it refers most likely to an oral proof (or testimony) of two men as in *lebende urkunde* (IV 22). In other cases it may well refer to a written document, as in *urkunde von gote* (II 61), where the Bible as textual proof is certainly implied. In the passage *ouch gab uns got urkunde an eime phenninge*, the term indicates physical proof (III 42), but it can also mean an oral "notice, notification" (III 5).

96. *bricht is aber einen nuwen abegang da mite vorlust he sins landes nicht*: *Abgang* translates as a "backwater" which is defined as "a low-lying tract of ground with shallow pools onto which the overflow of a river deposits its alluvial waste" (*OED*). Schmidt-Wiegand translates the passage as *Bricht es (das Wasser) aber ein neues Flu-ßbett, dann verliert er sein Land nicht* (*Facsimile W*, vol. 2, 211). My translation of this chapter is based on the helpful suggestions of Lambertus Okken in personal correspondence.

97. This passage regulates the use of new, fertile land. When the water carries away land in one place and deposits fresh silt in another, the landholder has no recourse, but when this process creates new, unclaimed land, users' rights are adjusted.

98. *in lediglicher gewere* means "free, inherited right of possession" according to Ishikawa (69). It can also translate as "enfeoffment," which in practical terms is a condition quite like ownership because the term *gewere* is never used with a leasehold (Ishikawa, 70). Hence, according to this passage, one person may hold land from another, and that person from yet a third, and so on. The last in this series is the primary, or enfeoffed, holder. The secondary holders may control the land (i.e., work it), but they only have subsidiary usage rights, never "possession." In contrast, the primary holder has enfeoffment or "possession" (*gewere*), meaning that rents and dues are paid to him.

99. *Ab der man keinen lenerben enhat noch sime tode*: mention of a feudal heir indicates that *der man* here really does mean "vassal."

100. The phrase *vordient gut* literally means "reaped property" or "revenues" and refers to the fiefholder's income based on the yields of the land.

101. *Nu vornemet wen is vordient si*: "Now hear when it is reaped, [i.e., collected] by the lord." The phrase refers to the specified days when the tithe on the peasants' agricultural production is paid.

102. *zins und phlege*: "rents and dues." The *phlegehaften* are those tenants who pay dues as wards of the king.

103. This feast was known as *wurzmesse*.

104. See II 48.

105. This means that if the minor attains majority before the rent is due on St Urban's day, the revenues are given to him and not to the lord.

106. *Anegevelle* is that which devolves upon someone either as inheritance or according to feudal law. In this case, the lord has right to the revenues of the child's property until he comes of age.

107. These two statements are proverbs and were perhaps even placed together in the text because they share the principle of "first come, first served" formulated using parallel syntax. The rule regarding the mill is still well-known today.

108. Here "peace" (*vride)* means "safety" or "freedom" from injury as in "peace days" (see II 66 and glossary).

109. I have translated *banvürsten* as "game preserves." They were proscripted forests because they were the royal hunting preserves.

110. The first hunting preserve is perhaps Koine near Guben, and the third may be Mosigkau near Reppichau (Eckhardt, *Lnr*, glossary of proper names, 251–53).

111. Anyone who trespasses in the royal hunting forest must pay the king's fine, called a *ban*.

112. According to Dalby, *winde*, and *windhund* refer to a "racer," a "greyhound" (311); *bracke* is a "tracker" (34); and (*jage-) hunt* is a large "running-hound" (104). Hounds are normally coupled by a strap (34).

113. *Grusen* means "to incite with the voice or with a hunting cry," not with a horn (Dalby, 71).

114. The source of this story is *Corpus juris civilis*, Dig. III 1 *De postulando* 1 ¶ 5. Calefurnia, or Cafarnia was a woman who allegedly brought bold and unjustifiable claims to the court official and beleaguered him until an edict against women was established (cf. Eckhardt, *Lndr*, 181, n. 44.) Here *riche* must refer to the emperor himself.

115. She can prove the rape with the witnesses who answer the alarm.

116. *Schaden* usually means "disadvantage" in legal procedure, but here it refers to a "fine."

117. No specific wergeld is mentioned for a male child in the tables, which means that it must have been the same as a man's (see III 46).

118. *mit der guten knechte willekor des landes*: *knecht* here refers to the princes of the realm; *gut* as attribute means they are the capable and respected servants of the realm. This phrase is repeated from the *Imperial Landpeace of Mainz*. However, this entire chapter corresponds very closely to Heinrich IV's *Truce of God* and its later versions. See Heinrich's text in Henderson's *Select Historical Documents*, 208–11.

119. Translated as "peace," "safety," or "immunity," *vride* refers to protection from injury to person and property.

120. Peace or binding days prohibit violence in certain places and against certain people on specified days of the week (II 10, 12, 61) See "land peace" and "peace days" in glossary.

121. The verb *mern* means "to eat by dipping bread in wine, to share a meal" (Lexer), and here it refers to the celebration of the Last Supper.

122. The phrase *des suntagis worde wir vorsunet mit gote umme Adams* shows *Adam* with a possessive *s* but without the following noun. Schmidt-Wiegand adds *missetat* ("sin") from H and O, to make it read "Adam's sin," but this is not in W or its closest precursor, D (*Facsimile W*, vol. 2, 220).

123. The phrase *als hi vor gesprochen ist* ("as was said earlier") indicates the oral nature of the legal process retained even into the fourteenth century. Instead of a temporal reference, today we would expect "as explained above," a phrase that implies a text in which one may move forward and backward. Additional discussions of peace violations follow below; see also III 14, 61, 66, 69.

124. *Gelobter vride* is a truce sworn between two parties in conflict. This is often imposed by the court itself (see III 36).

125. *Richten*: "to judge" usually, but here "to try."

126. A *burg* is a "castle" and not necessarily a fortified town because W distinguishes between town (*stete*), castle (*burg*), and village (*dorf*). Towns and villages may also be fortified or walled.

127. A *knecht* can be a free or unfree servant or serf.

128. This chapter should be numbered 72, but the scribe evidently skipped a number.

129. *unde engeben si si nicht her abe zu rechte*: *Zu recht* does not, as Ignor suggests, mean "for the purpose of a court trial" because the phrase *vor gerichte* already occurs with that meaning. Rather, it contains the idea of handing someone over for justice or judgment, a slightly more abstract concept indicating not the procedure, but the goal of achieving justice (Ignor, 144–45).

130. *Rat und tat* ("advice and aid") is the phrase used to describe the aiding and abetting of a person engaged in criminal activity.

Book III

1. Terms for rape are *genotzaget, genotigetit, notnunft*; all have to do with forcing someone.

2. The building is not mentioned, but the entire context clearly implies that it has been condemned by the court ruling. Razing a building appears to be a rather extreme and expensive measure. If actually practiced, it would have deterred women from prosecuting for rape for fear of creating serious hardship for the entire family whose building was razed.

3. I seriously doubt that this law requiring the beheading of all living things present at the rape was actually enforced because animals were dear. If the law was indeed taken seriously, it would have forced women to deny rape, for no woman could admit to a rape if it meant losing her family's farm animals. Opinions vary, however. Rudolf His proposed that the animals were punished for failing to aid the victim (18), and Karl von Amira thought the beheading created a taboo (*Todesstrafen*, 231).

4. Normally a person is fined for bringing charges against someone without evidence (I 62).

5. This refers to the immunity of certain groups secured in the royal and territorial landpeaces; see "landpeace" in glossary.

6. *Anevangen*: "to initiate a suit for recovery of owned property by grasping the item" (II 34); see "recover property" in glossary.

7. The term used is *urkunde*, "notice, notification." The primary connotation is that an *urkunde* provides facts, or certain knowledge about something. It may be oral or written in form in the mid-fourteenth century (see II 54, 61; III 42; IV 22).

8. According to Kisch, the king's overlordship and rights of the Jews originated in Roman times. After the conquest and destruction of Jerusalem, the surviving Jews lost their rights and became slaves of Emperor Vespasian. Eventually he granted them legal protection as a reward for the medical services of one Flavius Josephus who had cured the imperial prince Titus of the gout. Consequently the *Sachsenspiegel* texts reiterate that the German kings, as successors to the Roman emperors, continued to protect the Jews (*Jews*, 154).

9. The term used is *bucher* ("books"). Given the context, it could mean any type of liturgical text, but it probably implies Bibles (personal correspondence, Paul Brand).

10. *Vride*: "Immunity" from assault; see "land peace" in glossary.

11. *Wen swer den vorsten vride globet unde en truwe phlichtig is bricht he den vride man sal uber en richten*: I translated *richten* as "to try and sentence" because I understand the statement to stress both the judicial process and the punishment.

12. *Bescheiden tagen*: "specified day, specified time."

13. *Swer uffe den anderen clait unde iener wider uf en der alrest clait der enhat ieme nicht zu entwerten he ensi von im alrest ledig*: The pronouns stand without clear antecedents, but the passage means that lawsuits were to be dealt with in the sequence in which they were brought before the court.

14. This refers to the thirtieth day after the funeral, which was also the day the estate was divided among the heirs.

15. Outlaws could not bring a claim or suit to court because their rights and privileges had been withdrawn (I 38; III 34); see "outlawry" in glossary.

16. *Des riches dinstman* refers to imperial ministerials in this context.

17. *deme riche hulde tun*: "to perform feudal service to the king" (IV 4).

18. *Ere* translates as "public reputation" and not "personal honor."

19. *Vride dar uber geworcht si* means that an oath of truce or peace between the parties had been imposed by the court. Thus if the person who lost the case plows nonetheless, he is guilty of breaking his oath (II 71; III 8); see "sworn peace" in glossary.

20. *Wasserurteil* ("trial by water") is here considered to be different from the boiling water mentioned in I 39 (Lieberwirth, *Entstehung*, 33). The illustration in W shows a naked man lying in a large basin of water.

21. *Verfestung* is "limited outlawry"; i.e., limited to the judicial district that outlaws the person.

22. Proper procedure is discussed I 64; II 4; and III 36.

23. D not only completes the sentence but fills in chapters 25–39, which are missing from W.

24. *Der kunig is richter ubir al*: There is some dispute whether *ubir al* refers to people, as in "over everyone," or whether it is to be understood in its spatial meaning, "everywhere." Given the spelling and syntax, the latter is more likely, but the context, since it is more concerned with class privileges and offices, has led me to read it as "all people." The primary point here is that the king is the central power from whom all law and judicial authority emanates, and therefore royal justice extends to all people and all places. The thirteenth-century *Schwabenspiegel* reception changes the wording to "all people": *uber eins ieglichen menschen lip und gut* (Janz, *Rechtssprichwörter*, 109).

25. See "family estate" in glossary.

26. *Gescheidung, scheidung* means "divorce" or "annulment" and not merely a separation.

27. *swen man unecht sait von geburt oder ammechte: Unecht* here is used meaning *rechtlos*, which I normally translate as "deficient in legal capacity." The term *ammechte* in combination with *unecht* demonstrates that the concept of disreputable occupations existed and that it limited a person's legal capacity (I 50, 51). For a discussion of all laws pertaining to these people, see Danckert; see also "legal incapacity" and "disreputable occupation" in glossary.

28. *sin echt unde sin recht*: "his legal capacity and his rights"; see "legal capacity" and "legal incapacity" in glossary.

29. See I 51 and "family estate" in glossary.

30. The borrower must account for the items only if the heirs bring a suit for recovery of property.

31. *Swer die gewere hat an einen manne*: *Gewer* ("right of possession") is almost the equivalent of ownership and indicates having possession of a bondman or serf because of the context, but the term *man* itself means simply "man." See "possession" in glossary.

32. This rule is apparently intended to safeguard the lord's rights so that one master cannot easily take a serf from another, and it is also consistent with rules of possession; namely, that having possession presupposes the right of possession and is therefore easier to prove.

33. *Sich vor gericht zu eigen geben*: "to place oneself into servitude." Entering into bondage, probably because of poverty, seems to have been common; see discussion of the origins of servitude (III 43).

34. *Kindere . . . di he nach der gabe gewan*: The phrase here simply refers to the transaction or gift (*gabe*) of having given himself into serfdom.

35. *mit zwen sinen inburtigen eigenen mannen*: "men born in servitude on his land."

36. See "outlawry" and "attainder" in glossary.

37. *Oberacht* ("superior outlawry") indicates that degrees of outlawry existed. *Oberacht* is graver because it cannot be lifted. It is imposed if the person does not release himself from royal or imperial outlawry within the specified year and a day. See "attainder" in glossary.

38. *So wirkt man en beiden vride*: "thus one establishes peaceful conduct for both parties." This is a sworn truce accomplished with a binding oath (II 71: III 20); see "sworn peace" in glossary.

39. The wife had no control over her morning gift until after her husband's death. This means that if she died first, there was no morning gift for her to pass on, according to Rummel (148). This interpretation is supported by the fact that the morning gift is mentioned together with the divisible food stores which, naturally, would not be considered divisible while both spouses were alive. It is consistent then, in case of divorce, that she takes no morning gift with her (III 74). This means that both the morning gift and the food supplies were intended to provide support for the widow. See "inheritance" in glossary.

40. The W text resumes here.

41. *di mus der cleger gezugen selb sibende uf en*: *Gezugen* indicates that the six others are witnesses and not merely oathhelpers.

42. The chapter number 40 is missing in W.

43. The term used is *gewerde* (n.f.), which means "an article of value," but it may also be a synonym for *gewer* (n.f. and n.), "security" (Lexer). Here the person may be attempting to pay with an item of like value rather than cash.

44. *Urfehde*: "peace"; that is, a cessation of hostilities promised by the injured party (I 8). See "truce" in glossary.

45. *Dinstliute* is best translated as "unfree people or servants" in this general context rather than as "ministerials," who are also referred to as *dinstman*. The text is probably referring to ministerials, but that is not clear. What follows is Eike's discussion concerning the origin of bondage.

46. *da man ouch recht sazte von erst da enwas kein dinstman*: *Dinstman* must here, too, be translated as generic "unfree person" or "servant" because it is unclear whether the text distinguishes between ministerials and serfs in this chapter. See "ministerial" in glossary.

47. *Eigenschaft* translates as "servitude, bondage"; see "bondman" in glossary.

48. *ouch nicht in unseme rechte*: The statement makes little sense unless the negative is omitted. The law referred to is III 33.

49. *Losunge* refers to periods of redemption when pardons were given by the king; see "pardon" in glossary.

50. Lev. 25:39–41.

51. The reference is to the emperor's image on coins from Matt. 22:19–21.

52. The text alludes to Wisd. of Sol. 2:23; Lev. 25:42, 55.

53. *vor rechte haben will*: "to accept as right." Here the text implies that custom

and tradition are not always correct, and that one must recognize the occasional example of "bad tradition" in the hope of eradicating it. Kern claims that all traditional law was considered good because it had been handed down by the ancestors (23–29), but Kroeschell has shown that Eike's critical evaluation of tradition is consistent with canon law ("Rechtsaufzeichnung," 364–67). See also Kolb's discussion of this entire chapter as a formal theological *quaestio* (300–305).

54. The land referred to is Greece; *des landes has* ("hatred of the land") I translate as "people's anger."

55. *rujan* designates the island of Rügen (Eckhardt, *Lnr*, 253).

56. Schmidt-Wiegand equates the *lasin* with "half-free peasants" who had been leaseholders but gradually became bound to the soil (*Facsimile W*, 245; see "bondman" in glossary).

57. The payments in the table listed here were usually awarded in compensation for personal injury or damages, called *buse*. An additional sum could be added to the compensation in punitive damages if the court found it warranted. Thus it is difficult sometimes to determine whether a payment mentioned in W is a fine or is intended to indemnify a person. See "compensation" in glossary.

58. Females received 50 percent of what a male who enjoyed the same legal status would have received. Since a female was valued separately in obtaining justice before the court, she was not hindered in any way by the possible lower status of a guardian.

59. Thus in marriage, husband and wife shared the same rights and legal status (I 45). In addition, evidence from tax lists indicates that the wife continued to represent her husband's rights and affairs long after his death (Kuchenbuch, 160–62).

60. *in gastis wise*: "like guests." The king's tenants have no land of their own but are free. Because they are not tied to the land, they are evidently not considered full members of the village community but rather as guests. See "tenant farmer" in glossary.

61. *vadem*: a "fathom"; a measure of length or depth, approximately six feet.

62. *zu eigen geben*: "to give in ownership."

63. Paid champions were those who could be hired to fight in a trial by combat. It was considered a disreputable occupation (see I 50, 51; III 28; see also "champion," and "disreputable occupation" in glossary.

64. Brooms and scissors were both symbols of a conviction and sentence.

65. *Varndes wib* meant "an itinerant woman minstrel." These women were generally considered prostitutes, and some actually were, but not every female performer earned her living that way. Helttampt's list of payments made to entertainers includes women for the years 1290–92 (see 140–44).

66. *An varnden wiben unde an siner ameien mag der man sinen lip vorwirken, ab he si ane dang belegit*: "A man may forfeit his life with an itinerant woman or his lover if he lies with her against her will." Curiously enough, this sentence describes the act of rape but refers to it as "intercourse." The *Sachsenspiegel* does not define what constitutes rape, but this sentence certainly associates rape with the woman's refusal. If we can rely on the term *not* in the table of contents as accurately designating the act described, then that act was definitely considered rape.

67. See the wergeld table for animals (III 52).

68. *dar zu behelt ienir sin vie des is er was*: Ownership in this passage is expressed according to time of possession. The person who had had the animal earlier keeps it.

69. *alse hi vor geredit is*: "as discussed earlier." The "earlier" is interesting because it reflects the oral frame of reference in which speech is experienced in time, not as stretched out on a page. The reference is to III 48 above.

70. *Stellente*: a live duck used by hunters as a decoy.

71. *uf den stul komt*: "installed on the throne."

72. *den kunig kusit man zu richtere uber eigen unde uber len unde uber iclichs mannes lip der keiser enmag aber in allen landen nicht gesin unde alle ungerichte nicht gerichten zu aller zit*: This alternation of the terms *kunig* ("king") and *keiser* ("emperor") seems to be stylistic in these statements because they refer to the same office. With the exception of the very beginning of this chapter, the text does not distinguish between the two roles and thus interchanges the terms seemingly indiscriminately. This lack of distinction is a typical feature of vernacular epic as well and may have come about because the German ruler was frequently but not always emperor and king at the same time. R. Schmidt has pointed out that according to this chapter, the German king already had the right to imperial authority as soon as he was elected king (89). His interpretation implies that distinguishing between the two offices was rarely necessary.

73. A *van len* is "a banner or territorial estate" conferred by the king's authority on the major princes of the realm who owe fealty directly to the king (see III 52, 58, 60).

74. The investiture of the *Schultheiss* becomes most important in cases of legal abuse by the count himself (I 2, III 45); see "*Schultheiss*" in glossary.

75. An *echtes ding* is a "regularly scheduled court session."

76. *Schult* translates here as "duties, responsibilities."

77. *Burgreve* ("burgrave") is the magistrate who rules by hereditary right a German castle and its adjacent lands (IV 78). See "burgrave" and "margrave" in glossary.

78. W contains two chapters numbered 53. I have labeled the second 53a.

79. The term is *van len*. These banner fiefs were held directly from the crown; see "banner estate" in glossary.

80. This passage refers to the *Leihezwang*, the requirement of granting out judicial and imperial fiefs within the year and a day time limit. Scholars today question whether this rule was actually enforced (*LexMA* 4, c. 1857); see III 60.

81. This chapter is misnumbered 64 in W. The correct numbering resumes with 55.

82. See "fief" in glossary.

83. "Franconian law" here is a geographic designation. The custom referred to was that the king had to be elected, crowned, and anointed on Franconian soil and could only be tried there. The commonly held idea that Frankish freemen enjoyed certain immunities does not apply here (*LexMA* 4 c. 742–43, *HRG* 1, c. 1208–10).

84. *so enmus nimant richten wen der echte vronebote*: *Richten* means "to execute" in this statement.

85. *Vride* usually means "peace" but translates as "immunity" in this instance.

86. *erstatelaege, erdstadelich* ("cut, standing grain") refers to grain that had been harvested, bound in sheaves, and then placed upright (see II 48).

87. The concept of German identity implied here is remarkable. The idea as stated in W is quite old and consistent with earlier manuscripts cited in Eckhardt. Bohemia is unquestionably part of the empire according to IV 4. But even though the king of Bohemia is an imperial prince and one of the four court officers, he does not have a vote because he is not German. According to Eckhardt, the king of Bohemia voted only to break a tie (*Lndr*, 242, n. 57).

88. See IV 20, 78.

89. As immediate vassals of the emperor, both groups owed fealty directly to him.

90. This refers to the required granting out of judicial fiefs and banner territories within the limitation period of a year and a day called *Leihezwang*, see III 53b and the accompanying footnote.

91. *lant* usually means "territory, region," but it indicates a judicial district in this passage.

92. *Burg*: "castle" or "fortified town."

93. *Echte hove*: the "true" or "authentic court" is the imperial court.

94. According to W, the place-name spellings are *gruna, werle, gosler, walhusen, alstete, merseburg*.

95. *leuenu* ? in W is illegible. Aschersleben is consistent with the list in D and the early manuscripts in Eckhardt, *Lndr*, 246–47.

96. Actually, four archdioceses are named. The archdioceses of Mainz and Cologne are themselves clearly not located in Saxony but are listed because some of their dioceses are. The total number of bishoprics named equals fifteen.

97. This is a reference to the Donation of Constantine, but the source of the particular fine is unclear. For sources see Eckhardt, *Lndr*, 248, n. 66.

98. See "advocate" in glossary.

99. See II 13; III 52; and "royal judicial authority" in glossary.

100. *Ban liet man ane manschaft*: "Authority is invested without a compliment of supporters or workers." These men are most likely vassals because *manschaft* refers to the act of homage (IV 22). See "homage" in glossary.

101. See IV 86, and "military shield" in glossary.

102. *binnen der erden*: "within the ground," but apparently only partially underground.

103. The *zunen* (n. pl.) may be a "fence" or a "hedge" (see II 50).

104. The text makes explicit that no one was to eat any breakfast before a court hearing.

105. *unde zie is da hes durch zien sal*: This means that the person offering the new judgment presents it before the authority of the court for acceptance or rejection (see II 13).

106. As Willoweit explains it, this chapter refers to the margrave's court, not the local court, and certainly not the count's court because the margrave does not judge under the king's judicial authority, but under his own (II 12; III 65). Since everyone in the margrave's court could be called upon to hand down a judgment, Willoweit reasons that ethnic tensions were avoided by not asking a German to hand down a judgment on a Wend and vice versa (89–92). Consequently, only under the king's judicial authority did the German *Schöffen* normally hand down judgments on Germans and Wends alike (Willoweit 85–88; see III 69).

107. Here it becomes clear that language was a significant problem when dealing with the Wends. Since the court was normally conducted in German, the spokesman functioned as an interpreter for Wends (Willoweit, 88).

108. See I 3; IV 1, 2; and "military shield" in glossary.

109. These people are also free; see "tenant" and "sharecropper" in glossary.

110. Bishop Wichmann (1152–92) was known for giving settlers personal freedom. Often the landholdings of his peasants became their owned property (Rösener, 231). He is also mentioned in the *Sächsiche Weltchronik* with respect to this rule for establishing the legal status of children.

111. Here *dinstman* appears to refer to ministerials in their status as unfree servants.

112. *Dinstlute*: "servants." Again, ministerials are most likely meant because the issue seems to be of gaining freedom for the next generation by means of marriage. With regard to inheriting status from father or mother, see III 33, which states that in order to establish one's free status, one had to list free ancestors on both the father's and mother's side.

113. *Bumite*: literally a "tax for building a house" but designates a "general wedding tax."

114. *Vrische pheninge*: "departure fee," paid when a Wend woman divorced a man.

115. *was si zu irme manne brachte*: literally, "what she brought to her husband" upon the union.

116. This passage refers to her wedding gift, promised to her by the husband upon the marriage, which is not the same as the morning gift.

117. The term *gedinge* refers to an enfeoffed holding having predetermined conditions and delayed possession: a "fief in reversion." A woman who cannot pass on a fief in inheritance fits the definition. See "fief" and "fief in reversion" in glossary.

118. *len*: "property held in fief."

119. Missing text is supplied from D fol. 52r–53v, containing chapters 77–84.

120. I think this statement refers to the primary holder who ultimately receives all rents and dues, and not to the lessor; for the sequence of subleasing, see II 57.

121. *Man* implies "vassal, member of household" consistently in this chapter because the topic pertains to the responsibility of man to lord, and lord to man. However, I continue to translate it as "man."

122. *Swo abir ein man in einer reise is unde nicht ein houbitman is riten luite an en unde an di sinen tut he schadin sime herrin odir sime manne oder sime mage odir sweme das si ane sinen rat unde ane sine tat gewerit hes uf den heiligen he blibit is ane gelt unde ane lastir*: My translation is based on the assumption that *tut he scadin* was intended as a plural and refers to the attackers.

123. *Erbezinsrecht*: "the right to inherit the rented land."

124. *sinen dinstman oder sinen eigenen man*: This statement distinguishes between an unfree ministerial and a servile person. The remainder of the chapter refers also to ministerials when *dinstman* occurs; see I 38; II 42; III 19.

125. *zuget abir der schephin*: *Zuget* means "perish, die out." Since the *Schöffen* office is hereditary, the passage is concerned not with a single death but with the demise of an entire male line, and that event is what necessitates creating a new *Schöffen* family. The ministerials appear to be the beneficiaries of such losses. This

passage would appear to support the commonly held theory that the ministerials rose to freedom and power in the twelfth and thirteenth centuries as a result of the wars that extinguished a number of family lines. But according to Arnold, ministerials of the crown were often highly respected at the imperial court and were customarily rewarded with large and small fiefs (43–45). In contrast, Kroeschell supports the thesis of Otto von Zallinger that the once free landowning families gave up their freedom to become ministerials but did not relinquish their allodial lands nor their rights as judgment finders ("Rechtswirklichkeit," 5).

126. *Das suln si besizzin dri tage* literally means that "they must sit on it for three days" because keeping something in one's possession eventually turns into ownership.

127. W resumes here.

128. *Wartunge* ("expectancy") is a promise to invest a person with the first available property (see IV 34, and "expectancy" and "fief" in glossary). The "Imperial Landpeace of Mainz" contains detailed laws against patricide and attempted usurpation of a kinsman's property (see fol. 1r, 1v,l).

129. *Swo me lute den einer zusamne globin ein wergelt oder ander gelt alle sin sie das phlichtig zu leistene di wile is unvorgoldin is unde nicht ir iclich allis me wen also vil alse menlicheme gebort unde alse verre man en da zu getwingen mag von gerichtis halben der deme das da gelobit is oder der das mit im gelobete ab hes vor in vorgoldin hat*: The "pledge of several people" concerns payment of a sum either to the creditor or to the person who had agreed to pay the sum for the debtor and then had to be repaid.

130. *vor dem oberstin richtere*: It is unclear which judge is meant by "highest judge."

131. A *geburschaft*, translated as "peasant community," appears to have become a peasant corporation by the end of the fourteenth century.

132. *rechtis weigirt der richter*: "the judge circumvents the law or justice," or "refuses to carry out the law." This does not mean he breaks the law, because no crime has been committed; III 87. Failure to comply is punishable, however.

133. *rechtis weigirt der man*: "a man circumvents the law." The constraints or duties of complying with the law are enforced on a person who is accused of something or has a judgment against him.

134. The correct number is 90 but the W text and the table of contents have 100 because they omit the "X" from "XC." Otherwise the numbering is consecutive.

135. The term *anevangen*, "to grab," is the legal remedy for recovery of owned property (II 33, 34). See "recover property" in glossary.

136. *binnen sinen geweren*: literally, "in his possession," but here it refers to the shelter or care the helper provides (Ishikawa, 60–61).

137. W contains no chapter number 92, but I have added it in brackets because the table of contents lists it separately but labels it chapter 102.

Book IV

1. The seven orders of knighthood are referred to as *herschilt*; see "military shield" in glossary; also I 3; II 22; III 59; IV 83.

2. *der bischove man* may also be translated as "the bishops' vassals."

3. The term *volge* means "the right to have a fief renewed or confirmed" by a new lord if one's own lord dies or fails in his duty. It also entails the right to pass the fief to an heir. The issue in a feudal property contract is whether the relationship between lender and vassal is limited to those specific individuals or whether the fiefholder can renew his right to the fief with the original lord's successor and also pass it on as inheritance (see III 14, 63; IV 4, 10, 26, 30, 59, 67, 81; and "renew" in glossary.

4. This passage means that a fiefholder of non-knightly status may not refuse to accept as his lord anyone who succeeds his original lord. In contrast, a vassal with knightly status does not have to accept a new lord who is below the rank of his original lord (see IV 21, 26, 56, 86).

5. On the investiture of women, see III 59; IV 57, 58, 81.

6. *des riches dinst*: "military service for the empire" (see IV 38, 48).

7. *sal he dinen bi phlicht binnen duczschir zungen di romischeme riche undirtan is*: "He is duty-bound to serve within the German tongue [i.e., territory] that is subordinate to the Roman Empire." The formulation here marks the German portion of the empire only by means of language and thus reveals the lack of a clear concept for the geopolitical territories loosely bound under the aegis of the German king and emperor.

8. *schat rowe*: "a rest for the lance shaft."

9. See III 57 for list of electors and procedure.

10. The obligation to participate in the emperor's entourage is called a *herfahrt*, a term normally designating a military campaign.

11. *Gewer* means "right of possession"; that is, legally protected possession or control of a property. See "possession" in glossary.

12. *Zcwen mannen mag der herre ein gut lien also das einer di gewer dar an habe unde der andire das gedinge*: "A lord can invest two men with one property such that the first has right of possession and the other the reversion." *Gedinge*, meaning "reversion," is investiture but with a delayed possession that is contingent upon the property reverting to the lord upon the death of the first fiefholder. At that point the lord grants right of possession to the fiefholder with reversion (see IV 6, 7, 38; and "fief in reversion," "fief" in glossary.

13. This is formulated as a maxim: *an gedinge is kein volge*. *Gedinge* is "reversion," and *volge* refers to the right to "renew" a feudal contract with the lord's successor. See "reversion," "renew" in glossary.

14. *ein gut liet sinem manne*: "[If a lord] enfeoffs his man with a property." It seems that *lien* (v.) indicates a "pledge to enfeoff" and does not always designate actual enfeoffment, as it does when a person is enfeoffed with a reversion (IV 5), and need not entail the actual transfer of control over the property, which is a separate process called *wisunge* ("investiture") (IV 10). The first person mentioned here has received only a pledge for the first available property. The other person has actually been enfeoffed with a specific fief in reversion under the condition that possession is taken when the fiefholder dies without an heir. Hence the condition of "first available property" cannot take precedence over a specified fief in reversion. See IV 8, and "fief in reversion," "investiture" in glossary.

15. *Husgenos* literally means "member of the household," and in this case, since the context is property held in fief, it translates best as "fellow vassal" (see IV 25, 43, 49, 70b).

16. *In einer sache von eime lene enmugen si zcwene nicht gezug sin, di wile si an deme lene nicht beteilt ensin*: "In a suit regarding a fief, the two parties cannot validate their own testimony with an oath." The text does not make clear whether the two hold the fief jointly or whether they are opponents in a legal case.

17. See IV 14, 20, 43, 70, 78, 82; and "revoke" in glossary.

18. See "spokesman" in glossary.

19. *etliche lute sagen das man kein gedinge lien muse ane iens bete der das gut in geweren hat des enis nicht (10) wen der man gezcuget sine lenunge ab hes bedarf unde nimandes bete*. The phrase in chapter 10 forms the conclusion of the previous idea and should probably read: "Some people say that no one may bestow a fief in reversion without the request of the person who has right of possession to the property, but that is not so because the man proves his enfeoffment with witnesses when necessary and not by request." However, the manuscript divides the sentence with a capital letter and a chapter number, and I reproduce this break by maintaining the original chapter division. Continuation of a thought across chapter boundaries is a recurrent stylistic trait in the entire text but nowhere else does it occur in midsentence.

20. *Is ouch ein man belent von sime herren mit eime phunde oder mit zcwen wo is im erst ledig wirt lenrecht hat he dar an deme is geligen unde benant wirt*. Other manuscripts and editions have an additional clause to read: *Is ok en man belent van sime herren mit eneme punde oder mit twen, swar it eme erst ledich wert, lenrecht hevet disse dar an deme it gelegen under benumet wert* (Eckhardt, *Lnr*, 10). The underlined phrase clarifies the meaning of the passage: "If a man is granted by his lord rent of one pound or two, as soon as it is free, he has a legal entitlement to this; all the more is this the case when he has been enfeoffed in a specified place" (translation by Paul Brand, personal communication).

21. *Swen aber der herre weigert zu bewisene so getan gut als he im geligen hat swo is im ledig si sunder bewisunge*: "but if the lord refuses to invest someone in the property once he had enfeoffed him where it is available without investiture." *Bewisunge* refers to the investiture procedure. I interpolate from the context since subject and verb are missing in W, D, and O. Eckhardt's edition reads: *Swen aver de herre weigert to bewisene so gedan gut alse he eme gelegen hevet de man underwinde sek so gedanes gudes, alse eme de herre gelegen hevet swar it sime herren ledich si, sunder bewisunge* (*Lnr*, 10). See "investiture" in glossary.

22. See "royal jurisdiction" in glossary.

23. The procedure here is that witnesses are asked one by one until seven are found who support the claim, but no more than twenty-one men may be asked (see II 22).

24. *die wile he sins gutes sinnen sal odir is uszcien sal*: "while he must claim his property or clear it." The term *us czien* means here to "clear" or "release" a property from incumbrance or seizure and to "reinstate" full rights to it (see IV 45, 46, 47, 52, 70, 70a, 78, 82; and "seize a fief" in glossary.

25. *Morgen*: a "measure of land" varying in size from .6 to .9 acres; see "hide" in glossary.

26. The sequence of subinfeudation is outlined here. A discussion of successive lessees, each holding a property from another, is found in II 57. See "possession" in glossary.

27. *Sagit ein man im gut von einem anderen herren an in sins herren keginwarte von deme hes hat, hat is der herre gezuk siner manne an deme gute enhat der man kein recht mer iener enbehald es von deme hes im zusagete*: "If a man claims he holds land from a second lord in the presence of his lord from whom he holds it, if the lord has witnesses among his men, then the man has no longer right to it unless the other, from whom he claimed it, acquires it."

28. The "man" referred to here is the overlord's immediate vassal.

29. The term for "attornment" or "transfer" of a man to another lord for homage and service is *wisunge*.

30. *Enzcagen* ("to repudiate") refers to breaking or canceling the feudal contract of mutual fealty and so it could be translated as "breach of contract." A lord may have done it in order to recover control of the property itself. See IV 46, 82. and "fief," "homage," "repudiate" in glossary.

31. See III 58.

32. The aspect of homage important here is that the voluntary subordination to another of equal status can lower the status of that person causing serious legal consequences such as loss of vassals (see IV 26, 56, 86).

33. *binnen und tage* probably should read *binnen jare und tage*, "a year and a day," the limitation period for legal action. The complete phrase is in Eckhardt's text, which includes the Bremen manuscript (*Lnr*, 22), and also in Schmidt-Wiegand's edition, taken from H and O (*Facsimile W*, IV 22).

34. *das he die sulle wegen*: It is likely that the *die* as pronoun refers to hands.

35. The term here is *manschaft*, "oath of subordination and obedience," and entails feudal service (see IV 24, 26, 86; and "homage" in glossary.

36. *Lebende urkunde*: "living proof," meaning "witnesses." *Urkunde* is used in a number of ways meaning "proof," "notification," and "knowledge based on evidence" (II 54, 61; III 5, 42).

37. In this text and until the beginning of the twentieth century, *kint* tended to refer to male children only, but rather than render too precise and exclusive a meaning, I translate "child" and "children." It was, of course, possible for unmarried and married women to be enfeoffed, but the property did not devolve upon their children.

38. The term *genosin* (pl.) means "mates, peers, fellow vassals" (see IV 7, 43).

39. The criteria and procedures for a legal excuse are the same in feudal and territorial law (see I 38, 70; II 7, 42, 71).

40. On the knightly status relationship between lord and vassal, see IV 21, 56, 86.

41. The term *jarzcale* translates as "time limit" or "limitation period" and refers specifically to the fixed duration of one year and six weeks in which the vassal was permitted to have his fief renewed or have himself reinstated in it. See I 38, 70; IV 30, 37, 43, 46, 47, 52, 59, 66, 70, 86; and "limitation period" in glossary.

42. *sinnen*: to "request" or "petition formally" for the renewal or confirmation of one's feudal property.

43. This statement refers to the feudal obligations of the grantor inherent in

the contract when he bestows a fief on someone. See "fief," "homage," "repudiate" in glossary.

44. *Jarzcal* usually indicates the standard limitation period, but here we have young heirs who have until they reach the age of thirteen to confirm their inherited fief in feudal law.

45. *mit vingeren unde mit zcungen geloben*: "To swear with fingers and tongue" refers to the complete act of oath-taking that requires the formal gesture and the spoken word (see II 4; IV 55).

46. *Anegevelle*: "that which devolves upon someone either as inheritance or right of use according to feudal law." See II 58; IV 29, 30, 78; and "right of use" in glossary.

47. The lord is the child's guardian only for the specific property the child holds from him. Normally the child would also have a guardian who cares for him and his owned property.

48. That is, the child continues to fulfill his feudal obligations as grantor.

49. *Mit rechte brechen*: "to cancel lawfully."

50. *Lasin*: "to transfer." The implication seems to be that the lord wishes to parcel out property in smaller segments.

51. This statement continues the topic of the previous chapter and implies that the lord himself divides the man's feudal property. In such a case the man has the right to require confirmation directly from the overlord.

52. See the parallel formulation in I 14, where this law is in conflict with territorial law.

53. On the age of enfeoffment of children, see IV 28.

54. *imande der des wartende is*: "someone who is waiting for it." The noun is *wartunge*, meaning "contract of expectancy" (III 84; IV 59). See "fief," "expectancy" in glossary.

55. *Veter*: "father's brother" (see I 5).

56. The phrase *noch gesazteme rechte* refers specifically to enacted laws and not to custom.

57. See IV 5, 7, 20.

58. The point here is that the father, by transferring property held in fief to his son, changes the rights connected with the fief so that it can no longer be passed on by inheritance.

59. The text inserts a chapter number here that is not in the table of contents.

60. *Ungetruwelich*: "disloyally, traitorously." Mutual trust and loyalty are an essential part of the feudal contract. See IV 22, 57, 82; and "homage," "repudiate" in glossary.

61. See IV 7, 49.

62. *Wasserurteil* ("trial by cold water"), as in III 21.

63. This is the only mention of a *gotes orteil* in the entire manuscript.

64. See IV 14.

65. See "seize a fief" in glossary.

66. *is deme manne des riches dinst geboten mit orteiln*: Imperial service (*riches dinst*) normally means military service (see IV 4, 38). *Orteil*, from *erteilen* ("to proclaim") translates here as "decree, proclamation."

67. The reason for the conviction is that the man failed to join the troops when summoned.

68. *von munde zu munde mit orteiln*: "from mouth to mouth by proclamation." Left unsaid is that the man fails to appear in court and can therefore be convicted in feudal court.

69. According to this passage, the fiefholder must pay 10 percent of his own revenues that are produced annually by the fiefs he holds from the lords.

70. Some fiefs lack men and yet provide income.

71. *Sweme dirre manne zcuste unde doch zu deme herschilde geboren is also ho das he lenrecht getun mag des herren husgenose si nuczen di man in der manne stat swo he ir bedarf di da man sin da sin gut hingehort.* I follow here the Schmidt-Wiegand translation: *wer selbst keine mannen hat aber doch so hoch zum Heerschild geboren ist, daß er Lehenrecht gewahren kann, der bedient sich, wenn er ihrer bedarf, an Stelle eigener Mannen der Gefolgschaftsleute des Herrn, die dort (als) Mannen (belehnt) sind, wo sein Gut hingehört* (facsimile W).

72. Several leaves of W containing chapters 50–70 are missing. I supply them from D folios 73r–80v in italics.

73. *Volge* ("to renew") implies here "by the overlord."

74. Since W had already numbered the previous chapter as 50, I note this chapter with "a." I keep here the numbering of the D manuscript as the translation shifts to D to fill in the passages missing from W. This numbering also coincides with the numbering in the table of contents in W.

75. *Uber mer*: "across the sea." The sea is the Mediterranean, and the phrase refers specifically to the Holy Land in the context of the crusades.

76. *Mit fingere unde mit zungen*: "with finger and tongue" refers to the hand gesture and words necessary for a valid oath (II 4; IV 28).

77. Two issues are important here. First, since the system is hierarchical, the lord can lower his knightly status only by pledging homage to an equal. Second, vassals who lose a lord have a right to another who is equal in status to the previous one (see IV 21, 26, 86).

78. This implies that the new lord is of lower status than the previous one.

79. *wirt einen manne gut geligen uf sine truwe*: "if a man is granted property based on his honorable word." I conclude from the rest of this chapter that this grant of property is given as security until the lord can pay off his debt.

80. *selp sibende gezugen*: "to prove with himself and six others" (see I 8, 15).

81. *manschaft*: normally, "homage," but here more specifically, "upon condition of feudal service."

82. *Truwe* in this and the next sentence translates best as "loyalty" or "goodwill."

83. D has only a truncated sentence (*geligene sazczunge*), but O completes it: *dat nis weder len noch sattunghe* ("that is neither enfeoffment nor property in pledge") (Lübben, *Facsimile O*, IV 55).

84. The terms are *recht len* ("proper fief"), *erbelen* ("heritable fief"), *burglen* ("castle fief"), and *gedinge* ("fief in reversion"). See "fief," "fief in reversion," "homage" in glossary.

85. *Herschilt* ("military shield") here refers to the right and ability to provide military service as part of knightly status.

86. See IV 57 above.

87. *mit gesamenter hant*: "jointly, with joined hands."

88. *Vluchtsal*: "the fraudulent transfer of property with intent to harm creditors."

89. *Alle len ane gewere darben der volge unde alle gewere ane liunge is unrecht sie enhabe ein man beide so sin si beide unrecht*: "All enfeoffment without investiture lacks right of renewal, and all investiture without enfeoffment is unlawful. Unless a man has both, the grant is unlawful." The main point here is that a man must be enfeoffed with feudal property and invested (*gewere*) with the property for the contract to be legally binding, hence the rules prohibiting the feudal tenant from giving up right of possession (or investiture) in 61 above. The term *gewere* means "right of possession," but according to Ishikawa, it can also translate as "investiture" (81).

90. The statement implies that this lord has been accused and found guilty of granting property without right of possession.

91. Six weeks is the legal limitation period noted here because it is the period between regular court sessions.

92. *dulden durfe; durch recht liden durfe*: "to have to suffer it, to have no legal remedy."

93. A man loses legal capacity for a conviction or outlawry (see "legal incapacity" in glossary). Women and priests were in a separate category because they did not have membership in the judiciary.

94. *len ane gerichte*: "a fief with judicial powers."

95. The term used is *ammechtman* ("steward, estate manager").

96. *wen im sin herre alle sin gut in sine gewere bevolen hat*: *Gewer* is best translated as "control of property." The steward does not have right of possession of his lord's fief, but as steward, he does indeed have control over the property. See "possession" in glossary.

97. The term is *manschaft* ("feudal service") but it is usually translated as "homage."

98. *dinstmann*: "ministerial"; and not "servant" in this chapter.

99. *Hoverecht* designates the rules that apply to the household of a manor or court, especially of an ecclesiastical foundation. It was distinct from feudal law (*DWB*, vol. 4.2, c. 1696; *BMZ* vol. 2.1, c. 624). See "household law" in glossary.

100. *sal iclich dinstman geboren sin trucsesse odir schenke*: literally, "each ministerial shall be born a seneschal or butler."

101. I assume this refers to the decision about whether the case is valid.

102. *volge*: the "consensus" needed to confirm a judgment or verdict; see II 13; IV 75; and "consensus" in glossary.

103. A portion of text appears to be missing. I have completed the sentence based on the parallel structure of the following sentence.

104. *ab he es noch under im hat*: "if he still has it [the rent] in his possession."

105. It is apparently necessary to attest with an oath the judgment finders' inability to determine a judgment.

106. For possible court venues, see I 59, 62; IV 78.

107. W resumes here.

108. *Sint da aber dorf oder hove di in eine burgwere oder in einen hof gehoret swo der*

herre sich des hoves underwint da mite hat he sich underwunden al der huven unde al der burgwere di in den hof gehort: The meaning here is not transparent. A castle can be held as a fief by itself, or it may be attached to a surrounding large estate. The first part of the sentence mentions a fortification as being independent of an estate, and in the last section, it is part of one.

109. The term is *steber* ("the court official who administers the oath").

110. *swelches tages der man sime herren den stegereif helt*: To hold the stirrup is a sign of subordination and service to one's lord (see I 1).

111. This chapter is misnumbered; it should be number 73. Chapter 74 picks up the correct sequence.

112. *so bitte der man vorsprechen unde gespreches*: "then the man requests a spokesman and deliberation." With the judge's permission, the litigant leaves the hearing to confer with his spokesman, family, and friends but must remain in the vicinity so that he may be recalled (see I 62; IV 74, 75).

113. See III 30.

114. *czinsgenosen*: "fellow tenants."

115. See III 46, 47 for wergeld tables.

116. See "consultation" in glossary.

117. See II 13.

118. See corresponding guidelines in II 13.

119. See IV 48, 70.

120. I render the sense following W strictly. According to Schmidt-Wiegand, however, the phrase *das he ime phlichtig is zu tunde von des riches gute* ("he is required to serve him for the imperial holdings") has been transposed in copying to several lines below but actually belongs here. Consequently her edited text reads: "A man is required to perform the same service for his lord when he holds the lord's allod in fief as the person who holds royal property is required to serve on peace days" (*Facsimile W*, IV 75). See note 121.

121. I have attempted to render the text of W strictly because it makes sense. According to Schmidt-Wiegand, however, the phrase found here, *das he ime phlichtig is zu tunde von des riches gute* ("he is required to serve him for the imperial property"), has been transposed from above (see previous note 120). One may correct the text as Schmidt-Wiegand does by omitting the phrase to read: "If peace days hinder so that the judgment cannot be determined within the proper time limit, then the judgment shall be handed down in six weeks time once the peace days end" (*Facsimile W*, IV 75).

122. I assume this means "and he fails to have that decision overturned."

123. The reference is to III 21. This passage appears to have nothing to do with feudal law and may be a novella inadvertently added here because novellas were often inserted between chapters (Kroeschell, "Rechtswirklichkeit," 4).

124. See I 57, 71; II 13; III 52; and "royal judicial authority" in glossary.

125. *Burger*: "castleholder, holder of a castle fief"; plural is "castle men." Both the original term and the translation remain a bit ambiguous. They appear to imply that the castle is held by a sole holder, but according to the text, a castle may be held by one or by several men in fief who together form the military guard. See "castle fief" in glossary.

126. *anegevelle*: "that which devolves upon someone, right of use" (see II 58; IV 28; and "right of use" in glossary.

127. See above in this chapter, p. 173.

128. See III 58; IV 20.

129. *Spricht ein herre ein vrouwen gut an das si in geweren hat oder imant der des herschildes darbet unde saget is im der herre ledig von sins mannes tode unde saget is ir di vrouwe zu von eime anderen der noch lebet gewert si der herre des gutes noch lenrechte di vrouwe behelt is*: "If a lord appropriates a lady's property when she has right of possession or someone who lacks the military shield, and claims that it becomes available when the man dies, and the woman claims the property for herself from another who still lives, and the lord accepts it in accordance with feudal law, then she retains it." The apparent function of the other, still living person is to prevent reversion of the property.

130. See IV 20, 46; and "repudiate" in glossary.

131. W reads *mit rate noch mit tage* ("with advice nor day") but D reads *tate* ("deed").

132. Manuscripts earlier than W lack this and the previous sentence, but this section in Eckhardt's edition reads *herren unde mannes valsche rat geliket wol ungetruwer dat* ("The false advice of man and lord is the same as a traitorous deed"). Eckhardt has taken this from later manuscripts (Eckhardt, *Lnr*, 117) and is most likely a fourteenth-century addition. The issue seems to be whether any word of advice, evil or not, may be taken for the action itself.

133. *schiltlen das ende mit deme schilde*: "a shield fief that ends with the shield." According to Lexer, this is a fief for which the fiefholder must fulfill military service (2, c. 740–41), but this definition does not distinguish it adequately from a regular fief. According to Grimm, *schildrecht, feudum scutiferum* was a fief for which one owed military service to ecclesiastical houses. If so, these men were possibly ministerials. The arrangement sounds much like the hiring of long-term mercenaries (*DWB*, 9, c. 136).

134. *gebulen ende alse der man da nicht uffe ensiczt*: "a building fief that ends when the man no longer inhabits it." I have not found this term used elsewhere.

135. This probably refers to those charged with a felony because that falls under territorial law.

136. *wil der here*: "if the lords wants," which I translate as "if the lord asks."

137. The statement compares the old lord's status to the new lord's status. A man does not have to accept a holding from a lord of lower rank than the one he had previously served (IV 21, 26, 56).

138. Text may be missing at the beginning of this sentence. Given what follows, the passage would make greater sense if the sentence read: "If the court finds against the man, then he must either renew with that lord or appeal the judgment."

Bibliography

Primary Texts

Auctor vetus de beneficiis archetypus. Ed. Karl August Eckhardt. (Monumenta germaniae historica: Fontes juris Germanici antiqui, n.s., vol. 2, pt. 2.) Hanover: Hahnsche Buchhandlung, 1962.

Deutschenspiegel und Augsburger Sachsenspiegel. Ed. Karl August Eckhardt and Alfred Hubner. Rev. ed. Hanover: Hahnsche Buchhandlung, 1933.

Die Dresdner Bilderhandschrift des Sachsenspiegels. Ed. Karl von Amira. 2 vols. Leipzig: Hiersemann, 1902.

Eike von Repgow. *Sachsenspiegel: Die Wolfenbütteler Bilderhandschrift Cod. Guelf. 3.1 Aug.2°*. Ed. and trans. Ruth Schmidt-Wiegand. 3 vols. Berlin: Akademie Verlag, 1993.

Der Harffer Sachsenspiegel vom Jahre 1295: Landrecht. Ed. Märta Åsdahl Holmberg. (Lunder germ. Forschungen, 32). Lund: Gleerup, 1957.

Die Heidelberger Bilderhandschrift des Sachsenspiegels: Kommentar und Anmerkungen. Ed. Walter Koschorreck. 2 vols. Frankfurt am Main: Insel Verlag, 1970.

Helttampt, Walfart. "Nota Liber Rationis." In: *Sammlung historischer Schriften und Urkunden*, ed. Freiherr von Freyberg. Stuttgart: J. G. Cottasche Buchhandlung, 1829, vol. 2, pp. 81–168.

Henderson, Ernst F. *Select Historical Documents of the Middle Ages*. London: Bell and Sons, 1896.

Das Landrecht des Sachsenspiegels nach der Bremer Handschrift von 1342. Ed. Conrad Borchling. Dortmund: F. W. Ruhfus, 1925.

The Laws of the Kings of England from Edmund to Henry I. Ed. Agnes J. Robertson. New York: AMS Press, 1925.

The Laws of the Salian Franks. Trans. Katherine Fischer Drew. Philadelphia: University of Pennsylvania Press, 1991.

"Leges Anglo-Saxonum." *Germanenrechte: Westgermanisches Recht*. Ed. Karl August Eckhardt. Göttingen: Musterschmidt, 1958.

Der Oldenburger Sachsenspiegel: Vollständige faksimile-Ausgabe im Originalformat des Codex Picturatus Oldenburgensis CIM 1410 der Landesbibliothek Oldenburg. Ed. Ruth Schmidt-Wiegand. 2 vols. Graz, Austria: Akademischer Druck-u. Verlagsanstalt, 1995.

Patriologiae Cursus Completus: Series Latina. Ed. Jacques-Paul Migne. Turnhout: Brepols, 1990 [1844–64].

Quellenverzeichnis zur deutschen Verfassungs-, Wirtschafts-, und Sozialgeschichte bis 1250. Trans. Lorenz Weinrich. (Freiherr von Stein Gedächtnisausgabe, 32). Darmstadt: Wissenschaftliche Buchgesellschaft, 1977.

Der Sachsenspiegel: Die Heidelberger Bilderhandschrift Cod. Pal. Germ. 164. Ed. Walter Koschorreck. Frankfurt am Main: Insel Verlag, 1989.

Sachsenspiegel Landrecht. Ed. Karl August Eckhardt. (Monumenta Germaniae historica: Fontes juris Germanici antiqui, n.s., vol. 1, pt. 1.) 3rd ed. Göttingen: Musterschmidt, 1973.

Sachsenspiegel Lehnrecht. Ed. Karl August Eckhardt. (Monumenta Germaniae historica: Fontes juris Germanici antiqui, n.s., vol. 1, pt. 2). Göttingen: Musterschmidt, 1973.

Sachsenspiegel: Landrecht und Lehnrecht. Ed. Friedrich Ebel. (Universal-Bibliothek, 3355). Stuttgart: Reclam, 1993.

Der Sachsenspiegel (Landrecht) nach der ältesten Leipziger Handschrift. Ed. Julius Weiske and V. R. Hildebrand. Leipzig: Reisland, 1911 [1877].

Der Sachsenspiegel, Landrecht und Lehnrecht Nach dem Oldenburger Codex Picturatus von 1336. Ed. August Lübben. Amsterdam: Rodopi, 1970 [1879].

Sachsenspiegel, Quedlinburger Handschrift. Ed. Karl August Eckhardt. (Monumenta Germaniae historica: Fontes juris Germanici antiqui in usum scholarum, vol. 8). Hanover: Hahnsche Buchhandlung, 1966 [1933].

Des Sachsenspiegels erster Theil nach der Berliner FHS. v. J 1369. Ed. C. G. Homeyer. 2nd rev. ed. Berlin: Dümmler, 1835–44.

Des Sachsenspiegels zweiter Theil, nebst den verwandten Rechtsbüchern. Ed. C. G. Homeyer. Berlin: Dümmler, 1842–61.

Spiegel van Sassen. Antwerp: Wilhelm Vorsterman, 1536.

The Treatise on the Laws and Customs of the Realm of England Commonly Called Glanvill. Ed. G. D. G. Hall. Oxford: Clarendon Press, 1993.

Weisthümer. Ed. Jacob Grimm. 3 vols. Göttingen: Dieterich, 1840–42; (Vols. 2 and 3 edited with Ernst Dronke and Heinrich Beyer; vols. 4–7 edited by Richard Schröder, 1863–70.)

Reference Works

Bayer, Erich. *Wörterbuch zur Geschichte*. Stuttgart: Kröner, 1974.

Black, Henry Campbell. *Black's Law Dictionary*. St. Paul, Minn.: West Publishing, 1933.

Dalby, David. *Lexicon of the Medieval German Hunt*. Berlin: Walter de Gruyter, 1965.

Die deutsche Literatur des Mittelalters, Verfasserlexikon. Ed. Kurt Ruh and Gundolf Keil. 2nd rev. ed. Berlin and New York: de Gruyter, 1978-.

Deutsche Rechtsregeln und Rechtssprichwörter: Ein Lexikon. Ed. Ruth Schmidt-Wiegand and Ulrike Schowe. Munich: Beck, 1996.

Deutsches Rechtswörterbuch: Wörterbuch der älteren deutschen Rechtssprache. Ed. Heidelberger Akademie der Wissenschaften. Weimar:Böhlau, 1974–83.

Deutsches Wörterbuch. Ed. Jacob Grimm and Wilhelm Grimm. Leipzig: Hirzel, 1854.

Dictionary of Doctrinal and Historical Theology. Ed. John Henry Blunt. New York: Longmans, Green, 1891 [1872].

Handwörterbuch zur deutschen Rechtsgeschichte. Ed. Adalbert Erler and Ekkehard Kaufmann. Berlin: Schmidt Verlag, 1971–93.

Hilfswörterbuch für Historiker: Mittelalter und Neuzeit. Ed. Eugen Haberkern and J. F. Wallach. 2nd ed. Bern: Francke, 1964.

Medieval Scandinavia: An Encyclopedia. Ed. Phillip Pulsiano and Kirsten Wolf. New York: Garland, 1993.

Mittelhochdeutsches Wörterbuch. Ed. Georg Benecke, Müller, and Zarncke. 3 vols. New York and Hildesheim: Georg Olm, 1986 [1854].

Mittelniederdeutsches Handwörterbuch. Ed. August Lübben. Darmstadt: Wissenschaftliche Buchgesellschaft, 1990 [1888].

Translations

Der Sachsenspiegel (Landrecht). Trans. Hans Christoph Hirsch. Berlin and Leipzig: Verlag Walter de Gruyter, 1936.

Der Sachsenspiegel (Lehnrecht). Trans. Hans Christoph Hirsch. Halle: Max Niemeyer, 1939.

Der Sachsenspiegel Eikes von Repgow. Ed. Clausdieter Schott. Trans. Ruth Schmidt-Wiegand and Clausdieter Schott. Zurich: Manesse, 1984.

Secondary Works

Adler, H. G. *The Jews in Germany from the Enlightenment to National Socialism*. Notre Dame, Ind.: University of Notre Dame Press, 1969.

Altenkirch, Christel, and Horst Kuntschke. "Rechte der Frau und Vormundschaftsrecht im 'Sachsenspiegel.'" In *Deutsches Recht zwischen Sachsenspiegel und Aufklärung: Rolf Lieberwirth zum 70. Geburtstag dargebracht von Schülern, Freunden und Kollegen*. Ed. Gerhard Lingelbach and Heiner Lück (Rechtshistorische Reihe, 80). New York and Bern: Peter Lang, 1991, pp. 27–36.

Amira, Karl von. *Die germanischen Todesstrafen*. (Abhandl. der bayr. Akad. der Wiss., phil.-philol. Kl. 31, Abt.3). Munich: Akademie der Wissenschaften, 1922.

———. *Germanisches Recht*. Ed. Karl August Eckhardt. (Grundriss der germanischen Philologie, 5). 2 vols. 4th ed. Berlin: de Gruyter, 1960–67.

Arnold, Benjamin. *Princes and Territories in Medieval Germany*. New York and Cambridge: Cambridge University Press, 1991.

Bar, Carl Ludwig von. *A History of Continental Criminal Law*. Trans. Thomas S. Bell. (Continental Legal History Series, 6). New York: Augustus M. Kelley Publishers, 1968 [1916].

Bertelsmeier-Kierst, Christa. "Text im Bild—Bild im Text. Beispiele hochmittelalterlicher Rechtsikonographie." In *Wolfram Studien XV: Neue Wege der Mittelalter-philologie*, ed. Joachim Heinzle, L. Peter Johnson, and Gisela Vollmann-Profe. Berlin: Erich Schmidt Verlag, 1998, pp. 373–95.

Bokonyi, Sándor. "The Development of Stockbreeding and Herding in Medieval Europe." In *Agriculture in the Middle Ages: Technology, Practice, and Representation*, ed. Del Sweeney. Philadelphia: University of Pennsylvania Press, 1995, pp. 41–61.

Bradley, Ritamary. "Backgrounds of the Title *Speculum* in Mediaeval Literature." *Speculum* 29 (1954): 100–115.

Bühler, Theodor. *Rechtsquellentypen*. Zurich: Schultheiß Polygraph Verlag, 1980.

Conrad, Hermann. *Deutsche Rechtsgeschichte: Ein Lehrbuch*. 2 vols. Karlsruhe: C. F. Müller, 1954.

Damm, Helmut. *Mundartliche Eigenarten im Sachsenspiegel*. Heidelberg: A. Grosch, 1969.

Danckert, Werner. *Unehrliche Leute: Die verfemten Berufe*. Bern and Munich: Francke Verlag, 1963.

Die deutsche Ostsiedlung des Mittelalters als Problem der europäischen Geschichte: Reichenau-Vorträge, 1970–71. Ed. Walter Schlesinger. Sigmaringen: Jan Thorbecke, 1975.

Deutsche Rechtsgeschichte Ein Studienbuch. Ed. Heinrich Mitteis. Berlin and Munich: Beck, 1966.

Dilcher, Gerhard. "Mittelalterliche Rechtsgewohnheit als methodisch-theoretisches Problem." In *Gewohnheitsrecht und Rechtsgewohnheiten im Mittelalter*, ed. Gerhard Dilcher, Heiner Lück, Reiner Schulze, Elmar Wadle, and Jürgen Weitzel. (Schriften zur Europäischen Rechts- und Verfassungsgeschichte, 6). Berlin: Duncker and Humblot, 1992, pp. 21–66.

——. "Mythischer Ursprung und historische Herkunft als Legitimation mittelalterlicher Rechtsaufzeichnungen zwischen Leges und 'Sachsenspiegel.'" In *Herkunft und Ursprung. Historische und mythische Formen der Legitimation*, ed. Peter Wunderli. Sigmaringen: Jan Thorbecke, 1994, pp. 141–55.

Dobozy, Maria. "From Oral Custom to Written Law: 'The Sachsenspiegel.'" In *Consolatia Philologiae: Festschrift für E. S. Firchow*, ed. Anna Grotans. Göppingen: Kuemmerle, 1999, pp. 31–40.

Drescher, Ulrich. *Geistliche Denkformen in den Bilderhandschriften des Sachsenspiegels*. (Germanist. Arbeiten zu Sprache und Kulturgeschichte, 12). New York and Bern: Lang, 1989.

Drew, Katherine Fischer. Introduction. In *The Laws of the Salian Franks*. Philadelphia: University of Pennsylvania Press, 1991.

Ebel, Friedrich. "Die deutsche Rechtsliteratur im mittelalterlichen Schlesien unter besonderer Berücksichtigung der Breslauer Quellen." In *Anfänge und Entwicklung der deutschen Sprache im mittelalterlichen Schlesien*, ed. Gundolf Keil and Josef Joachim Menzel. Sigmaringen: Jan Thorbecke, 1995, pp. 83–87.

Ebel, Wilhelm. *Geschichte der Gesetzgebung in Deutschland*. Göttingen: O. Schwartz, 1958.

——. "Über das 'ungezweite Gut' in 'Sachsenspiegel' Ldr. I 31." *ZRG GA*, 92 (1975): 184–89.

Eckhardt, Karl August. "Glossar der Wortbedeutungen." In *Lnr*, pp. 220–55.

Fricke, Friedrich-Wilhelm. *Das Eherecht des Sachsenspiegels: Systematische Darstellung*. Frankfurt: Haag und Herchen, 1978.

Gönczi, Katalin. *Ungarisches Stadtrecht aus europäischer Sicht: Die Stadtrechtsentwicklung im spätmittelalterlichen Ungarn am Beispiel Ofen*. Frankfurt am Main: Vittorio Klostermann, 1997.

Graus, Frantisek. "Die Problematik der deutschen Ostsiedlung aus tschechischer Sicht." In *Ostsiedlung*, pp. 31–77.

Hall, G. D. G. Introduction. In *The Treatise on the Laws and Customs of the Realm of England Commonly Called Glanvill*. Oxford: Clarendon Press, 1993.

Hatfield, George B. "The Bible in Mediaeval Civilization: The Saxon Code of Law in Illustration." *Historical Judaica* 5 (1943): 63–72.

Helbig, Herbert. "Die ungarische Gesetzgebung des 13. Jahrhunderts und die Deutschen." In *Ostsiedlung*, pp. 509–26.

Hirsch, Hans. *Die hohe Gerichtsbarkeit im deutschen Mittelalter.* Darmstadt: Wissenschaftliche Buchgesellschaft, 1958 [1922].

———. "Glossar." In *Der Sachsenspiegel(Lehnrecht)*, pp. 302–32.

His, Rudolf. *Geschichte des deutschen Strafrechts bis zur Karolina*. Darmstadt: Wissenschaftliche Buchgesellschaft, 1967 [1928].

Homeyer, Karl Gustav. *Die deutschen Rechtsbücher des Mittelalters und ihre Handschriften*. Rev. ed. Ed. Conrad Borchling, K. A. Eckhardt, and Julius Gierke. Weimar: H. Böhlaus Nachfolger, 1931–34.

Houtte, J. A. van. *Europäische Wirtschaft und Gesellschaft von den großen Wanderungen bis zum Schwarzen Tod*. (Handbuch der europäischen Wirtschafts- und Sozialgeschichte, 2). Stuttgart: Klett-Cotta, 1980.

Huebner, Rudolf. *A History of Germanic Private Law*. Trans. Francis S. Philbrick (Continental Legal History Series, 4), New York: Augustus M. Kelley, 1968.

Hüpper, Dagmar. "Die Bildersprache. Zur Funktion der Illustration." In *Facsimile W*, vol. 3, pp. 143–62.

———. "Ehe, Familie, Verwandtschaft—Zur Widerspiegelung von Begrifflichkeit in der Bildtradition des 'Sachsenspiegels.'" In *TBI*, pp. 128–44.

———. "Funktionstypen der Bilder in den Codices Picturati des 'Sachsenspiegels.'" In *Pragmatische Schriftlichkeit im Mittelalter—Erscheinungsformen und Entwicklungsstufen*, ed. Hagen Keller, Klaus Grubmüller, and Nikolaus Staubach. Munich: Fink, 1992, pp. 231–49.

———. "Poesie und Recht aus einem Bette." *Frühmittelalterliche Studien* 27 (1993): 87–123.

Ignor, Alexander. *Über das allgemeine Rechtsdenken Eikes von Repgow*. Munich and Zurich: Ferdinand Schöningh, 1984.

Ishikawa, Takeshi. "Die Gewere im 'Sachsenspiegel.'" In *Festschrift für Hans Thieme zu seinem 80. Geburtstag*, ed. Karl Kroeschell. Sigmaringen: Thorbecke, 1986, pp. 59–82.

Jacoby, Michael. *Germanisches Recht und Rechtssprache zwischen Mittelalter und Neuzeit unter besonderer Berücksichtigung des skandinavischen Rechts: Gegenthese zu Jacob Grimm und zu romantischer Auffassung im 20. Jahrhundert.* New York and Bern: Lang, 1986.

Janz, Brigitte. *Rechtssprichwörter im Sachsenspiegel: Eine Untersuchung zur Text—Bild—Relation in den Codices picturati*. (Germanistische Arbeiten zu Sprache und Kulturgeschichte, 13). New York and Bern: Lang, 1989.

———. "'Wir sezzen unde gebiten . . .' der Mainzer Reichslandfriede in den Bilderhandschriften des 'Sachsenspiegels.'" *Beiträge zur Geschichte der deutschen Literature* 112 (1990): 242–66.

Jaritz, Gerhard. "Material Culture of the Peasantry in the Late Middle Ages: 'Image' and 'Reality.'" In *Agriculture in the Middle Ages: Technology, Practice, and Representation*, ed. Del Sweeney. Philadelphia: University of Pennsylvania Press, 1995, pp. 163–90.

Johanek, Peter. "Rechtsschrifttum." In *Geschichte der deutschen Literatur* vol. 3/2, ed. Ingeborg Glier. Munich: C. H. Beck, 1987, pp. 396–431.

Kern, Fritz. *Recht und Verfassung im Mittelalter*. Darmstadt: Wissenschaftliche Buchgesellschaft, 1992 [1952].

Kisch, Guido. "Biblical Spirit in Medieval Law." *Speculum* 14 (1939): 38–53.

——. *The Jews in Medieval Germany: A Study of Their Legal and Social Status*. Chicago: University of Chicago Press, 1949.

——. *Sachsenspiegel and Bible*. Notre Dame, Ind.: University of Notre Dame Press, 1941.

——. "Sachsenspiegelbibliographie." *ZRG* 90 (1973): 73–100.

Köbler, Gerhard. *Bilder aus der deutschen Rechtsgeschichte von den Anfängen bis zur Gegenwart*. Munich: Beck, 1988.

——. *Das Recht im frühen Mittelalter. Untersuchungen zu Herkunft und Inhalt frühmittelalterlicher Rechtsbegriffe im deutschen Sprachgebiet*. Vienna and Cologne: Böhlau, 1971.

——. "Vorstufen der Rechtswissenschaft im mittelalterlichen Deutschland." *ZRG GA* 100 (1983): 75–118.

Kocher, Gernot. "Die Rechtsikonographie." In *Facsimile W*, vol. 3, pp. 107–17.

Kolb, Herbert. "Über den Ursprung der Unfreiheit. Eine Quaestio im 'Sachsenspiegel.'" *ZfdA* 103 (1974): 289–311.

Koziol, Geoffrey. "Lord's Law and Natural Law." In *The Medieval Tradition of Natural Law*, ed. Harold J. Johnson. (Studies in Medieval Culture, 22). Kalamazoo, Mich.: Medieval Institute Publications, 1987, pp. 103–17.

Kroeschell, Karl. *Deutsche Rechtsgeschichte*. 3 vols. Reinbeck bei Hamburg: Rowohlt, 1972–89.

——. "Germanisches Recht als Forschungsproblem." In *Festschrift für Hans Thieme zu seinem 80. Geburtstag*, ed. Karl Kroeschell. Sigmaringen: Thorbecke, 1986, pp. 3–19.

——. "Rechtsaufzeichung und Rechtswirklichkeit. Das Beispiel des 'Sachsenspiegels.'" In *Recht und Schrift im Mittelalter*, ed. Peter Classen. (Vorträge und Forschungen, 23). Sigmaringen: Thorbecke, 1977, pp. 349–80.

——. "Rechtswirklichkeit und Rechtsbücherüberlieferung. Überlegungen zur Wirkungsgeschichte des 'Sachsenspiegels.'" In *TBI*, pp. 1–10.

——. "Der 'Sachsenspiegel' in neuem Licht." In *Rechtsgeschichte in den beiden deutschen Staaten (1988–90). Beispiele, Parallelen, Positionen*, ed. Heinz Mohnhaupt. Frankfurt: V. Klostermann, 1991, S. 232–44.

Kubinyi, András. "Zur Frage der deutschen Siedlungen im mittleren Teil des Königreichs Ungarn (1200–1541)." In *Ostsiedlung*, pp. 527–66.

Kuchenbuch, Ludolf. "Links Within the Village: Evidence from Fourteenth Century Eastphalia." In *Agriculture in the Middle Ages: Technology, Practice, and*

Representation, ed. Del Sweeney. Philadelphia: University of Pennsylvania, 1995, pp. 138–62.

Kunze, Konrad. *Himmel in Stein: Das Freiburger Münster*. Freiburg: Herder, 1980.

Lade, Ulrike. "Dorfrecht und Flurordnung in den Illustrationen der Sachsenspiegel-Bilderhandschriften." In *TBI*, pp. 171–88.

Lieberwirth, Rolf. *Eike von Repchow und der Sachsenspiegel*. (Sitzungsberichte der Sächsischen Akad. der Wiss. zu Leipzig, Phil.-hist. Kl., 122). Berlin: Akademie Verlag, 1982.

———. *Eike von Repgow und sein Sachsenspiegel. Entstehung, Inhalt, Bedeutung*. Köthen: Heimatmuseum Köthen, 1980.

———. *Über die Glosse zum Sachsenspiegel*. (Sitzungsberichte der Sächsischen Akad. der Wiss. zu Leipzig, Phil.-hist. Kl., 132), Berlin: Akademie Verlag, 1993.

———. "Vorrede von der Herren Geburt." In *Buch*, pp. 1–18.

Lindner, Gustav. "Der *Schwabenspiegel* bei den siebenbürger Sachsen." *ZRG GA* 6 (1885): 86–141.

Long, Pamela O., ed. *Science and Technology in Medieval Society*. (Annals of the New York Academy of Sciences, 441). New York: New York Academy of Sciences, 1985.

Mess, F. "Wartburgkrieg und 'Sachsenspiegel.'" *ZRG GA* 74 (1957): 241–56.

Milde, Wolfgang. "Kodikologische Einführung." In *Facsimile W*, vol. 2, pp. 11–30.

———. "Zum Wolfenbütteler Sachsenspiegel: Lagenfolge mit Inhalt und Ausstattung, Einband, Erwerbung." In *TBI*, pp. 207–13.

Mitteis, Heinrich, *Die Rechstgeschichte und das Problem der historishen Kontinuität*. (Abhandl. der deutschen Akademie der Wissenschaften, Berlin, phil.-hist. Kl. Nr.1). Berlin: Akademie Verlag, 1948.

Müller, Bärbel. *Die Berliner Sammelhandschrift Mgf 10 und ihre Bedeutung für die überlieferungskritische Ausgabe des Sachsenspiegels*. (Germanistische Arbeiten zu Sprache und Kulturgeschichte, 19), New York and Bern: Lang, 1991.

———. "Kapitelverzeichnisse und 'Sachregister' zum 'Sachsenspiegel' in Mgf 10 und in der Wolfenbütteler Bilderhandschrift: Ein Vergleich." In *Buch*, pp. 143–68.

Nowak, Elisabeth. "Die Verbreitung und Anwendung des 'Sachsenspiegels' nach den überlieferten Handschriften." Diss. Hamburg, 1965.

Oppitz, Ulrich-Dieter. *Deutsche Rechtsbücher des Mittelalters*. 3 vols. Cologne: Bohlau, 1990.

Ott, Norbert. "Rechtsikonographie zwischen Mündlichkeit und Schriftlichkeit. Der 'Sachsenspiegel' im Kontext deutschsprachiger illustrierter Handschriften." In *Facsimile W*, vol. 3, pp. 119–42.

———. "Vorläufige Bemerkungen zur 'Sachsenspiegel'-Ikonographie." In *TBI*, pp. 33–44.

Piirainen, Ilpo Tapani, and Winfried Waßer. *Der Sachsenspiegel aus Oppeln und Krakau*. (Schriften der Stiftung Haus Oberschlesien, Landeskundliche Reihe, 10). Berlin: Gebr. Mann Verlag, 1996.

Planck, Julius Wilhelm von. *Das Deutsche Gerichtsverfahren im Mittelalter nach dem Sachsenspiegel und den verwandten Rechtsquellen*. New York and Hildesheim: Georg Olms Verlag, 1973 [1879].

Pollock, Frederick, and Frederic William Maitland. *The History of English Law before the Time of Edward I*. Cambridge: Cambridge University Press, 1895.

Posse, Otto. *Die Notwehr im Sachsenspiegel*. Coburg: Tageblatt-haus, 1937.

Recht und Gerechtigkeit im Spiegel der europäischen Kunst. Ed. Wolfgang Pleister and Wolfgang Schild. Cologne: DuMont Buchverlag, 1988.

Rösener, Werner. *Peasants in the Middle Ages*. Trans. Alexander Stützer. Cambridge: Polity Press, 1992.

Rummel, Mariella. *Die rechtliche Stellung der Frau im Sachsenspiegel-Landrecht*. (Germanistische Arbeiten zu Sprache und Kulturgeschichte, 10). New York and Bern: Lang, 1987.

Der Sachsenspiegel als Buch. Ed. Ruth Schmidt-Wiegand and Dagmar Hüpper. New York and Bern: Lang, 1991.

Schadt, Hermann. *Die Darstellung der Arbores Consanguinitatis und der Arbores Affinitatis*. Tübingen: Verlag Ernst Wasmuth, 1982.

———. "Zum Verwandtschaftsbild und der Weltalterlehre des 'Sachsenspiegels.' Kunstgeschichte als Hilfswissenschaft der Rechtsgeschichte." *Frühmittelalterliche Studien*, 10 (1976): 406–36.

Scheele, Friedrich. *"Di sal man alle radebrechen": Todeswürdige Delikte und ihre Bestrafung in Text und Bild der Codices picturati des Sachsenspiegels*. 2 vols. Oldenburg: Isensee Verlag, 1992.

———. "'Spillute . . . di sint alle rechtelos.' Zur rechtlichen und sozialen Stellung des Spielmanns in Text und Bild des 'Sachsenspiegels.'" In *Buch,* pp. 315–57.

Schlesinger, Walter. "Zur Problematik der Erforschung der deutschen Ostsiedlung." In *Ostsiedlung*, pp. 11–30.

Schlosser, Hans. *Die rechtsgeschichtliche Exegese*. Munich: Beck, 1993.

Schmidt, Roderich. "Kaiser, König und Reich in der Wolfenbütteler Bilderhandschrift des 'Sachsenspiegels.'" In *Facsimile W*, vol. 3, pp. 87–95.

Schmidt-Wiegand, Ruth. "Bilderhandschriften des 'Sachsenspiegels' als Quelle der Kulturgeschichte." In *Buch*, pp. 219–60.

———. "Die Bilderhandschriften des 'Sachsenspiegels' als Zeugen pragmatischer Schriftlichkeit." *Frühmittelalterliche Studien*, 22 (1988): 357–87.

———. "Eid und Gelöbnis, Formel und Formular im mittelalterlichen Recht." In *Recht und Schrift im Mittelalter*, ed. Peter Classen (Vorträge und Forschungen, 23). Sigmaringen: Thorbecke, 1977, pp. 55–90.

———. "Eike von Repgow, 'Sachsenspiegel.'" In *Wolfenbütteler Cimelien: Das Evangeliar Heinrichs des Löwen in der Herzog August Bibliothek*. Wolfenbüttel: Acta Humaniora, 1989, pp. 197–203.

———. "Gebärdensprache im mittelalterlichen Recht." *Frühmittelalterliche Studien* 16 (1982): 363–79.

———."*hantgemaelde* (Parzival 6,19): Rechtswort und Rechtssinn bei Wolfram von Eschenbach." In *Studien zu Wolfram von Eschenbach. Festschrift für Werner Schröder zum 75. Geburtstag*, ed. Kurt Gärtner and Joachim Heinzle. Tübingen: Niemeyer, 1989, pp. 333–42.

———. "Kleidung, Tracht und Ornat nach den Bilderhandschriften des 'Sachsenspiegels.'" In *Terminologie und Typologie mittelalterlicher Sachgüter: Das*

Beispiel der Kleidung. Vienna: Österreich. Akademie der Wissenschaft, 1988, pp. 143–75.

——. "Die mitteldeutschen Bilderhandschriften des 'Sachsenspiegels' und die sprachgeschichtliche Stellung des Elb-Saale-Raums im 14. Jahrhundert." In *Festschrift für Rudolf Große zum 65 Geburtstag*, ed. Sabine Heimann, Gotthard Lerchner, and Ulrich Müller. Stuttgart: Hans-Dieter Heinz, 1989, pp. 93–101.

——. "Recht und Dichtung." In *HRG*, vol. 4, c. 232–49.

——. "Recht und Gesetz im Spannungsfeld zwischen Schriftlichkeit und Mündlichkeit im Mittelalter." *Frühmittelalterliche Studien* 27 (1993): 147–66.

——. "Rechtsbücher als Zeugen pragmatischer Schriftlichkeit. Ein Forschungsprojekt im Sonderforschungsbereich 231 der Universität Münster." *Niederdeutsches Wort* 29 (1989): 1–11.

——. "Rechtssprichwörter und ihre Wiedergabe in den Bilderhandschriften des 'Sachsenspiegels.'" In *Text und Bild: Aspekte des Zusammenwirkens zweier Künste in Mittelalter und früher Neuzeit*, ed. Christel Meier und Uwe Ruberg. Wiesbaden: Reichert Verlag, 1980, pp. 593–629.

——. "Der Rechtswortschatz." In *Facsimile W*, vol. 3, pp. 219–32.

——. "Der 'Sachsenspiegel' Eikes von Repgow als Beispiel mittelalterlicher Fachliteratur." *Zeitschrift für Literaturwissenschaft und Linguistik*, 51–52 (1983): 206–26.

——. "Sprache und Stil der Wolfenbütteler Bilderhandschrift." In *Facsimile W*, vol. 3, pp. 201–18.

——. "Text und Bild in den codices picturati des 'Sachsenspiegels' -Überlegungen zur Funktion der Illustration." In *TBI*, pp. 11–32.

——. "Die Wolfenbütteler Bilderhandschrift des 'Sachsenspiegels' und ihr Verhältnis zum Text Eikes von Repgow." Public lecture. Wolfenbüttel: Herzog August Bibliothek Wolfenbüttel, 1983.

——. "Die Wolfenbütteler Bilderhandschrift im Kreis der Codices picturati des 'Sachsenspiegels.'" In *Facsimilie W*, vol. 3, pp. 1–16.

——. "Überlieferungs- und Editionsprobleme deutscher Rechtsbücher." In *Methoden und Probleme der Edition mittelalterlicher deutscher Texte*. Tübingen: Niemeyer Verlag, 1993, pp. 63–81.

——. "Von der autornahen zur überlieferungskritischen Ausgabe des 'Sachsenspiegels.'" In *Deutsches Recht zwischen Sachsenspiegel und Aufklärung. Rolf Lieberwirth zum Geburtstag*, ed. Gerhard Lingelbach und Heiner Lück, Bern/New York: Peter Lang, 1991, pp. 13–25.

Schulze, H. K. "Rodungsfreiheit und Königsfreiheit. Zu Genesis und Kritik neuerer verfassungsgeschichtlicher Theorien." *Historische Zeitschrift* 219 (1974): 529–50.

Schulze, Reiner. "'Gewohnheitsrecht' und 'Rechtsgewohnheiten' im Mittelalter-Einführung." In *Gewohnheitsrecht und Rechtsgewohnheiten im Mittelalter*, ed. Gerhard Dilcher, Heiner Lück, Reiner Schulze, Elmar Wadle, and Jürgen Weitzel (Schriften zur Europäischen Rechts- und Verfassungsgeschichte, 6). Berlin: Duncker und Humblot, 1992, pp. 9–20.

Schulze, Ursula. *Lateinisch-deutsche Parallelurkunden des 13. Jahrhunderts: Ein Beitrag zur Syntax der mittelhochdeutschen Urkundensprache*. (Medium Aevum 30). Munich: Wilhelm Fink, 1975.

Shinn, Gerald Harris. "Text and Illuminations of the D ms of the 'Sachsenspiegel' in Relation to their Weltanschauung und Zeitgeist." Ph.D. diss. Duke University, 1964.

——. "The Eschatological Function of the Iconography of the Dresden Manuscript of the 'Sachsenspiegel.'" In *Contemporary Reflections on the Medieval Christian Tradition: Essays in Honor of Ray C. Petry*. Durham, N.C.: Duke University Press, 1974, pp. 53–64.

Stutz, Ulrich. *Das Verwandtschaftsbild des Sachsenspiegels und seine Bedeutung für die sächsische Erbfolgeordnung*. Aalen: Scientia, 1973 [1890].

Text—Bild—Interpretation: Untersuchungen zu den Bilderhandschriften des Sachsenspiegels. Ed. Ruth Schmidt-Wiegand. Munich: Fink Verlag, 1986.

Text-und Sachbezug in der Rechtssprachgeographie. Ed. Ruth Schmidt-Wiegand. Munich: Fink Verlag, 1985.

Theuerkauf, Gerhard. "Sachsenrecht im Übergang von der 'Lex Saxonum' zum 'Sachsenspiegel.'" In *Gesellschaftlicher und ideengeschichtlicher Wandel im Reich der Salier*, ed. Stefan Weinfurter and Hubertus Seibert. (Die Salier und das Reich, 3). Sigmaringen: Thorbecke, 1992, pp. 415–23.

Willoweit, Dietmar. "Gericht und Urteil über den Wenden." In *Festschrift für Hans Thieme zu seinem 80. Geburtstag*, ed. Karl Kroeschell. Sigmaringen: Thorbecke, 1986, pp. 83–95.

Index

www.ingramcontent.com/pod-product-compliance
Lightning Source LLC
LaVergne TN
LVHW102010210926
848483LV00015B/451/J
* 9 7 8 0 8 1 2 2 3 4 8 7 9 *